NOSH ON THIS

"Lisa Stander-Horel is a great baker and a mensch. With *Nosh on This*, she has created a bevy of reci-pes for gluten-intolerant folks who still want the foods they ate as want one of everything, please!" —SHAUNA JAMES AHERN

"What could be more comforting than a book of noshable treats not!—can enjoy? *Nosh on This* provides delicious gluten-free recipe
—KYRA BUSSANICH, *Cupcake Wars*–winning founder of Kyra's Bake Shop and author of *Sweet Cravings*

"*Nosh on This* is a wonderful, carefully crafted, and must-have cookbook not only for gluten-free Jewish-American bakers, but for all gluten-free bakers. It is a unique resource that brings gluten-free Jewish baked specialties into the realm of deliciousness!"
—JEANNE SAUVAGE, author of *Gluten-Free Baking for the Holidays*

"Had Lisa Stander-Horel simply taken traditional Jewish holiday recipes and made them gluten-free, it would have been enough. Instead, she added incredible flavor and flair to gluten-free baking, ensuring whatever you make will be devoured. The recipe photos will convince you gluten-free also means gorgeous presentation. *Nosh on This* is a total reinvention of bubbe-style goodies that everyone could enjoy. Maybe it should be subtitled: you don't have to be gluten intolerant to enjoy this book because the baking is simply uncompromised, irresistible goodness."
—MARCY GOLDMAN, bestselling author of *A Passion for Baking*, *A Treasury of Jewish Holiday Baking*, and *The Best of BetterBaking.com*

"This book provides wonderful gluten-free alternatives to classic Jewish baking, and it's so modern! Many of our diners request gluten-free dishes—it's nice to have *Nosh on This* as a new authority to turn to for inspiration and instruction." —ELLEN KASSOFF GRAY, co-author of *The New Jewish Table* and co-owner of Equinox Restaurant

"A must-have cookbook for the gluten-free baker who craves traditional Jewish baking for holidays and every day. Enjoy an amazing array of gluten-free noshes that anyone following a GF diet can finally enjoy!"
—NORENE GILLETZ, author of *The New Food Processor Bible* and *Norene's Healthy Kitchen*

THE EXPERIMENT

BECAUSE EVERY BOOK IS A TEST OF NEW IDEAS

NOSH ON THIS

Gluten-Free Baking
from a Jewish-American Kitchen

LISA STANDER-HOREL AND TIM HOREL

WITHDRAWN

THE EXPERIMENT

NEW YORK

The Experiment, LLC
260 Fifth Avenue
New York, NY 10001-6408
www.theexperimentpublishing.com

Nosh on This includes a variety of gluten-free recipes, as well as dairy-free alternatives. While care was taken to provide correct and helpful information, the suggestions in this book are not intended as dietary advice or as a substitute for consulting a dietician or medical professional. We strongly recommend that you check with your doctor before making changes to your diet. The authors and publisher disclaim all liability in connection with the use of this book.

Many of the designations used by manufacturers and sellers to distinguish their products are claimed as trademarks. Where those designations appear in this book and The Experiment was aware of a trademark claim, the designations have been capitalized.

The Experiment's books are available at special discounts when purchased in bulk for premiums and sales promotions as well as for fund-raising or educational use. For details, contact us at info@theexperimentpublishing.com.

Library of Congress Cataloging-in-Publication Data

Stander-Horel, Lisa.
Nosh on this : gluten-free baking from a Jewish-American kitchen / Lisa Stander-Horel and Tim Horel.
pages cm
ISBN 978-1-61519-086-7 (pbk.) -- ISBN 978-1-61519-178-9 (ebook)
1. Gluten-free diet--Recipes. 2. Jewish cooking. I. Horel, Tim. II. Title.
RM237.86.S73 2013
641.5'676--dc23
2013012379

ISBN 978-1-61519-086-7
Ebook ISBN 978-1-61519-178-9

Cover design by Susi Oberhelman
Cover photographs by Tim Horel
Author photograph courtesy of the authors
Text design by Pauline Neuwirth, Neuwirth & Associates, Inc.

Manufactured in the United States of America
Distributed by Workman Publishing Company, Inc.
Distributed simultaneously in Canada by Thomas Allen and Son Ltd.

First printing August 2013
10 9 8 7 6 5 4 3 2 1

With love to our daughters and the ZZ boys

CONTENTS

Chocolate Nut Two-Bite Tarts (page 124)

FOREWORD

FORTUNATELY, I don't have a problem with gluten, a kind of protein found in bread, cake, cookies, pasta—all those delicious foods that are made with wheat, the most plentiful source of gluten in the United States. But I think I can relate in a very small way to not being able to eat the things you crave. When I was young, and all Jewish delicatessens in Brooklyn were kosher delicatessens and thus closed for the eight days of Passover because of holiday dietary restrictions, one couldn't get a pastrami sandwich for that whole week. A whole week! It killed me. Naturally, I who loved pastrami in every season, and certainly more than any other meat, craved it most intensely during Passover when I couldn't get it.

I am sure people, even Jews, can live without rugelach, mandlebrot, strudel, and challah. But when you can't possibly eat them because you have celiac or Crohn's disease, or a wheat or gluten allergy—I mean you would get very sick if you did eat them—and, on top of that, you've grown up with a grandmother who baked all day and egged you on to nearly daily submission to her sweets with a plaintive "Eat a little something, darling"—well, the craving must be unbearable.

In fact, Lisa Stander-Horel did have such a grandmother, and both she and Tim Horel, her husband and coauthor of this authoritative book, did find their cravings unbearable. What happened in their family is typical—broken bones and other obscure symptoms took their toll for eight years before the final diagnosis of celiac disease, an autoimmune response to gluten, which is one of those genetically transmitted diseases that afflict a large number of Eastern European Jews among other groups. (Although, as you likely know because it's in the news all the time, Americans of every ethnicity are, for various reasons, also following gluten-free diets.) The shelves of my kosher supermarket in Brooklyn have many more gluten-free products than the mainstream markets do. For Passover, there are now even gluten-free matzos and matzo products. The tragic irony is that we Jews are a people with an extensive repertoire of high-gluten delicacies, many of which we regard as cultural icons. It's like, I love rugelach, therefore I am Jewish. We even have special prayers that we say before eating pastry and bread.

Naturally, the first thing Lisa did—expert baker that she is, a woman from a serious baking family in the Eastern European tradition—was figure out how she could enjoy "noshes," as her family refers to all those beautiful baked things. This was not easy. Flours used for gluten-free baking—rice flour and tapioca flour, to name two—don't behave the same way as wheat flour. Gluten is, with the obvious pun actually a point of etymology, the glue that holds them together. Experimentation, manipulation, and, I am sure, many sweet duds led to this great collection of recipes. Not all the recipes are from Stander-Horel's Eastern European tradition, but they all have their roots there. Lisa has contemporized many, added more or different flavors, or just changed the technique so that you get a superior product with the special ingredients needed to bake gluten-free. There is nothing like *Nosh on This*, and I don't know any bakers as dedicated as Lisa and Tim to this repertoire or to gluten-free baking in general.

I have to admit: I don't enjoy baking as much as cooking, because baking requires precision and cooking is more forgiving. You can always add seasoning at the end of a stew, a soup, a braise, or even a quick sauté. You can judge cooking time by looking, smelling, and tasting. Baking without gluten requires even more precision than baking with wheat flour, which is why Lisa and Tim have offered metric weight measurements for their ingredients, the most precise way to measure ingredients for baking. It's what professional bakers always do. You will get the best results when you follow this example, so I urge you to weigh everything, too. I live by the scale myself, even when I cook. Do read the amazing introduction, with its hand-holding advice, admonitions, charts, and vital information about ingredients and techniques. Then have a good time, enjoy Lisa's family stories, and "Eat hearty," as my grandfather used to say as we started a meal, or even a little nosh.

ARTHUR SCHWARTZ is an award-winning cookbook author whose *Jewish Home Cooking: Yiddish Recipes Revisited* was named best American-subject cookbook by the International Association of Culinary Professionals (IACP).

NOSH ON THIS

Tim's second birthday

INTRODUCTION

SOMEWHERE AROUND the time Bill Clinton was about to win his first presidential election and my kitchen was filled with wheat flour, rye flour, and chocolate malt, we discovered, literally by accident, that gluten was causing some serious health issues in our family. We knew something was wrong when Tim fractured both elbows simultaneously in a stumble, despite being a young man. Fortunately we were able to find a physician who stuck with us. Unfortunately it took another eight years to get a definitive diagnosis. The cause of his prematurely brittle bones? Gluten. Although good health returned quickly once we were eating gluten-free, the unseen long-term damage took years to remedy. That is how celiac disease works—sometimes silently.

Meantime, trying to figure out how to navigate gluten-free back in the days when it meant a truly limited diet was not only confusing, but often amusing. "Why yes! We have gluten-free options—the chef will leave the potatoes off your plate." Or the more awkward moment when your boss brings in a homemade birthday cake happily reporting it is totally flourless. Just as you are about to hug her with gratitude and take a bite, she announces with sincerity, "Only one tablespoon of flour in the whole cake!" as your fork drops (not) accidentally to the floor.

The day our kitchen became gluten-free was the day I promised that no cookie, strudel, brownie, pie, cake, tart, or treat would be left behind. The first recipes to meet the gluten-free conversion were the ones that had never been committed to paper in the first place—all the Jewish family recipes. With the very expensive—and only—brand of gritty white rice flour available at the market, I used every combination of tricks imaginable to create *mandelbrot* (Jewish biscotti) that, once baked, didn't dissolve into a sand dune.

One day, a second brand of flour showed up next to the first and from there it only got better. Today, more great tasting gluten-free ingredients are available in almost every grocery store or by mail-order, including some fantastic flours that are every bit as good as any wheat flour. There are nuances that can make gluten-free baking challenging when starting out, but after a while, it becomes just baking. And the recipes in this book will serve as proof that gluten-free baking need never be taste-free or texture-challenged.

During the great recipe conversion to gluten-free, it was the family classics that were the heart and soul of our efforts. Great-Grandma Goldie's Romanian Jewish legacy to her family was that food was love doled out in several noshes a day. I grew up in a world where if a sprinkle of something was a good thing, then a tablespoon (or two) of that same thing would be even better. A nosh was about as important as breathing.

"Oy vey, bubbala (tsk tsk). You look tired. Nosh something. Oy gevalt— you're so skinny. Nosh something. No one ever died eating two desserts. Nosh. I slaved all day making this. Try a bissel. Dinner's not for five more minutes. Nosh on this!"

Our tiny kitchen was Mom's favorite place in her house. It was Nosh Central, where she carried on the tradition of teaching me how to bake the family recipes. Tradition included: If it tastes good, more of any ingredient is always better than less; there can never be too many raisins in strudel; and finally, to actually write down a family recipe is meshuga. That last one would result in finger-wagging with the threat of being sent to live with the fabled Great-Aunt Hilda, a recluse who lived in a place called far-far-away-somewhere-else.

Although my first-generation Jewish American mother wore circa 1960s modern pillbox hats and made me a fashionable handcrafted poodle skirt for nursery school, she still channeled her inner Goldie by baking classic noshes almost every day. From toddling around the kitchen, following my mother's flour-dusted fancy red shoes, to being tall enough to watch her roll strudel dough so thin you could read the newspaper through it, I learned the bona fides of our family's recipes—and some more good lessons along the way. First, every nosh should be made with love. And second, eighty servings can be made as easily as ten, so why not make enough to feed a village? One just never knows who (or which entire neighborhood) is going to be dropping by.

And after losing my mother well before I could thoroughly memorize the family recipes, it was important to me that no future generation should have to pull the recipes out of thin air. I'm guessing that Great-Grandma Goldie wouldn't mind that the recipes are now both gluten-free and committed to paper as long as we made sure to include her rugelach along with some of the newer classics, like Cory-O Sandwich Cookies, named after her great-great-granddaughter.

Also, it is only fair to give you some warning. I come from a long line of bakers who are slightly obsessed with ingredients, odd baking pans, and reading cookbooks or recipes like some people read novels. Some of our baking techniques undoubtedly make genuine pastry chefs gasp and fall faint with astonishment (or amusement). Although we've been told over the years that *smooshing* the dough is not a technical term, nor is making a cake by *tossing* all the ingredients in a bowl and *beating it into submission* a proper way to bake, we submit that those are all Goldie-approved, time-tested methods in creating the perfect nosh.

Welcome to *Nosh on This,* a collection of Jewish-American recipes that bring the nosh back into our gluten-free lives.

GLUTEN-FREE FLOUR MATTERS

In baked goods, flour should be like a neutral canvas, providing substance and structure. It should never be the star of the final product. Flour, even gluten-free (GF) flour, should be seen and not heard. Never settle for less.

Superfine gluten-free flours are exceptionally neutral, and the ticket to some of the best homemade goodies. Our Nosh AP GF Flour blend (on the following page) is simple: brown rice flour, white rice flour, and tapioca starch, all superfine. That's it. We believe that all additives (e.g., salt, milk powder, xanthan gum, or guar gum) should be added by the baker only when necessary and not by the manufacturer because not every recipe requires the same exact amount of any of these—if any at all. The majority of our recipes are gum-free and several are dairy-free.

Superfine rice flours are milled to have zero grit and are silky smooth. Many people cannot tell the difference between regular all-purpose (AP) flour and GF superfine rice flours because they're almost indistinguishable from each other in texture. *Superfine* refers to a milling process. Unfortunately, whizzing flours in a machine with a sharp blade won't create superfine flours at home. Our favorite brands and retailers can be found in the Resources section (see page 249).

Although, these days, many AP GF blends are now available commercially or as mixes to prepare at home, many are *not* useful for every purpose. In fact, many blends begin with starches and not whole grains. Too much starch or gum can make a product gluey and the resulting crumb could be gummy or dense. Flour blends containing beans or other savory grains may be high in protein but they also have strong flavors.

Because the recipes in *Nosh on This* were developed and tested using our simple mix without any additives or a whole lot of starch, you'll find that if you prepare the recipes using other AP GF flour mixes that are heavy on the starch and gum, your results may vary.

The Nosh AP GF blend, made from Authentic Foods superfine flours (see page 254) unless otherwise stated, is two parts brown rice flour to one part each white rice flour and tapioca starch. The 2-1-1 ratio is measured by weight. A weight-to-volume one-cup measure should always be equal to 130 grams per cup (our standard), and for the best accuracy we have also given you charts showing the volume conversion for standard amounts used in our recipes. Note: You may mix up our blend using varieties other than our recommended brands of brown rice flour, white rice flour, and tapioca starch (see page 254). The flavor will probably be very similar, though the texture may be slightly different.

Gluten-free flours are nothing if not prolific. Almost anything that is not wheat (including spelt), barley, rye, or (most) oats can be gluten-free flour. In our kitchen, baking gluten-free means that we intend to end up with a really tasty baked good that is virtually indistinguishable from its gluten counterpart. Some flours that we use as ingredients are meant to be helpers or taste enhancers to baked goods. Nut flour, for example, is a fine addition in small amounts to build flavor layers, which is what baking is all about.

One last helper used in many gluten-free breads is a special starch called Expandex Modified Tapioca Starch. We find that a small amount is very useful in some recipes, primarily ones that also use yeast. It allows us to reduce the amount of xanthan gum used in the recipe and helps create that nice bendy tear we all know and miss in many gluten-free breads. Expandex will last a long time and it keeps quite well. Your breads will thank you.

NOSH AP GF FLOUR BLEND

TABLE 1: MAKING THE NOSH AP GF FLOUR MIX

	BY WEIGHT (GRAMS)				BY VOLUME (CUPS)		
Cups	Total	Brown	White	Tapioca	Brown	White	Tapioca
1	130	66	32	32	½	¼	¼
2	260	130	65	65	1	½	½
3	390	196	97	97	1½	¾	¾
4	520	260	130	130	2	1	1

TABLE 2: GENERAL FLOUR VOLUME TO METRIC CONVERSIONS

AP GF FLOUR VOLUME TO WEIGHT CONVERSION: 130 GRAMS/CUP						
Cups		¼	⅓	½	⅔	¾
		33 g	43 g	65 g	87 g	98 g
1	130 g	163 g	173 g	195 g	217 g	228 g
2	260 g	293 g	303 g	325 g	347 g	358 g
3	390 g	423 g	433 g	455 g	477 g	488 g
4	520 g	553 g	563 g	585 g	607 g	618 g

GENERAL FLOUR TIPS

- Weighing flour is most accurate, but when using volume measures, stir the flour (only) if it is compacted, and then spoon into the cup, creating a heaping peak, and level off the top with a spoon or knife, for best results.
- When creating the blend, be sure to use a whisk to blend all the flours together so they are light, not compacted, and well mingled with one another. No need to whisk again before using.
- Mix up a large batch of your homemade Nosh AP GF Flour Blend and store in a sealed container, and you will always be ready to bake.
- Nut flours should smell like freshly ground raw nuts and be refrigerated for best flavor.

SPEAKING BAKE FLUENTLY: TERMS

BAKING TIME is the oven time (or range) for baking the item in a conventional oven.

BLIND-BAKING TIME is the amount of time to bake a pastry crust prior to filling.

CHILLING the dough means placing it in the refrigerator. Otherwise, the recipe will indicate that it needs to chill in the freezer. GF dough that is chilled is more cooperative than floppy warm GF dough. You can make cutouts, form crusts, and bake chilled dough, resulting in a cookie that keeps its form and has a great crumb. Chilling is a baker's friend.

CLEAN TOOTHPICK is the best way to determine when a baked good is done. Poke it with a toothpick. If batter drips from the toothpick, bake it more. If the toothpick is dry, get it out of the oven immediately. If it comes out with crumbs that look almost dry, then it is perfectly done.

ICING THE CAKE refers to applying the frosting by using a spatula or by piping. Piping is important enough to have its own category (see "Piping," below). Icing is added to a cooled cake and the first application is called a *crumb coat*, which seals in all the pesky crumbs that a cake seems to shed. The crumb coat also helps even out all the cake divots. Once the crumb coat is dry, you can apply the final top coat of icing and decorate it any way you want.

IN THE BOWL:

- **BEAT** means to mix with vigor, and usually with an electric mixer.
- **FOLD** means to bring the ingredients from the bottom of the bowl up to the top with a swoop of a silicone spatula and repeat until everything is combined. When folding anything with whipped egg whites, fold *gently* until combined. When folding after something is mixed, fold from the bottom to mix in every last rogue dry ingredient that still lurks. Even the best of electric mixers miss some dry stuff at the bottom of the bowl.
- **MIX** means to combine ingredients any way that gets the job done. Usually this will mean using a hand or stand mixer or a boatload of elbow power.
- **SCOOP** is something that is done to dough or batter. Cookie or batter scoops are handy because they are premeasured and useful for making same-size portions.
- **STIR** means exactly that, going in a circular pattern—over and over again.
- **WHIP** means to use that arm and wrist with a whisk or electric mixer to incorporate lots of air into the mixture, making it increase in volume.
- **WHISK** is what you use to mix or whip things together. It's a tool and a verb. You'll often see references to whisking together dry ingredients—this is so they are light and combine more easily.

KNEAD WITH THE HEEL OF YOUR HAND is a way to make sure the dough ingredients are fully mixed. Smear the dough together using the heel of your hand, as if you were pushing it. Round it up and smash with the heel of your hand a few more times until it looks like dough. This is also known in my house as *smooshing* the dough.

PIPING refers to using little metal or plastic piping tips attached to a plastic bag meant for getting stuff on a baking sheet quickly and efficiently or putting decorating and festive touches on a cake. In a pinch, a resealable plastic bag with a tiny corner cut off will do. Filling, however, requires a special piping tip called a Bismarck (see "Disposable Piping Bags," page 10). Piping requires a good strong fist to squeeze the bag of dough or batter. Piping decorations on a cake can be fun, and if you make a mistake, it is easy to scrape off the icing, restuff the bag, and pipe again.

PULSE refers to the pulse button on your food processor. *Pulse a few times* means to press the button, wait, press, wait, press. Pulse as many times as needed to get the job done, but no more than that or you risk the wrath of dough that is no longer in a ragged ball but one big smear. GF dough balls are always ragged, some crumbly and ragged, others smeary ragged. Where applicable, I have listed which texture to look for.

REFRESHING most gluten-free baked goods in the oven makes them (almost) taste like fresh-baked. Place the items on a baking sheet (close together is fine) and set the oven to preheat at 350°F. Set the baking sheet in the oven right away and when the oven beeps because it has reached 350°F, turn it off and set the timer for 3 to 5 minutes. Good as new-ish. However, this will only work for breads, cookies, fruit pies, hand pies, and most pastries (other than custard- or cream-filled).

ROUGHLY CHOPPED is how chocolate and nuts should be prepared. It refers to cutting the nuts or chocolate into uneven pieces by hand. The nuts still look like nuts and not crumbs or coarse nut flour, and the majority of the chocolate still has some shape to it with just a small amount of shavings. Roughly chopping chocolate is often easiest with a serrated knife.

SIFT means to run dry stuff (flour, sugar, or cocoa) through a mesh strainer, pushing it through with a spoon or clacking the edge of the strainer with the same spoon to get the material sifted into the bowl. This eliminates stray lumps.

SPRINKLE seems obvious but can be tricky. It means to shower something over the batter, dough, or ready-to-bake items. Don't sprinkle things from a short distance. Drop them like rain so that the scatter pattern is random and they get all over. A small plop of dough will require a smaller rainstorm than will a whole cake pan or baking sheet full of dough.

STORING baked goods will most often mean in a tin. A tin is not plastic, nor is it a resealable plastic bag or plastic wrap. It really isn't even foil. There are many places to find inexpensive cookie tins, including discount stores or online. Over the years we have found that these are the best for storing GF baked goods. If they go in crispy, they stay that way. If they go in soft, they might get just a little more soft. If they're gooey, layer them with parchment.

WEIGH means getting that little $20 kitchen scale. I wish the book could come packaged with a scale. It is by far the most important kitchen tool. If you do nothing else with this book but learn how to weigh all your ingredients, then send me a note and I will buy you coffee. I was once a volume measurer. But then I got a scale and stumbled through a few months of being awkward at using it. I was never convinced a scale was smarter than the cup, so I double-checked everything. The scale was indeed very smart. So smart that I started paying attention and now I can think in grams. To avoid baked goods that are dry, crumbly, and dense, the weight of the dry ingredients (especially the flour) matters.

SPEAKING BAKE FLUENTLY: INGREDIENTS

BUTTER, VEGETABLE SHORTENING, AND OIL: Always use unsalted butter. You want to have control over the amount of salt in the recipe. Butter is not necessarily interchangeable with shortening measure for measure. Any differences will be noted in each recipe. Vegetable shortening is a great nondairy choice for fats in baked goods. Use products that have no trans fats and that are preferably organic, for best results. I use Spectrum Organic brand shortening for all of my baking. While we use canola oil for the majority of the recipes, any neutral vegetable oil will do and can be exchanged one for one. Caution: Peanut and other nut oils can have strong flavors, so avoid those unless you are using them because of the added flavor. While butter might provide a bigger flavor in say, a cupcake, using shortening as a nondairy option will make almost no difference in the quality. In fact, vegetable shortening–based "buttercream" frosting will last longer and doesn't need refrigeration. It will also hold up well in warm weather when the butter-based frosting will wilt in the heat. We still get to call it buttercream because who would order a cupcake with shortening cream?

CHOCOLATE: I could write for days about chocolate as long as I have a pile of chocolate to snack on while I type. Chocolate is as essential to baking as noshing was to my great-grandmother. Having a varied selection of chocolate at the ready means you are one serious baker, or just someone who loves chocolate. Dark chocolate bars, semisweet chocolate bars, chocolate chips, chocolate discs (pistoles or melting wafers), enrobing chocolate, unsweetened chocolate, and mini chocolate chips should all be in your baking supply cupboard. They won't lead you astray. In fact, almost everything is better with chocolate. We've listed resources (see page 254) from which you can order chocolate and not pay a fortune. I like to do that in the colder months because shipping is safer and less expensive and then I have a long-lasting supply.

COCOA POWDER: A variety of unsweetened Dutch processed cocoa powders can be used successfully in these recipes. Dutch processed cocoa is less acidic than other cocoa powders and mixes more easily with liquids. Hershey's dark or regular cocoa is Dutch processed and can be found in most grocery stores at a reasonable price. I also buy Valrhona or Guittard cocoa in bulk and use those sparingly for special occasions because they cost more.

DECORATING HELPER TOPPINGS: Favorite toppings including sprinkles, sugar, candy, espresso beans, and anything else should always be confirmed GF by reading the label or calling the manufacturer. When in doubt, leave it out.

EGGS: All of our recipes use extra-large eggs. Extra-large eggs help support gluten-free baking because it needs a little assistance—liquids in general, and liquids that provide extra proteins to help binding (read: less crumbling), which is a problem with a lot of gluten-free baked goods.

FLAVORINGS–VANILLA EXTRACT, BEAN, AND BEAN PASTE; CITRUS OILS; ALMOND AND OTHER EXTRACTS: The most common flavoring is vanilla. Use pure vanilla extract—the best you can afford. Don't ever buy imitation vanilla because the flavor is harsh and artificial and it contains unnecessary additives. All flavorings should be pure. Citrus oils can be interchangeable with a citrus extract in a pinch. Fiori di Sicilia is an indispensible flavoring with hints of vanilla and citrus. This is the one you want to use so that your baked goods smell like you just collected them from the bakery. The small bottle will not break the bank or come close to wreaking havoc on the college fund, and it lasts for years.

GLUTEN-FREE LITTLE HELPERS: Xanthan gum, a common additive in many foods, is also known in the medical world as a laxative. It is used extensively in GF baking because it is thought to help the flours act more stretchy and gluten-like. For our purposes, xanthan gum will only be utilized when absolutely necessary, usually in bread. Guar gum is a second cousin to xanthan gum in the gluten-free baking world. Guar gum is more subtle and doesn't seem to impart the flavor or gummy mouthfeel that xanthan gum does. If it's on the ingredients list, you can be assured that we have used the minimal amount needed for the recipe to work successfully.

HONEY: Cheap everyday supermarket-brand honey is probably not entirely honey and could very well be faux honey from places afar. Rashes of contaminated honey from some parts of the world have been making their way into honey that is available in the grocery because they are sold by way of third-party distributors. I like to buy honey that is produced locally. Local farmers' markets are great places to find many varieties of pure honey. You will enjoy baked goods best when they are prepared with 100 percent pure honey.

INSTANT ESPRESSO POWDER: Just like instant coffee, not ground espresso beans. Don't mistakenly use freshly ground coffee beans in anything unless you like crunching on your cup of coffee in a baked good. A decaf version of instant espresso powder is fine to use. Also, remember that brewed coffee or decaf is a liquid and not interchangeable with instant espresso powder.

LEAVENING AGENTS: Helpful leavening agents (other than yeast) are baking powder and baking soda. Baking powder should be one of those double-acting deals where it puffs up as soon as the liquid hits the dry stuff and once again when it all heats up. Double-acting baking powder is like using an umbrella with a hooded raincoat. Sometimes a little redundancy is good. What you don't want in your baking powder is any aluminum or gluten, so please read labels. Baking soda is used when there is also a corresponding acid in the recipe, like sour cream or buttermilk. Or just because you want it to have that elementary school science fair volcano effect. It's the same idea, only with a much smaller amount so that the baked good gets some puff but doesn't actually blow up in the oven.

LIQUEURS: Distilled, quality liqueurs are considered gluten-free because the distilling process removes the gluten from the product. That said, liqueurs with unidentifiable flavorings, natural flavors, caramel coloring, or anything that doesn't sound like a real food ingredient should be suspect. When in doubt, always call the manufacturer and ask. If you are sensitive to liqueurs or wish to not imbibe, substitutions are listed in each recipe.

MILK AND DAIRY-FREE MILK: There are nondairy alternatives for most recipes in this book. But dairy milk contains proteins that help make dough rise and keeps the crumb soft in cookies and cakes, and in a few recipes there is no good substitute. In most other recipes, almond milk is a fine choice, but get the unsweetened variety without flavorings for baking. Coconut milk may seem an odd choice in some recipes but it turns out to be rather neutral in flavor once it is baked. Choose full-fat canned coconut milk, stirred thoroughly, because it is *only* coconut milk, which, by the way, is a good fat.

NUTS: Unless specified, these are interchangeable. If you hate almonds, use hazelnuts or walnuts. If pecans make you happy, use those. Always toast raw nuts before using. It only takes a few minutes but lends great flavor to the final product (see page 251 for toasting instructions). Also, there are a few recipes where I use packages of store-bought roasted and salted nuts in place of toasting raw nuts—just for the zing and convenience (see page 255). Be sure to purchase nuts that are confirmed GF.

READING LABELS: This may not be an actual ingredient but it cannot be stressed more. Every single one of the recipe ingredients in this book can be located GF, but many varieties are not GF. Always read labels. Suppliers change and ingredients lists change. Look online for the company's FAQs, where allergen information is often discussed. Also, call the company. I've found most to be friendly and helpful and these days they are used to gluten-free callers' questions.

SALT: All of our recipes should be made with coarse kosher salt (Diamond brand). It is a larger salt crystal and has way better flavor but also will dissolve quickly and has no additives as table salt does. Salt that is used as a topper on savories will usually also be a coarse salt—sea salt or kosher salt.

SUGAR—SUPERFINE, CONFECTIONERS', GRANU- LATED, BROWN, COARSE: Superfine sugar is also called baker's sugar and can be found in cartons that look as if they should hold milk, not sugar. It's a finer granulated sugar that dissolves faster.

Confectioners' sugar (also known as powdered sugar) should always be sifted prior to using. The stuff notoriously clumps into tiny little hard lumps and if you don't sift it, those will be in your icing. Measure first, and then sift. Don't substitute granulated or superfine sugar for confectioners' sugar. Organic confectioners' sugar usually contains tapioca starch. Most nonorganic brands contain cornstarch.

When brown sugar is called for you can use either golden (light) or dark brown.

Coarse sugar is often called decorating sugar. It is a larger crystal that is sprinkled on top of baked goods and generally doesn't change color when baked.

YEAST: Instant or bread machine yeast is the kind you want for GF bread making. All yeast is not created equally. Be picky. I like to use Red Star or SAF, which can be found at bulk prices. Store extra yeast in the freezer for long-term use.

See Resources (page 249) for select ingredients and retailers, as well as notes on commonly used ingredients and substitutions.

SPEAKING BAKE FLUENTLY: EQUIPMENT

BAKING PANS AND BOWLS are some of my favorite things. These are the pans that are important in the Nosh kitchen.

- 9- to 10-inch cast-iron skillet
- 9½ × 4½-inch loaf pan
- 8- or 9-inch square cake pan
- 8- or 9-inch round layer cake pans (2)
- 12-count muffin pans (2)
- 24-count mini muffin pan
- 13 × 18-inch rimmed baking sheets (2)
- Metal or ceramic pie pan
- Variety of large and small tart pans
- 8-inch springform pan
- Tube pan (also known as an angel cake pan) with a removable bottom
- 9-inch tart pan with a removable bottom
- Specialty pans and rings: regular-size donut pans (2), canoe pan, English muffin rings (12)
- Metal baking pans: Dark-colored nonstick baking pans are not all that nonstick in the end, and the dark stuff makes things bake funny. I like USA Pans because they are ridiculously sturdy and will be the kind you'll hand down to some worthy heir.
- A gaggle of small, medium, and large metal mixing bowls will be workhorses that will last almost longer than vintage candy corn. I have many, including the originals we got when we were first married, which was when Jimmy Carter was famous for fireside chats.
- A double boiler is a heatproof metal or glass bowl set tightly over a small saucepan, and you probably already have one in your kitchen.

BENCH SCRAPERS AND PASTRY BLENDERS help you mix up and handle pie, tart, and pastry dough. When using a bench scraper, you can slice off a finger as easily as you can cut into dough, so take care. It is the best tool for scraping up rugelach or strudel dough. It can also unstick dough from the countertop in a flash. A pastry blender is a handheld tool that can blend the fat or some liquids into pie, pastry, or tart dough. It's the alternative to using a food processor. The best ones have comfortable padded handles.

COOLING RACKS are as necessary as baking sheets. You will have to cool the baked goods on something that doesn't collect moisture, which will happen if you place hot cookies, cupcakes, cakes, or anything from the oven on a flat surface. Cooling racks allow the air to circulate. They are cheap, and if you have a matchbox kitchen, there are some that stack.

CUPCAKE LINERS are the holy grail of beautiful cupcakes. Use greaseproof as much as possible. First, it keeps the liner looking festive and keeps all the grease from the baked item in the liner and not on your hands or clothes. Part of the cupcake charm is the look. The taste matters, but so does the package.

DISPOSABLE PIPING BAGS are plastic bags of varying sizes, all shaped into a V. You can buy them at a restaurant or baking supplier for a fraction of the retail price. Piping tips are not only fun to collect but they can also help alleviate baking stress. Load up the bag with icing and pipe anything on a baking sheet. Then scrape it up and get serious. For piping out butter cookies, you will want the largest star tip you can find. Couplers are handy because they allow the piping tip to be changed without losing all the icing in the piping bag. Get a long, skinny Bismarck piping tip for gooey filled items.

FOOD PROCESSORS make quick work of most pastry, pie, and cookie doughs and fillings. If you can only get one appliance, get this thing. Get the biggest one you can afford. More bowl space is useful, not because you want to fill it to the rim, but because it has the power to deal with whatever you throw in it. If you can swing it, get an extra bowl and even an extra blade at a kitchen supply store. My food processor is almost as old as the day we went gluten-free, which makes it more than twelve years old. I also own a small food processor called a mini-prep that costs under $40 and that I use more than the large one.

GLUTEN-DETECTING TEST STRIPS are handy to have available at home. We keep a small supply to test ingredients. Sometimes an ingredient should be GF but a manufacturer will not say with certainty that it is—we test. Conversely, sometimes a product is supposed to be GF, but might be suspect. We test.

HAND MIXERS are handy if you don't have a stand mixer. I bought mine at the red-circle-with-red-dot store. It was cheap but it works well. I love that the beaters pop off with a click of the button.

INSTANT-READ THERMOMETERS are digital probes and an important kitchen investment. We use the workhorse sold by Thermoworks because of the speed and accuracy with which it measures the temperature. You want that bread out of the oven right away if it is done, or the chocolate off the heat before it gets too hot. This digital instant-read is the way to go.

MEASURING CUPS have their place. The best function they have is as batter scoops. If you are using them for measuring, the metal kind seems to be more precise.

MEASURING SPOONS are still useful. Our spoons are not metric (ml), but we list those equivalents in Resources (see page 249). If you have more than one set of spoons, check that they all measure about the same because not all spoons (or measuring cups) are created equal, depending on where they were manufactured. Though the differences are small, some are more precise than others—metal sets seem to be more consistent than plastic or ceramic.

MESH STRAINERS are inexpensive and have multiple uses in the kitchen. Use them for sifting, straining, and rinsing. A 3-, 5-, and 8-inch set will serve all your needs.

OFFSET SPATULAS are the best thing since really good gluten-free sliced bread. They are perfect for applying icing or glaze, removing tender cookies from the baking sheet, or releasing the edges of cakes from pans, because they are thinner and kinder to your baked goods than any knife. Use restaurant supply websites or visit a warehouse—the price difference could send your child to Harvard. Get lots of very small and fewer larger offset spatulas. You won't regret it and in fact will wonder how you ever baked without them.

PARCHMENT PAPER, FOIL, AND PLASTIC WRAP are a baker's best friends. Parchment paper will line the baking sheets for most of the recipes. It also serves as a surface for rolling out dough. It's an easy task to slide the parchment with rolled dough onto a baking sheet and chill it. Foil is good for wrapping some things. Freeze-tite plastic freezer wrap is great for helping with the rolling job. It peels right off dough, especially chilled dough. This plastic wrap is stronger than the stuff at the store and less expensive in bulk.

PASTRY WHEELS OR FIVE-WHEEL BICYCLES are what the for-real pastry chefs call these tools. Otherwise these are known as a multi-wheel accordion cutter. Think pizza cutter quintuplets. They are mighty sharp and make cutting crackers or other square-ish cutout cookies a breeze. You can live with the pizza cutter, but if you start to make lots of things that require several even-steven-size pieces, a five-wheeler is your friend.

PIZZA CUTTERS roll through rugelach, strudel, and biscuit dough without crushing the edges. If you are buying one for the first time, get the best you can afford and make sure the handle is comfortable and the blade big and sharp.

SCALES are what you want to have on your kitchen counter for weighing all your ingredients because they save time, cleanup effort, and eventually lots of money, because you won't waste ingredients on recipes that don't work out because you used too much (or too little) flour by volume. Get one that you'll be inclined to keep on your countertop for easy access. Some are as small and cute as a smart phone.

SERRATED KNIVES in all sizes are a baker's helper. They can cut through thick chocolate bars, brownies, and other bar cookies, raw cookie dough rolled into logs, cakes, and bread. They might even be good on a tomato. Two sizes are particularly helpful: one with a 5-inch blade and the other with a 9-inch blade.

SILICONE SPATULAS should be replaced every once in a while. They can only go through a dishwasher a certain number of times before they turn into gooey messes that never feel clean. Avoid ones with wooden handles because of the cross-contamination issue and the fact that the handles are tough on the hands. Skinny spatulas are your friend when it comes to stuffing the piping bag. Fat spatulas are great for weighty dough and batter. Nice soft ergonomic handles are not a waste. When you get to the age where arthritis is approaching, you'll be happy to have them.

STAND MIXERS make quick work of mixing, whipping, or beating batter or dough. Get the highest wattage power you can afford. If you can, buy one that was made when Aunt Mabel was a girl. Those were made to last forever. The paddle attachment is useful for most batters and sometimes icing. The whip is used to make many frostings,whipped cream, and my favorite— marshmallows. The dough hook is sometimes used to make bread, but it is usually the one that gets left in the drawer most of the time.

WOODEN SPOONS are a little controversial. If your kitchen is totally gluten-free, you're fine. But if your kitchen is not all gluten-free, you might be inviting disaster—otherwise known as cross-contamination. The cracks that form in wood are susceptible to sucking up little bits of gluten and never letting it go. If you are baking for someone gluten-free and you are not gluten-free, just avoid wooden implements altogether and stick to plastic or stainless steel—or clean hands. Or buy new wooden spoons, store them separately, and use them only for GF baking.

See Resources (page 249) for select equipment and retailers.

Mom, with her famous
red shoes, baking

GLUTEN-FREE BAKING CONUNDRUMS ANSWERED

About Gluten-Free

Can a tiny bit of regular flour really hurt?

Plenty of people are eating gluten-free because they say it makes them feel better. While a tiny bit of gluten might not bother them, anyone with celiac disease, an auto-immune disease, will be harmed by that same tiny amount.

In the United States, the proposed industry standard is no more than 20 ppm (parts per million) gluten. Picture it: One teaspoon sitting in a container that holds more than a thousand cups by volume—a 55-gallon drum or, say, your favorite cast-iron bathtub filled with GF flour. Add one teaspoon of regular flour to that bathtub—that's all it takes to make someone with celiac quite ill.

Do I need to do anything special to my kitchen to bake gluten-free, and what does cross-contamination mean?

If your kitchen is not already gluten-free, think of it as you would for kosher preparation, like for Passover. You'll want to do a deep cleaning and make sure the utensils you use for baking gluten-free are clean and free from all gluten crumbs or dust. Using metal or ceramic bowls, silicone spatulas or spoons, or metal spoons are safe choices. Leave the wooden implements, including spoons, boards, and bowls, tucked away because they can carry forward small amounts of gluten. Or buy new wooden spoons that are used only for gluten-free baking. Use separate work spaces if you are preparing gluten and gluten-free in the same kitchen.

Make use of plastic wrap or parchment paper to contain your dough. Think of prepping the kitchen for baking gluten-free as you would if preparing a meal for someone allergic to nuts or sensitive to dairy. Serve your gluten-free guest first to avoid any chance of cross-contamination and make sure no gluten-free item is near any gluten items when serving. If you take these easy precautionary steps, your gluten-free guest will appreciate your efforts all the more. And everyone will be happy. Think kosher, bake gluten-free.

Navigating GF Recipes

Can I make substitutions and will the recipe work?

If you use the ingredients listed and their corresponding quantities, and follow the directions that accompany the recipe, you should be happy with the result and it should look similar to the accompanying photo. If there are substitutions that will work and have been tested, they will be listed (see The 411 on Frequently Used Ingredients, page 250). If you use other ingredients that aren't listed in the recipe or incorrect measures, it becomes a different recipe at that point. When I meet a new recipe, I like to try it exactly as written the first time or so. Then I may make adjustments to fit my preferences, if necessary.

Troubleshooting a recipe?

To troubleshoot a recipe, take a photo and use it to look for clues where there might be differences between the recipe you made and the photo in the book. Check off all the ingredients to make sure you used exactly what is listed in the recipe—including the amounts. See what might have been missed, left out, or altered. Substitutions are the number one reason, and the wrong amount of an ingredient is the second reason that recipes fail. Be sure to double-check how you measured the dry ingredients—especially the flour. Read over the section Gluten-free Flour Matters (see page 3) for a refresher. Then read over the instructions, line by line. Did you happen to miss a step or have you checked your oven's temperature accuracy lately? Forget to chill the dough? Missing or skipping a step in the instructions is the third most frequent reason why recipes fail. After you've examined all that, if nothing comes to mind, we are happy to help; feel free to e-mail us at glutenfreecanteen@gmail.com.

Of course, if you have a cake in pieces all over your counter right now, this advice might help you next time. But taste it. If it tastes good, proceed to the Cake Wreck Parfaits recipe (page 211) because even a cake wreck is an opportunity to be creative.

I'm new to baking gluten-free. Are there tips I should keep in mind?

Whether you are new to baking gluten-free or just need a baking refresher, these are good things to keep in mind.

- Read each recipe all the way through— at least twice.
- Plan ahead. Many types of GF dough need time to rest and chill overnight and some baked goods just taste better the next day after flavors get to mingle. Be sure to also allow enough time to complete a recipe.
- It isn't a bad idea to prep and have everything ready to go (*mise en place*).

- Ingredients should be at room temperature unless otherwise indicated in the recipe.
- Always sniff spices, seeds, nuts, and nut flours to check for freshness.
- Use an oven thermometer to double-check your oven's temperature settings.
- All recipe temperatures and times are for a conventional oven.

What's with using multiple flavorings or extracts in a single recipe?

It's because we like to layer flavors in certain recipes. This way, each bite gets more complex and the finish is something else from where the flavor began—quite on purpose. Gluten-free baking should be full of whimsy and flavor. Think of it as chasing the flavor. It's usually a trio of pure extracts: vanilla, almond, and citrus. If nothing else, you'll find that the flavor layers lend a unique complexity to what might otherwise be ordinary.

What's with all the sifting?

It's because of a syndrome called clumping. No, really, clumping is real. When confectioners' sugar settles, it makes little tiny clumps, and the same thing happens with cocoa powder. Weigh or measure, then sift. Use a simple mesh strainer and a metal soup spoon to push the stuff through and prepare to be amazed at the clumps left behind. You would not want those in your buttercream frosting.

Why does everything have to rest or be chilled? I'm hungry now.

That's why freezers were invented. Cookie dough (already scooped) freezes well. Pop that scooped dough onto a baking sheet and you can have a cookie (or two) in minutes.

For that other just-made dough, let it rest. It'll be less cranky for it. There is a trick to GF that makes things taste really good, even if you use less than great flours. It's the resting time. The longer it rests, the more the rice flours and starch absorb the liquids and the fats. The amylase is released from the remaining germ in the grain and helps develop the flavors, too. I call it the mingle. When a recipe calls for a chilled rest or freeze time, call on your patience. By letting the dough sit, the flavor and texture are improved, at times nominally, but at other times the result is phenomenal and changes the entire product from meh to OMG.

Why do gluten-free baked goods mostly look beige and never seem to brown?

Bake a cake made with rice flour, shortening, and nondairy products and it will be beige unless it begins as chocolate. Bake the same cake with eggs, butter, and milk or brush it with a little egg or milk wash, and it will turn deliciously golden-ish.

Why is gluten-free dough always so sticky?

Most GF dough should start off pretty gooey. It's because the flour and starches are a little slower to hydrate than regular AP flour is. Give it a little time and chilling. Overnight is best because all the particles will absorb the liquids by then and the sticky dough you initially put in the refrigerator will be very different than what comes out. This is especially true for nut flours.

Keep it chilled when working with the dough. Chilling before baking helps for so many reasons and will result in a better, flakier product. Many of the recipes are better tasting because they are chilled in advance of baking. It's good to read through a recipe to know whether you need to plan ahead to take advantage to get the best result possible.

About Baking Equipment

Do I really need a double boiler to melt chocolate?

Melting chocolate in the microwave is not hard, but it can be risky if you don't pay attention or get distracted, because chocolate burns easily. A double boiler keeps chocolate from getting scorched if you melt it slowly, on low heat. No one needs to buy a special double boiler—you already have one right in your kitchen if you have a metal or heatproof glass bowl that fits snugly on top of a small saucepan. You just want to heat a little bit of water in the saucepan over low heat until it is barely simmering but not boiling. Place the chocolate in the bowl and set it on top of the simmering water in the saucepan. The fit should be tight without the water touching the bottom of the bowl, and no steam should escape.

Good grief! I only have a hand mixer. Can I still make these recipes?

Yes. Yes, you can. It is best to work with larger bowls when using a hand mixer. Also, set the bowl on a wet towel or a silicone hot pad on the countertop to keep it from spinning. That will give you better control. You will be mixing a little bit longer than if you were using a stand mixer, but it should get most jobs accomplished successfully.

Will elbow grease do?

There are very few recipes that absolutely require an electric mixer or food processor. Pastry crusts, batters, and many doughs can be mixed by hand, giving the baker a good bicep workout. Be sure to take advantage of hand tools designed for the job. Pastry blenders (see page 10) can be handy when making up pastry dough, and whisks can beat egg whites to lofty peaks. Don't let the lack of power tools deter you from any baking adventure.

Why is weighing so freaking fantastic?

So glad you asked. First, cleanup is a whole lot easier if you aren't tossing every little ingredient into different bowls. You get to use one bowl most of the time when you weigh. And other times you might have to use two (one for dry, one for wet). Compare that to getting out, oh say, molasses and pouring that sticky stuff into a measuring cup, whereupon you turn that over and pour it into the mixing bowl, where it promptly takes 40 minutes to empty and even then stuff is left behind. If you were weighing it, you'd put the main bowl on the scale, zero it out, and flip the molasses container upside down (carefully—don't drop it into the bowl) and weigh in the appropriate measure.

Weighing is particularly important when using gluten-free fours. All of them—different types, including homemade and commercial AP GF blends, and even the same types from brand to brand—weigh different amounts. And that translates into a cup of one not being the same as a cup of another. Too much or too little flour in a recipe matters. And, just for fun, flour weight (and volume measurement) is different in differing climates. The best way to make sure your recipe outcome is successful is to weigh that flour—on a scale.

COOKIES and MACAROONS

These recipes would make Great-Grandma Goldie, the cookie maven, quite proud. Even the more modern cookies, like Cory-O Sandwich Cookies or Mallo Bites, would please a very picky Goldie, who loved to bake cookies and macaroons so the family would always have plenty of noshes. Every Jewish holiday seems to require a macaroon of some sort. Passover, especially, is a big showcase for macaroons. Macaroons are among the easiest gluten-free small-bite snacks to make on a moment's notice, and they store well for a long time. If you are a coconut fan or just love macaroons, this assortment offers plenty of choices—and the cookie monsters in your family won't go hungry, either.

SPECIAL EQUIPMENT

Rolling pin, cookie cutters, cookie scoops, spatulas, piping bags and tips, plenty of bowls, mixing spoons

TIPS

- Gluten-free cookie dough may look quite sticky and un-cookie-dough-like when first mixed, but chilling it will turn the dough into a more cooperative product.
- The refrigerator and freezer are your cookie dough's best friends, so just chill: overnight when possible, to help the GF flour hydrate fully and for the full flavor to develop; periodically while rolling or forming cookies, so they're easier to handle; and right before baking to help cookies hold their shape.
- Rolling out GF cookie dough between sheets of plastic wrap or parchment paper will make life easier.

- Separating eggs is easiest while they are cold, but for macaroon baking make sure egg whites are at room temperature before using.
- Macaroons taste best when baked until they look just golden, which means they have dried enough but will still have some chew.
- Coconut macaroons are best formed loosely so they bake easily and are not terribly dense and tough.

CHERRY CHOCOLATE MANDELBROT

This recipe was inspired by my best friend's mother, who was the guru of all things Jewish pastry and, luckily, our next-door neighbor. In the usual fashion of how Jewish recipes are shared, her note to me read, "add cherries and chocolate, then add more." We did, and this is the resulting recipe. The combination of cherry and chocolate is brilliant and makes a spectacular Mandelbrot. The cookies last for a week and the flavors improve with age.

1. Line a baking sheet with parchment paper.
2. Whisk together the flour, baking powder, and salt in a medium bowl. With a wooden spoon or strong silicone spatula, beat together the shortening and sugar in a large bowl. Beat in the eggs, vanilla, and almond extract. Stir in the dry ingredients and finish mixing the dough. Stir in the chocolate and cherries.
3. On the prepared baking sheet, with wet hands, form the dough into three logs 1 inch high and 3 inches wide. Cover loosely with plastic wrap and refrigerate for 2 hours.
4. Preheat the oven to 350°F.
5. Bake for 35 to 40 minutes. The logs will not be brown. Let cool thoroughly on the pan. Slice gently with a serrated knife into 1-inch-wide pieces. Place the slices ¼ inch apart on the baking sheet.
6. Return the pan to the oven, turn down the temperature to 300°F, and bake for 25 minutes. Turn off the oven. Leave the cookies in the oven for 20 to 30 minutes more to continue browning. Keep an eye on them and remove the pan once they are toasty brown. Transfer the cookies to a rack and let cool completely.

MAKES 21 TO 24 MANDELBROT

CHILLING TIME: 2 hours

BAKING TIME: 35 to 40 minutes (plus 25 to 55 minutes for the second baking)

DAIRY-FREE

Nosh AP GF flour (page 4)
390 grams | 3 cups

baking powder
2 teaspoons

kosher salt
½ teaspoon

shortening
150 grams | 12 tablespoons or ¾ cup

sugar
200 grams | 1 cup

eggs
180 grams | 3 extra-large

vanilla extract
1½ teaspoons

almond extract
½ teaspoon

bittersweet chocolate chunks or chips
170 grams | 1 cup

dried cherries
150 grams | 1 cup

ALMOND MANDELBROT

BAKING TIME: 30 minutes
(plus 40 to 45 minutes more
for the second baking)

DAIRY-FREE

Almond mandelbrot go especially well with that midmorning cup of coffee or tea. The back-note lemon flavor is a modern remake of this classic cookie from my childhood kitchen. The dough forms into logs best if you use your hands to pat it into shape. This recipe is the one that my mother made most often and is probably the most traditional. *Mandelbrot* translates literally to "almond bread," which would technically make this recipe almond-almond bread.

1. Preheat the oven to 350°F. Line a baking sheet with parchment paper.
2. Place the sugar in a small bowl. Work in the lemon zest with clean fingertips until the sugar is fully coated. Let the mixture rest for 15 minutes before using.
3. In a large bowl, whisk together the flour, baking powder, and salt. Add the sugar mixture and whisk to combine. In a small bowl, whisk together the lemon juice, vanilla, almond extract, lemon oil, canola oil, and eggs. Add the wet ingredients to the dry and stir. Stir in the almonds.
4. On the prepared baking sheet, with wet hands, form the dough into two logs ½ inch tall and 2 inches wide. Bake for 10 minutes. Turn down the temperature to 325°F and bake for 20 minutes more. The logs will not be brown. Let cool thoroughly on the pan. Slice the logs gently with a serrated knife into 1-inch-wide slices. Be gentle—they tend to crumble at this point. Place the slices on the baking sheet. Bake for an additional 10 minutes. Turn down the temperature to 275°F and bake for 30 to 35 minutes more, until golden brown. Transfer the cookies to a rack and let cool completely.

sugar
150 grams | ¾ cup

lemon zest, freshly grated
10 grams | 2 tablespoons

Nosh AP GF flour (page 4)
390 grams | 3 cups

baking powder
1 teaspoon

kosher salt
¼ teaspoon

fresh lemon juice
1 tablespoon

vanilla extract
1½ teaspoons

almond extract
½ teaspoon

lemon oil, Boyajian preferred
(see page 7)
¼ teaspoon
  or
lemon extract
½ teaspoon

canola oil
80 grams | ⅓ cup

eggs
180 grams | 3 extra-large

almonds, toasted (see page 251) and
roughly chopped
225 grams | 1½ cups

DOUBLE CHOCOLATE CHUNK MANDELBROT

This *mandelbrot* is for people who think one kind of chocolate in a cookie is just not enough. The chocolate chips will keep their shape, while the chopped bar chocolate will become melty and gooey as it bakes, the best of both chocolate worlds.

1. Line a baking sheet with parchment paper.
2. In a large bowl, whisk together the flour, baking powder, and salt. In a medium bowl, using a wooden spoon or a strong silicone spatula, beat together the butter and sugar. Beat in the eggs, vanilla, and almond and orange extracts. Stir the wet ingredients into the dry until combined. The dough will be sticky. Add the chocolate chips and chopped chocolate and stir in gently but thoroughly.
3. On the prepared baking sheet, with wet hands, form the dough into two logs 1 inch high and 3 inches wide. Cover loosely with plastic wrap and refrigerate for 2 hours.
4. Preheat the oven to 350°F. Bake for 35 to 40 minutes. The logs will not be brown. Let cool thoroughly and refrigerate so the chocolate hardens before slicing. Once the chocolate is set, slice gently with a serrated knife into 1-inch-wide pieces. Place the slices ¼ inch apart on the baking sheet. Return the pan to the oven, turn down the temperature to 300°F, and bake for 25 minutes. Turn off the oven. Leave the cookies in the oven for 30 to 35 minutes more to continue browning. Keep an eye on them and remove the pan once they are toasty brown. Transfer the cookies to a rack and let cool completely.

Nosh AP GF flour (page 4)
455 grams | 3½ cups

baking powder
2 teaspoons

kosher salt
½ teaspoon

unsalted butter, slightly softened
180 grams | 12 tablespoons
or ¾ cup

sugar
200 grams | 1 cup

eggs
180 grams | 3 extra-large

vanilla extract
1 teaspoon

almond extract
1 teaspoon

orange extract
½ teaspoon

semisweet chocolate chips
170 grams | 1 cup

bittersweet bar chocolate,
roughly chopped
275 grams | one 10-ounce bar |
2½ cups

KICHLACH

Nosh AP GF flour (page 4)
390 grams | 3 cups

sugar
400 to 500 grams | 2 to 2½ cups

kosher salt
½ teaspoon

eggs
360 grams | 6 extra-large

canola oil
115 grams | ½ cup

vanilla extract
1 teaspoon

almond extract
½ teaspoon

Kichlach are wonderfully crunchy, bow tie–shaped sugar-coated cookies with lots of puff. The trick to making these is to work quickly and avoid interruptions because the dough gets soggy while lazing around on the bed of sugar. Adapted from *Joan Nathan's Jewish Holiday Cookbook*, this recipe is a classic. The batter rest time is critical, and handling the dough requires a bit of care, but once you have the routine down they are easy to prepare.

1. In a large bowl, whisk together the flour, 1 tablespoon of the sugar, and the salt. Using an electric mixer on low speed, mix in the eggs, oil, vanilla, and almond extract. Raise the mixer speed to high and beat for 5 minutes (7 to 9, if using a hand mixer), scraping down the sides of the bowl occasionally. Scrape down the sides once more and cover the bowl with plastic wrap. Let the batter rest in the refrigerator for 2 to 3 hours.

2. Preheat the oven to 350°F and line two baking sheets with parchment paper.

3. Place half of the remaining sugar on a large parchment paper–lined surface. Gather the dough—it will be sticky—and drop it into the center of the sugared surface. Top the dough with most of the remaining sugar, reserving ½ cup (100 g) of sugar. Using clean hands covered in some of the remaining sugar, gently pat the dough flat. Cover with plastic wrap. Pat gently into a rectangle until ⅓ inch thick. Make sure the sugar on the bottom is keeping the dough from sticking to the surface. Remove the plastic wrap and sprinkle all the remaining sugar on top. The rectangle should be approximately 16 × 13 inches.

4. Working quickly, cut the dough into ½-inch strips, using a pizza cutter (also coated in sugar). Cut those strips into 2- to 3-inch pieces. Twist each dough piece so it looks like a bow tie—one twist turn will do it. Place the bow ties an inch apart on the prepared baking sheets. Half of the dough should fit on one baking sheet. Don't dawdle because the sugar will actually start to melt the dough.

5. Bake the *kichlach* for 15 minutes and rotate the pans for even baking. Bake for 15 to 25 minutes more, until they are lightly golden and dry. Some of the sugar may start to get very dark, but it is important for the *kichlach* to bake thoroughly. Let cool on the pans just until you can handle them and then transfer the cookies to a rack to cool completely.

Nosh AP GF flour (page 4)
185 grams | scant 1½ cups

superfine sugar
100 grams | ½ cup

unsweetened cocoa powder, sifted
65 grams | ⅔ cup

kosher salt
1 teaspoon

baking soda
½ teaspoon

baking powder
¼ teaspoon

cold unsalted butter
115 grams | 8 tablespoons or ½ cup

shortening
1 tablespoon

egg
60 grams | 1 extra-large

vanilla extract
1 teaspoon

orange extract
½ teaspoon

FILLING

shortening
130 grams | 11 tablespoons
or ⅔ cup

confectioners' sugar, sifted
330 grams | 3 cups

Nosh AP GF flour (page 4)
2 teaspoons

milk
1 to 2 tablespoons

kosher salt
½ teaspoon

vanilla extract
1 teaspoon

orange extract
½ teaspoon

CORY-O SANDWICH COOKIES

There was an Oreo thief in our house when our kids were small. We had to start hiding the cookies, but the little thief was clever and could find them with her Oreo X-ray vision. I don't think there was anyone ever who came close to loving Oreos as much as our youngest daughter. But there is also nothing like a homemade Oreo-like treat—deep, dark cookies that are slightly salty and not too sweet stuffed with a delicious smooth filling. I think the X-ray-proficient child, now all grown up, would agree.

1. In the bowl of a food processor, pulse to combine the flour, superfine sugar, cocoa, salt, baking soda, and baking powder. Cut the butter into tablespoon-size pieces. Add the butter and shortening and pulse until the mixture looks like coarse crumbs. Add the egg, vanilla, and orange extract. Pulse until the mixture forms a ragged ball. Turn out the dough onto plastic wrap. Knead with the heel of your hand until the dough becomes smooth. It won't take long. Divide the dough in half. Wrap each piece in plastic wrap and refrigerate for 4 hours—overnight is even better.

2. Preheat the oven to 375°F. Line two baking sheets with parchment paper. Remove the dough from the refrigerator. Sandwich the dough between sheets of plastic wrap and roll out each dough ball until it is ¼ inch thick. Slide the dough onto the prepared baking sheets and refrigerate for 15 minutes. While the dough is still cold, cut out 1½-inch circles and remove the scraps. Roll the scraps, chill in the refrigerator, and cut out more circles, using up all of the dough. Place the cutouts close together on the prepared baking sheets. Dock the dough by poking two sets of holes in each circle, using a fork. Bake for 8 minutes and rotate the pans for even baking. Bake for 2 to 3 minutes more. Remove the cookies from the oven. Let cool for a few minutes on the pan and then transfer the cookies to a rack to cool completely.

3. While the cookies cool, prepare the filling. Using an electric mixer beginning on low and finishing on high, whip

together the shortening, confectioners' sugar, flour, 1 tablespoon of the milk, and the salt, vanilla, and orange extract. If the filling is thicker than cookie dough, add up to 1 tablespoon more milk.

4. When the cookies are completely cool, top each with a scant teaspoon of filling by rolling the filling into a ball and placing it on the flat side of a cookie. Top with a matching cookie, flat side up. Press gently to flatten slightly, until the filling comes to the edge of the cookie.

BLACK & WHITE COOKIES

shortening
30 grams | 2 tablespoons plus 1 teaspoon

unsalted butter, at room temperature
95 grams | 6½ tablespoons

granulated sugar
175 grams | heaping ¾ cup

kosher salt
¼ teaspoon

eggs
120 grams | 2 extra-large

vanilla extract
1 teaspoon

Fiori di Sicilia (see page 7), strongly recommended but optional
¼ teaspoon

lemon extract
¼ teaspoon

Nosh AP GF flour (page 4)
300 grams | 2⅓ cups

baking powder
1 teaspoon

whole milk
120 grams | ½ cup

WHITE GLAZE

confectioners' sugar, sifted
330 grams | 3 cups

hot tap water
45 to 75 grams | 3 to 5 tablespoons

light corn syrup
½ teaspoon

vanilla extract
½ teaspoon

BLACK GLAZE

confectioners' sugar, sifted
330 grams | 3 cups

unsweetened cocoa powder, sifted
15 grams | 2 tablespoons

hot tap water
45 to 75 grams | 3 to 5 tablespoons

light corn syrup
½ teaspoon

vanilla extract
½ teaspoon

For anyone who has wandered into a Jewish bakery yearning for a black & white cookie, this gluten-free version you can make at home is as good as or better than you remember. The cookies are huge, at five inches around. Fiori di Sicilia, a citrus-vanilla flavoring, takes the cookie from great to extraordinary-fabulous-just-like-a-bakery-but-better. Do be tempted to get some, but don't be tempted to use more Fiori di Sicilia than the amount recommended in the recipe—it is very strong. Not only are these cookies from your own kitchen going to be popular, but they're also quite economical at less than $1 per cookie.

1. Preheat the oven to 325°F. Line two baking sheets with parchment paper.
2. In a large bowl, cream the shortening, butter, granulated sugar, salt, eggs, vanilla, Fiori di Sicilia, and lemon extract together until smooth and fluffy. In a medium bowl, whisk the flour with the baking powder. Add to the wet ingredients and mix just until smooth. Add the milk and mix thoroughly.
3. Scoop the batter with a ½-cup measure onto the prepared baking sheets, six mounds to a sheet. Using the back of a spoon or, even better, a small offset spatula, spread each mound into a 4-inch round with a slight dome in the center, giving the rounds room to spread just slightly.
4. Bake the cookies for 8 minutes and rotate the pans for even baking. Bake for 7 to 9 minutes more, or just until the edges look as if they are beginning to gain a golden color. Let them cool on the pan for a few minutes and then carefully transfer to a rack to cool completely before applying the glazes. They're fragile until they are completely cool, so handle them carefully.
5. To make the white glaze, sift the confectioners' sugar into a medium bowl. Stir in the hot water by the tablespoon just until the mixture runs off the spoon but seems very thick. Stir in the corn syrup and vanilla.

6. Place the rack on a baking sheet to catch the drips. Turn over the cookies to the flat side. Using a spoon and an offset spatula, apply the white glaze to one half of the top of each cookie. Make sure you apply enough glaze so that it is completely white and you cannot see the cookie through the glaze. Let the white glaze set while you prepare the black glaze.

7. To make the black glaze, sift the confectioners' sugar and cocoa into a medium bowl and whisk together. Add the hot water 1 tablespoon at a time and stir until the mixture is smooth and lump-free and drips off the spoon but is still rather thick. Stir in the corn syrup and vanilla.

8. Using a spoon and a clean offset spatula, apply the black glaze to the other half of each cookie top, all the way to the white glaze, overlapping slightly in a straight line along the center for the best look. Place the iced cookies far from one another on the rack and let the glaze harden completely. It will take at least an hour, depending on the humidity and temperature, but don't refrigerate them or you'll lose the shine on the glaze. You won't be able to stack them until the next day, when the glaze is thoroughly dry.

MALLO BITES

MAKES 12 COOKIES

CHILLING TIME: 5 to 24 hours
(marshmallows)

BAKING TIME: 8 to 9 minutes
(plus marshmallow and chocolate
coating setting times)

DAIRY-FREE

Mallomars were one of the cookies we missed most. Learning to make them took great patience and many wrecks. The biggest lesson was to make a manageable amount because the marshmallow is the boss of everything. Once it sets, everyone can just go home. Working on a batch of a dozen at a time, you can beat the clock and get them formed without the marshmallow turning into the shape of your piping bag. For best results, begin making the marshmallow after the cookie dough is formed and chilling in the refrigerator.

1. In the food processor, pulse the flour, sugar, baking powder, and salt. Add the shortening and pulse a few times. Add the vanilla, orange extract, and egg and pulse until the mixture comes together in a ragged ball. Turn out the dough onto plastic wrap. Knead with the heel of your hand to bring the dough together. Flatten the dough into a disk, wrap in the plastic, and refrigerate for 4 hours.

2. Preheat the oven to 325°F. Line a baking sheet with parchment paper.

3. Break off the dough into approximately ½-inch pieces and roll each in your hand until it is a smooth ball. Place them ½ inch apart on the prepared baking sheet. Flatten each cookie with clean fingers into a 1-inch round. Refrigerate the baking sheet while preparing the marshmallow. You will begin baking the cookies when you get to the end of step 5, whipping the marshmallow.

4. To make the marshmallow topping, place the gelatin in the bottom of a large bowl. Pour 175 grams (¾ cup) of the cold water over the gelatin and let the mixture sit without stirring or disturbing it for 5 minutes or so. You'll be using a mixer after the next step, so be sure to have it ready. In the meantime, in a small but deep saucepan, gently stir the sugar with the corn syrup, salt, and remaining 60 grams (¼ cup) of water once or twice just to combine. Without stirring it again, heat the mixture on medium heat, swirling the pan every once in a while, until it is

Nosh AP GF flour (page 4)
150 grams | 1 cup plus 2 heaping tablespoons

sugar
50 grams | ¼ cup

baking powder
1 teaspoon

kosher salt
½ teaspoon

shortening
70 grams | 6 tablespoons or ¼ cup plus 2 tablespoons

vanilla extract
½ teaspoon

orange extract
¼ teaspoon

egg
60 grams | 1 extra-large

MARSHMALLOW TOPPING

unflavored gelatin
14 grams | two ¼-ounce envelopes

cold water
235 grams | 1 cup

sugar
200 grams | 1 cup

light corn syrup
110 grams | ⅓ cup

kosher salt | ¼ teaspoon

vanilla extract
1 teaspoon

nonstick spray, for greasing

CHOCOLATE COVERING

semisweet bar chocolate,
roughly chopped
450 grams | 1-pound bar | scant 4 cups

240°F on an instant-read thermometer, about 5 minutes. The mixture will turn clear by the time it reaches 240°F. Remove it from the heat.

5. Begin mixing the gelatin and water in the large bowl on low speed. With the mixer on, pour the heated sugar down the side of the bowl, keeping it away from the beaters or it will splash. Be careful—the mixture is very hot. As soon as the sugar is incorporated, turn up the mixer speed little by little until the mixture begins to get frothy and fluffy. It will stink to high heaven, and you might want to not breathe much at this point. Keep going and turn the speed to high. Continue until the mixture gets huge in volume and turns marshmallow white with giant fluffy white peaks. It should take anywhere from 5 to 8 minutes in a stand mixer and 14 to 16 minutes with a hand mixer. Add the vanilla and whip just until mixed in thoroughly.

6. Bake the cookies for 8 to 9 minutes. They will look rather beige, though they are baked. Remove from the oven and apply the marshmallow topping (see step 7) while they are still warm. The marshmallow will not stick to the cookies unless you apply it while the cookies are warm. If your timing is not perfect, just warm the cookies for 1 minute in a 300°F oven before applying the marshmallow topping.

7. Fit a large plastic piping bag with a ½-inch regular tip (larger is fine). Grease the inside of the bag generously with nonstick spray. Grease a silicone spatula with nonstick spray so you can transfer the marshmallow easily into the prepared piping bag. Working quickly, scrape the marshmallow into the prepared piping bag. Immediately begin piping small "kiss" shapes on top of each cookie. Keep the tip pointed straight up and down while piping. Move quickly because the marshmallow will begin to set. If you have leftover marshmallow, pipe additional kisses onto a parchment paper sheet and let those set.

8. Let the cookies with marshmallow set on a rack for at least 5 hours or overnight. The longer they set, the less sticky they become.

9. To make the chocolate covering, temper the chocolate (see page 236) when ready to dip the cookies.

10. Line a baking sheet with parchment paper. Get your Mallo Bites ready to dip by placing them next to the chocolate bowl. Drop each Mallo Bite into the chocolate one at a time and flip it over to coat completely, using two forks or chocolate dipping forks (see page 236). Gently pop the Mallo Bite onto one fork, using the other to help, and rap it on the edge of the bowl to get rid of any extra drips. Place on the prepared baking sheet and repeat. Let the chocolate set and harden. Do not refrigerate or the chocolate will lose its shine.

11. If the chocolate has not set or hardened after a few hours, then the tempering didn't work. The Mallo Bites will still taste great, but you will want to place them in the refrigerator and not let them get back to room temperature, or the chocolate will soften—serve chilled.

CHOCOLATE CHIP MACAROONS

MAKES 16 TO 18 MACAROONS

BAKING TIME: 21 to 23 minutes

DAIRY-FREE

These macaroon cookies are made with just six ingredients. They may even be slightly good for you. Be sure to use unsweetened shredded coconut (see page 250). But if you can only find the sweetened stuff, use less sugar by about half, or to taste. Keep an eye on them while baking because they go from golden to well done in a flash.

egg whites
70 grams | 2 extra-large

sugar
150 grams | ¾ cup

unsweetened shredded coconut
170 grams | 3 cups

almond extract
½ teaspoon

kosher salt
¼ teaspoon

bittersweet or semisweet chocolate chips
170 grams | 1 cup

1. Preheat the oven to 350°F. Line two baking sheets with parchment paper.
2. In a large bowl, stir all of the ingredients except the chocolate chips until fully mixed. Let the mixture sit for 3 minutes. Stir again. Add the chocolate chips and stir to mix well. Using a ⅓-cup ice-cream scoop, place eight or nine mounds on each prepared baking sheet. Flatten each macaroon, using clean, damp fingers.
3. Bake for 15 minutes and rotate the pans for even baking. Bake for 6 minutes more for a deep golden toasted color, or 8 minutes more for a darker, crunchy macaroon.
4. Let cool on the parchment. You will have to peel the cookies from the parchment when they are cooled, but they will come off. Transfer to a rack to cool completely. Store in an airtight tin with parchment between the layers.

MOM'S DOUBLE CHOCOLATE GELT

granulated sugar
100 grams | ½ cup

Nosh AP GF flour (page 4)
130 grams | 1 cup

unsweetened cocoa powder, sifted
35 grams | ⅓ cup

baking soda
¼ teaspoon

kosher salt
¼ teaspoon

shortening
95 grams | 8 tablespoons or ½ cup

egg
60 grams | 1 extra-large

brewed coffee (decaf is fine)
1 teaspoon

vanilla extract
½ teaspoon

orange extract
¼ teaspoon

walnuts, roughly chopped
60 grams | ½ cup

semisweet mini chocolate chips
85 grams | ½ cup

coarse sugar, optional
125 grams | ½ cup

Before my mother ran off to her standing Saturday morning hair appointment, she would bake a batch of chocolate drop cookies. The cookie jar overflowed until one of my older brothers woke up. By the time Mom came back with her hair perfectly coifed, there were only crumbs, and sometimes not even that because one particular older brother liked to empty the cookie jar remnants onto his bowl of cereal. My mother did hide a few extra cookies for me, knowing I was last in line after three older (and much taller) brothers; but keeping four children in cookies was no easy feat in our house. These classic chocolate cookies remade remind me of Hanukkah *gelt* and they are so much easier to eat than those chocolate coins wrapped Houdini-like in foil. The dough is crumbly until it is kneaded together, so don't be fooled into thinking it needs additional liquid.

1. Preheat the oven to 350°F. Line two baking sheets with parchment paper.
2. In a large bowl, whisk together the granulated sugar, flour, cocoa, baking soda, and salt. Mix in the shortening. Add the egg, coffee, vanilla, and orange extract. Fold in the nuts and chocolate chips. Knead until the dough comes together.
3. Roll the dough into heaping teaspoon-size balls and flatten slightly into ¼-inch-thick disks. Roll the outside edges in coarse sugar—like rolling a penny on its edges in sand—if desired. Place ¼ inch apart on the prepared baking sheets. Bake for 12 to 14 minutes. Transfer the cookies to a rack and let cool.

DORABLE FUDGIES

MAKES 60 TO 65 SMALL
COOKIES

CHILLING TIME: 3 hours to 2 days
(dough)

BAKING TIME: 9 to 12 minutes

DAIRY-FREE OPTION AVAILABLE

These are the cookies that the women behind the counter at the neighborhood Jewish bakery used to give me if I looked especially cute while running errands with my mom. I instantly fell in love with these butter cookies, and whenever I see them in a bakery case, it brings back great memories. Pipe these into little stars and fill with chocolate for your very own homemade gluten-free Stella D'oro look-alikes. The recipe makes enough cookies for a small village. The very sticky dough is best made a day ahead and chilled, for best handling and flavor.

1. In a food processor, pulse together the confectioners' sugar, superfine sugar, and almond paste until smooth. Add the flour and salt and mix. Cut the butter into two or three pieces. Add the butter and shortening to the processor. Pulse until the mixture looks like coarse crumbs. Add the egg, egg white, vanilla, and almond and orange extracts and pulse until the dough is mixed. Scrape the sticky dough onto plastic wrap. Wrap and refrigerate the dough for at least 3 hours; overnight is better and it keeps in the refrigerator for up to 3 days.

2. Bring the dough to room temperature before piping. Place in a large piping bag with a ½-inch or larger star tip. Pipe 1-inch stars ½ inch apart directly onto unlined, ungreased baking sheets. Alternatively, using clean hands, roll the dough into heaping-teaspoon-size balls and flatten into disks on the baking sheet. Take one chocolate disc/wafer or pistole and place it in the center of each cookie. Press down on the chocolate so that it sits below the rim of the dough. Refrigerate for 30 minutes before baking to make sure the cookies keep their shape. Preheat the oven to 325°F.

3. Bake for 9 to 12 minutes, or just until starting to turn color on the edges. Leave the cookies on the baking sheet to cool without touching them because they are especially fragile. When cold, use an offset spatula to transfer the cookies to a rack.

confectioners' sugar
55 grams | ½ cup

superfine sugar
50 grams | ¼ cup

GF almond paste
30 grams | 2 tablespoons
  or
Almond Schmear (page 124)
45 grams | ¼ cup

Nosh AP GF flour (page 4)
230 grams | 1¾ cups

kosher salt
½ teaspoon

unsalted butter, slightly softened
90 grams | 6 tablespoons

shortening
110 grams | 9 tablespoons or
½ cup plus 1 tablespoon
  or
shortening (instead of butter and
shortening)
168 grams | 14 tablespoons or 1 cup
minus 2 tablespoons

egg
60 grams | 1 extra-large

egg white
35 grams | 1 extra-large

vanilla extract
½ teaspoon

almond extract
½ teaspoon

orange extract
¼ teaspoon

semisweet chocolate baking
discs (melting wafers or pistoles),
Guittard preferred
225 grams | 1½ cups

LINZER HEARTS

Nosh AP GF flour (page 4)
300 grams | 2⅓ cups

granulated sugar
100 grams | ½ cup

confectioners' sugar, sifted
30 grams | ¼ cup

ground cardamom
½ teaspoon

lemon peel powder, optional
½ teaspoon

kosher salt
¼ teaspoon

unsalted butter, slightly softened
180 grams | 12 tablespoons or ¾ cup

egg
60 grams | 1 extra-large

egg yolks
75 grams | 3 extra-large

almond extract
½ teaspoon

raspberry liqueur, Framboise
preferred, or raspberry flavoring
½ teaspoon

RASPBERRY FILLING

seedless raspberry jam, Bonne
Maman preferred
300 grams | 15 tablespoons

raspberry liqueur, Framboise
preferred
1 tablespoon
 or
raspberry flavoring
1 teaspoon

TOPPING

confectioners' sugar, sifted
55 grams | ½ cup

Similar to the French sugar or butter cookie, this is a wonderful gift-giving cookie. It can be cut into any shape you wish, but to get that pretty stained-glass look, be sure to protect the jam from loose confectioners' sugar while assembling the cookie. Keeping the dough chilled throughout the cookie-making process will make all the steps easy. The dough is best made ahead and chilled a day or so in the refrigerator, for better handling and flavor, which if you have a busy schedule, also breaks up the cookie-making effort into manageable blocks of time.

1. In a food processor, pulse together the flour, granulated sugar, confectioners' sugar, cardamom, lemon peel powder (if using), and salt until combined. Add the butter and pulse until the mixture looks like coarse, uneven, sandy crumbs. In a small bowl, whisk the egg, egg yolks, almond extract, and raspberry liqueur. Add to the flour mixture and pulse until it forms a sticky, ragged dough ball.

2. Place the dough on plastic wrap. Wrap and refrigerate the dough at least overnight; 2 days is even better.

3. Preheat the oven to 350°F. Line two baking sheets with parchment paper. Divide the dough in half. Sandwich each half of the dough between two layers of plastic wrap while still chilled and roll out until ¼ inch thick. Cut into thirty 3½ to 4-inch heart shapes, using a cookie cutter. Cut out the center of fifteen of the hearts with a 2-inch heart-shaped cutter. Chill the rolled dough if it becomes too soft to handle. Using an offset spatula, transfer the cutouts to the prepared baking sheets. Bake the cookies for 5 minutes and rotate the pans for even baking. Turn down the temperature to 325°F. Bake for 15 to 18 minutes more, or just until the cookies turn a pale golden brown.

4. Let the cookies cool for 30 minutes on the baking sheet without touching them—they will break if you move them while warm. Once cool to the touch, transfer to a rack to cool completely. Use the small heart cutouts for another purpose: a snack for the baker or treats for small kids.

5. To make the raspberry filling, in a small saucepan, mix the jam with the raspberry liqueur. Cook over low heat until the mixture simmers and reduces slightly, 5 to 6 minutes.

6. Let cool thoroughly. The mixture will thicken as it cools.

7. For the topping, keeping them far, far away from the whole cookies, line up all the cookies that have a heart cutout, bottom side (flat side) up, on a rack with a baking sheet under it to catch the excess sugar. Using a mesh strainer, shake confectioners' sugar in a deep layer onto the cutout cookies until they are all snowy white.

8. Turn the whole cookies bottom side up and place the jam on each cookie, almost to the edges, but leaving some breathing room. You will use a teaspoon of jam for each cookie, but make sure the center looks like a pool of jam. Place a sugar-coated cutout cookie top over a jam-covered whole bottom and gently push it down without disturbing the confectioners' sugar edging.

9. Handle the cookies along the edge to avoid disturbing the confectioners' sugar. Place on a rack to set for 2 to 4 hours. Try to not disturb them before they set, so the sugar does not fall into the jam.

CHOCOLATE DRIZZLE ALMOND MACAROONS

Macaroons made with coconut and almond flour and topped with chocolate are chewy and nutty and provide just the right finish to a great holiday dinner. They also might wake up Great-Aunt Sylvia after a long seder. Be sure to form loose haystacks so they aren't quite as dense as, say, foam pillows.

1. Preheat the oven to 350°F. Line two baking sheets with parchment paper.
2. In a large bowl, mix the egg whites, almond flour, sugar, almond extract, vanilla, salt, and coconut with a wooden spoon until fully incorporated. Using a scoop or wet hands, place ¼-cup mounds on the prepared baking sheets. Form into haystacks with wet fingers.
3. Let them sit at room temperature for 30 minutes. Place the baking sheets in the oven and turn down the temperature to 325°F. Bake for 20 minutes and rotate the pans for even baking. Turn down the temperature to 300°F. Bake for 10 to 15 minutes more, or until they are golden brown. Let cool thoroughly on the pans before adding the chocolate drizzle.
4. Melt the chocolate in a microwave on high in two 20-second bursts, stirring each time, or in a double boiler on the stove top over low heat. While the macaroons are on the parchment paper, drizzle the melted chocolate in random patterns over the completely cooled macaroons, using a small piping tip or a fork. Let the chocolate set for about 30 minutes.

egg whites
105 grams | 3 extra-large

GF almond flour
10 grams | 2 tablespoons

sugar
65 grams | ⅓ cup

almond extract
1 teaspoon

vanilla extract
½ teaspoon

kosher salt
¼ teaspoon

sweetened shredded coconut
375 grams | 4 cups

bittersweet or semisweet chocolate chips, melted
170 grams | 1 cup

LEMON ZEST MACAROONS

MAKES 20 TO 24 MACAROONS

BAKING TIME: 30 to 35 minutes

DAIRY-FREE

Every Passover we would buy a few cans of the popular store-bought brand of macaroons. That they were consumed at all is testament to the fact that my brothers would eat anything that looked like food. These macaroons are a vast improvement over any canned version and take little effort. This recipe uses sweetened coconut to best mimic those flavors we remember, but the macaroons are much tastier, especially after resting overnight.

1. Preheat the oven to 350°F. Line two baking sheets with parchment paper.
2. In a small bowl, mix the lemon zest into the sugar with your fingertips until thoroughly combined. Let the mixture rest for 15 minutes before using.
3. In a large bowl, mix the egg whites, lemon oil, vanilla, salt, and sugar mixture until fully combined. Stir in the coconut and mix thoroughly. Using a scoop or wet hands, place ¼-cup haystack piles of macaroons ½ inch apart on the baking sheets. Pinch the tops with wet fingers to accentuate the haystack look.
4. Let them sit at room temperature for 30 minutes before baking. Place the baking sheets in the oven and turn down the temperature to 325°F. Bake for 20 minutes and rotate the pans for even baking. Turn down the temperature to 300°F. Bake for 10 to 15 minutes more, or until the cookies are golden. If you like them slightly drier, place them back in a turned-off but still-warm oven for another 10 to 15 minutes. Transfer the cookies to a rack and let cool completely. They taste best on the second day, after the flavors mingle.

lemon zest, Meyer lemon preferred, freshly grated
 15 grams | 3 tablespoons

sugar
 65 grams | ⅓ cup

egg whites
 105 grams | 3 extra-large

lemon oil, Boyajian preferred (see page 7)
 ½ teaspoon
   or
 lemon extract
 1 teaspoon

vanilla extract
 ½ teaspoon

kosher salt
 ¼ teaspoon

sweetened shredded coconut
 375 grams | 4 cups

egg whites, at room temperature
140 grams | 4 extra-large

vanilla extract
1½ teaspoons

brewed coffee (decaf is fine)
1 teaspoon

orange oil, Boyajian preferred
(see page 7)
¼ teaspoon
or
pure orange extract
½ teaspoon

orange zest, freshly grated
5 grams | 1 tablespoon

confectioners' sugar, sifted
290 grams | 2⅔ cups

unsweetened cocoa powder, sifted
100 grams | scant 1 cup

kosher salt
½ teaspoon

toasted almonds, roughly chopped
(see page 251)
150 grams | 1 cup

dark chocolate orange bar,
Newman's or Fair Trade preferred,
roughly chopped
85 grams | one 3-ounce bar

FLOURLESS CHOCOLATE ORANGE COOKIES

We first met a similar cookie at a fancy Los Angeles hotel, where I begged the concierge to ask the chef for the recipe. Months later it came in the mail with a note saying the chef had no idea how to write the recipe for a home kitchen because he used baker's percentages and couldn't remember all the ingredients. I tucked the "recipe" away because, back then, it could have been written in Latin for all I could decipher it. This kindred cookie features orange as a partner to the chocolate. Every bite is a tasty reminder of why these two flavors work so well together, no Latin required.

1. Preheat the oven to 350°F. Line two baking sheets with parchment paper.

2. In a small bowl, whisk the egg whites until frothy (they must be at room temperature, or the batter won't spread) and add the vanilla, coffee, orange oil, and orange zest. In a large bowl, whisk the confectioners' sugar with the cocoa. Be especially accurate, because the addition of any extra confectioners' sugar or cocoa will make the cookie dry. Add the salt and whisk. Add the wet ingredients to the dry, and using a silicone spatula, keep stirring and folding until everything is incorporated. The mixture will look dry but suddenly becomes a wet batter. At that point, stir vigorously just until the batter is shiny and thick, and stop. The batter is just right when you push it aside and it gently fills back in like lava. Add the almonds and chocolate and gently fold in just until combined.

3. Using a 2-tablespoon scoop, place six or seven mounds on each prepared baking sheet. Carefully shake the baking sheets, keeping your fingers on the parchment so it doesn't slide, to flatten the batter into rounds. You can rap the pan on the countertop to further flatten them. If the batter isn't spreading on its own, use an offset spatula dipped in water to flatten the mounds and know they will come out a little more cakey than chewy.

4. Place the baking sheets in the oven and turn down the temperature to 325°F. Bake for 10 minutes and rotate the pans for even baking. Bake for 5 to 8 minutes more, or just until the tops start to crack and seem less glossy. Let cool completely on the parchment paper before removing, otherwise they will break apart. Once completely cool, carefully peel the cookies from the parchment paper.

FLOURLESS ALMOND PUFF COOKIES

MAKES 30 COOKIES

BAKING TIME: 35 to 40 minutes

DAIRY-FREE

If these cookies had been on the dessert sideboard during Passover when I was kid, I might not have minded being more patient through the long seder. Topped with a bit of crushed pistachio or even toasted almonds, these cookies are chewy and full of almond flavor, but also light and airy.

1. Preheat the oven to 300°F. Line two baking sheets with parchment paper. In a large bowl, whisk together the almond flour and superfine sugar. In another bowl, whisk the egg whites with the cream of tartar and salt until it forms very soft meringue peaks. Gently fold in the almond mixture until combined. Fold in the almond extract. The mixture will deflate somewhat.

2. Scoop by tablespoons or pipe using a ½ inch plain tip onto the prepared baking sheets, fifteen on each sheet. Top each cookie with an almond. Bake for 15 minutes and rotate the pans for even baking. Bake for 20 to 25 minutes more, or until the cookies look golden. Let cool thoroughly on parchment paper. Once cool, the cookies will peel away from the parchment paper.

GF almond flour
  150 grams | 1½ cups

superfine sugar
  100 grams | ½ cup

egg whites
  105 grams | 3 extra-large

cream of tartar
  ¼ teaspoon

kosher salt
  ½ teaspoon

almond extract
  1 teaspoon

whole almonds, toasted (see page 7)
  30 almonds

LEMON POPPY-SEED COOKIES

These cookies are a longtime family favorite. The original recipe was given to my mother by her cousin Ruthe when I was still a little sprout. We've updated them with an infusion of lemon in both the dough and the topping. Use plastic wrap and a big flat-bottomed glass to press the cookie dough as thinly as possible, and if you can wait, these taste best the next day after the flavors get to settle into the cookie. Be sure to sniff those poppy seeds to make sure they are fresh and use the resources in the back of the book to order them inexpensively in bulk (see page 255).

1. Line two baking pans with parchment paper.
2. In a small bowl, mix together the eggs, oil, lemon zest, vanilla, and almond extract. In a large bowl, whisk together the sugar, flour, almond flour, baking powder, salt, baking soda, and poppy seeds. Stir in the wet ingredients with a fork until incorporated. Using clean hands, finish mixing the ingredients until the dough is smooth.
3. Place 2 tablespoon–size balls on the prepared baking sheets, nine or ten to a pan. Flatten each ball, using plastic wrap and a large flat-bottomed glass, until they are thin and 3 inches in diameter. Let the dough rest at room temperature for 30 minutes.
4. Preheat the oven to 350°F.
5. To make the topping, work the lemon zest into the sugar, using your fingertips. Let the mixture rest for 15 minutes. After the dough has rested, beat the egg and brush a small bit of egg wash onto each cookie. Sprinkle generously with the lemon sugar.
6. Bake for 12 to 15 minutes, until golden brown. Transfer the cookies to a rack to cool completely.

eggs
120 grams | 2 extra-large

canola oil
115 grams | ½ cup

freshly grated lemon zest
5 grams | 1 tablespoon

vanilla extract
1 teaspoon

almond extract
½ teaspoon

sugar
200 grams | 1 cup

Nosh AP GF flour (page 4)
260 grams | 2 cups

GF almond flour
100 grams | 1 cup

baking powder
1 teaspoon

kosher salt
½ teaspoon

baking soda
¼ teaspoon

black poppy seeds
60 grams | 5 heaping tablespoons

TOPPING

lemon zest, freshly grated
5 grams | 1 tablespoon

sugar
65 grams | ⅓ cup

egg
60 grams | 1 extra-large

BARS *and* BROWNIES

I grew up thinking bars and brownies were the holy grail of baking—if anything good were to be baked, it would be a bar and it would contain chocolate and have a crunchy, chewy edge. Only as an adult did I learn to appreciate a wider world beyond chocolate that included new favorites: lemon and fig bars. Praise the bar.

SPECIAL EQUIPMENT

8- or 9-inch square baking pans, foil and parchment paper, serrated knives

TIPS

- Best-quality chocolate will result in best flavor.
- Lining bar and brownie baking pans with foil or parchment helps remove them easily for slicing.
- Expect brownies to be done when a toothpick comes out with gooey crumbs—this is the secret to dense, chewy brownies. They will continue to be gooey until they are completely cooled, which can take hours.
- Brownies and some bars taste best when allowed to be chilled or rested overnight after baking so flavors develop fully.

O'FIGGINZ BARS

confectioners' sugar
110 grams | 1 cup

GF almond flour
200 grams | 2 cups

GF oat flour
150 grams | 1½ cups

unsweetened cocoa powder
1 teaspoon

kosher salt
1 teaspoon

ground cloves
½ teaspoon

ground cinnamon
½ teaspoon

shortening
85 grams | 7 tablespoons or ¼ cup
plus 3 tablespoons

egg
60 grams | 1 extra-large

nonstick spray, for greasing

fig preserves, Bonne Maman
preferred
370 grams | 1 cup

dried figs, finely chopped
300 grams | 1½ cups

dried apricots, finely chopped
40 grams | ¼ cup

Nosh AP GF flour (page 4)
1 tablespoon

lemon zest, freshly grated
5 grams | 1 tablespoon

fresh lemon juice
2 tablespoons

dark rum
1 tablespoon
   or
rum flavoring
1 teaspoon

egg, beaten separately, for brushing
60 grams | 1 extra-large

When flavorful figs and oats meet Linzer, you get an O'Figginz Bar. It might remind you of a Newton but an O'Figginz is so much figgier, and slightly more chunky. These are at their most flavorful after resting overnight.

1. In the bowl of a food processor, pulse together the confectioners' sugar, almond flour, oat flour, cocoa, salt, cloves, and cinnamon.

2. Add the shortening and pulse until coarse crumbs form. Add the egg and pulse until the mixture becomes a ragged ball of dough. Wrap the soft dough in plastic wrap and chill for 4 hours or overnight.

3. Grease a 9-inch square pan with nonstick spray and line with parchment paper that overhangs like a sling, one piece in each direction. Grease the parchment with nonstick spray.

4. Split the dough into two pieces, one slightly larger than the other. Sandwich the larger piece of dough between sheets of plastic wrap. Roll into a 10-inch square. Remove the top sheet of plastic wrap. Flip over the dough onto the prepared pan so that dough comes up the sides like a piecrust, using the plastic wrap as an aid. Remove the plastic wrap carefully and press the dough into place. Expect it to be sticky. Refrigerate the dough for 30 minutes for easier handling. Roll out the remaining dough into a slightly oversize 9-inch square, using the same method. Slide the top crust, still encased in plastic wrap, onto a baking sheet and refrigerate while preparing the filling.

5. Stir together the fig preserves, figs, apricots, flour, lemon zest, lemon juice, and rum. Place over the chilled bottom crust, spreading the filling to the edges. Top the filling with the chilled top crust. Press the top and bottom crust edges together to seal. Refrigerate for 30 minutes. Meanwhile, preheat the oven to 350°F.

6. Brush the upper crust with the beaten egg. Poke holes in the top of the dough with a fork to create vents. Bake for

35 minutes and rotate the pan for even baking. Bake for 20 to 25 minutes more, or until the center is bubbling with filling through the vents and the crust is well browned. Let cool completely in the pan overnight, if possible. Using the parchment sling, transfer from the pan to a cutting board. Cut into bars once thoroughly cooled.

Mom, in her favorite room of the house, beginning a baking day

MOM'S BROWNIES

My mother was the queen of brownie baking in our neighborhood. Her brownies were the calling card presented to new neighbors; she was the welcome wagon long before it became fashionable. She never served the edge pieces to company because they were not as pristine, a lucky break for us. Consequently, I grew to love the chewy texture of the brownie edge. Woe is the person who tries to eat the corner pieces in my house.

1. Preheat the oven to 350°F. Butter an 8-inch square pan. Line the bottom of the pan with parchment paper. Butter the parchment and dust the pan with cocoa.

2. In a double boiler over low heat, melt the butter and all of the chocolate together and set aside to cool. Mix the superfine sugar with the eggs in a medium bowl. Stir in the vanilla and brewed coffee. Stir in the flour and salt until just mixed. Add the cooled chocolate mixture. Stir until the mixture is shiny and pulls away from the edge of the bowl. Scrape the batter into the prepared pan, pushing the batter into the corners. Rap the pan on the countertop to remove any air bubbles.

3. Bake for 10 minutes, then turn down the temperature to 300°F and bake for 25 minutes. You want a toothpick to come out with a few gooey crumbs. The top will look slightly dry and crackly. Let cool in the pan on a rack until cold. Invert the pan onto a cutting board and peel away the parchment. Cut into squares. As is true for most things chocolate, the brownies taste best on the second day. Store in an airtight container.

cold unsalted butter, plus more for greasing
 90 grams | 6 tablespoons
 or ¼ cup plus 2 tablespoons

unsweetened cocoa powder, for dusting pan

unsweetened baking chocolate
 56 grams | one 2-ounce bar

bittersweet chocolate
 28 grams | one 1-ounce bar

superfine sugar
 200 grams | 1 cup

eggs
 120 grams | 2 extra-large

vanilla extract
 1 teaspoon

brewed coffee (decaf is fine)
 1 teaspoon

Nosh AP GF flour (page 4)
 65 grams | ½ cup

kosher salt
 ½ teaspoon

MARZIPANY GOOEY BROWNIES

Plan at least one day ahead for this recipe. The prep and baking actually goes rather quickly—it's the waiting that takes time. For best flavor, these dense, chewy, gooey chocolate marzipanny brownies have to be refrigerated overnight and then they are all yours.

1. Preheat the oven to 350°F. Line a 9-inch square baking pan with foil.

2. Cut the butter into two or three pieces. Combine the butter and chocolate in a double boiler over low heat just until melted and smooth. Don't overheat. Set aside to cool slightly.

3. In a small food processor, pulse the sugar with the almond paste and salt until it is quite smooth. Place the mixture in a large bowl. Add the eggs and mix until thoroughly combined. Add the vanilla, hazelnut liqueur, and coffee. Stir again. Add the flour and mix until combined. Add the chocolate mixture and beat until the mixture is shiny and begins to pull away from the edge, about 45 seconds. Stir in the mini chocolate chips.

4. With a silicone spatula, scrape the batter into the prepared baking pan and smooth the top. Rap the pan on the countertop to remove any air bubbles. Bake for 25 to 35 minutes, or just until a toothpick comes out with a few gooey crumbs. The top should look a bit crackly and dry—which is perfect. Remove from the oven and let the brownies cool completely in the pan on a rack. Wrap the pan thoroughly with foil once cool and refrigerate overnight, for best flavor.

5. Remove the pan from the refrigerator. Remove the foil cover, then remove the insert from the pan by grabbing the foil and peeling it away from the cold brownies. Slice while cold. Store covered tightly with foil in the refrigerator, for best flavor.

cold unsalted butter
115 grams | 8 tablespoons or ½ cup

unsweetened chocolate, roughly chopped
150 grams | 5 ounces | 1¼ cups

sugar
200 grams | 1 cup

GF almond paste, Love'n Bake preferred (see page 255), cut into pieces
200 grams | ¾ cup

kosher salt
½ teaspoon

eggs
120 grams | 2 extra-large

vanilla extract
1 teaspoon

hazelnut liqueur, Frangelico preferred, or hazelnut or almond extract
1 tablespoon

brewed coffee (decaf is fine)
1 teaspoon

Nosh AP GF flour (page 4)
70 grams | heaping ½ cup

semisweet mini chocolate chips
170 grams | 1 cup

NUTELLA CHEWY BITES

These are little bites of Nutella heaven. Inspired by one of Abby Dodge's recipes in her four-ingredient book *Desserts 4 Today*, they can be made with any of your favorite fillings—chocolate chips, chopped dried fruit, or nuts. They are also reminiscent of the original gluten-free-style recipes one could find on the Internet about a dozen years ago that featured just peanut butter, sugar, eggs, and baking soda.

1. Preheat the oven to 350°F. Generously grease a 24-count mini muffin pan with nonstick spray or place two dozen mini muffin liners on a baking sheet.
2. In a medium bowl, mix the Nutella with the eggs. Stir in the flour, almond flour, cocoa, vanilla, hazelnut liqueur, and salt. If desired, stir in one optional filling.
3. Fill the prepared mini muffin pan or liners two-thirds full.
4. Bake for 12 to 14 minutes, or until a toothpick comes out with gooey crumbs and the tops are puffed up into domes. Let the pan cool on a rack for a few minutes before placing the bites directly on the rack to cool completely. Be sure to let them cool before eating the whole batch. Sharing is nice.

nonstick spray, for greasing

Nutella
370 grams | 1¼ cups |
one 13-ounce jar

eggs
120 grams | 2 extra-large

Nosh AP GF flour (page 4)
25 grams | 3 tablespoons

GF almond flour
25 grams | 4 tablespoons or ¼ cup

unsweetened cocoa powder
15 grams | 2 tablespoons

vanilla extract
1 teaspoon

hazelnut liqueur, Frangelico preferred, or hazelnut or almond extract
1 teaspoon

kosher salt
½ teaspoon

OPTIONAL FILLINGS
- maraschino cherries, chopped
  80 grams | ½ cup
- nuts, roughly chopped
  40 grams | ⅓ cup
- semisweet mini chocolate chips
  85 grams | ½ cup
- dried fruit, finely chopped
  75 grams | ½ cup

CHOCOLATE CHUNK CHERRY BROWNIES

Chewy tart dried cherries go with deep dark chocolate like an apple goes with pie. These are quite fudgelike (read: messy) and are not the cakey variety. Big gooey brownies equal happy people.

1. Preheat the oven to 350°F. Butter a 9-inch square baking pan. Line the pan with an extra-long sheet of parchment paper, creating a handle or a sling that will help remove the brownies from the pan. Butter the bottom of the parchment and dust with unsweetened cocoa.
2. Cut the butter into two or three pieces. In a double boiler over low heat, combine the butter with the semisweet and unsweetened chocolate and heat until melted and smooth. Let cool slightly.
3. In a medium bowl, combine the eggs, superfine sugar, salt, vanilla, and cherry liqueur. Add the flour and stir to incorporate. Add the chocolate mixture and stir to combine. Fold in the chocolate chips and dried cherries. Pour the batter into the prepared pan. Rap the pan once on the countertop to remove any air bubbles.
4. Bake for 20 minutes and rotate the pan for even baking. Bake for 12 to 15 minutes more and remove when a toothpick comes out with slightly gooey crumbs.
5. Let cool completely in the pan on a rack. Then cover with foil and refrigerate overnight, for best flavor.
6. When ready to serve, remove from the refrigerator and use the parchment handles to set the baked slab on a cutting board. Slice into servings with a sharp knife. Serve chilled.

cold unsalted butter, plus more for greasing
180 grams | 12 tablespoons or ¾ cup

unsweetened cocoa powder, for dusting pan

semisweet bar chocolate, roughly chopped
150 grams | one 5-ounce bar | 1¼ cups

unsweetened bar chocolate, roughly chopped
75 grams | one 3-ounce bar | ⅔ cup

eggs
120 grams | 2 extra-large

superfine sugar
200 grams | 1 cup

kosher salt
½ teaspoon

vanilla extract
1 teaspoon

cherry liqueur or maraschino cherry liquid
1 tablespoon

Nosh AP GF flour (page 4), sifted
130 grams | 1 cup

semisweet chocolate chips
85 grams | ½ cup

dried cherries, tart preferred
75 grams | ½ cup

MARSHMALLOW SWIRL COCOA BROWNIES

Cocoa brownies can be as chewy and dense as their chocolate bar counterparts, especially if they are refrigerated. These are swirled with melted marshmallow fluff that makes them taste almost like s'mores filling in a bar, and the 8-inch square pan helps give them their height.

1. Preheat the oven to 325°F. Line an 8-inch square pan with foil (a bigger pan will yield flat brownies) and coat with nonstick spray.

2. Cut the butter into two or three pieces. In a small saucepan over low heat, or in a microwave-safe container, melt the butter until just warm. Remove from the heat. In a medium bowl, combine the superfine sugar, cocoa, espresso powder, salt, and baking soda. Add the warm melted butter and stir. Add the vanilla and eggs and stir. The batter will feel very thick. Stir until the batter pulls away from the sides and is shiny. Add the flour and stir again until the batter is very thick and shiny, and your arm feels as if it will fall off—less than a minute.

3. Add the Marshmallow Fluff to the batter, and using a butter knife, gently marble the mixture, leaving streaks of white throughout. Less is more in this case.

4. Scrape the batter into the prepared pan and, using a wet silicone spatula, even out the top so that it is smooth. Bake for 20 minutes and rotate the pan for even baking. Bake for 15 to 18 minutes more, or just until a toothpick comes out with chocolate crumbs that look more baked than wet. The top will be crackly dry except where there is marshmallow, which will remain gooey. Set the pan on a rack and let cool completely—at least 2 to 3 hours, and overnight in the refrigerator is even better. Cut into bars and serve.

nonstick spray, for greasing

cold unsalted butter
135 grams | 9 tablespoons or
½ cup plus 1 tablespoon

superfine sugar
200 grams | 1 cup

unsweetened cocoa powder, sifted
100 grams | 1 cup

instant espresso powder
(decaf is fine)
1 teaspoon

kosher salt
½ teaspoon

baking soda
¼ teaspoon

vanilla extract
1 teaspoon

eggs
120 grams | 2 extra-large

Nosh AP GF flour (page 4)
65 grams | 1½ cups

Marshmallow Fluff or Creme
100 grams | ½ cup

BETTY'S LEMON BARS

MAKES 16 SQUARES

CHILLING TIME: 30 minutes

BAKING TIME: 30 minutes (crust) and
25 to 35 minutes more (filling)

There is no one on this planet who loves lemon more than my lemon-loving in-laws. They've been known to add lemon to anything, even chocolate chip cookies. My mother-in-law, Betty, makes a version that is similar, but I bet these actually have more lemon and might be slightly tarter. But don't tell her I said that.

1. Grease a 9-inch baking pan with nonstick spray. Line the pan with an extra-long sheet of parchment paper, creating a handle like a sling, which will help you remove the bars from the pan. Spray the parchment paper.

2. In a food processor, pulse together 195 grams (1½ cups) of the flour, the confectioners' sugar, and the salt. Cut the butter into tablespoon-size pieces. Add the butter and pulse until the mixture looks like coarse cornmeal.

3. Pour the coarse crumbs into the prepared pan. Press the crumbly dough into the bottom of the pan until it is solid. Refrigerate for at least 30 minutes. Meanwhile, preheat the oven to 325°F.

4. Remove from the refrigerator and bake the crust for 30 minutes, until it is lightly browned.

5. While the crust is in the oven, prepare the filling. In a medium bowl, mix the granulated sugar and lemon zest with the tips of your fingers until the zest is fully worked into the sugar and it turns lemony yellow. Let it sit for 15 minutes to flavor the sugar. Stir the lemon sugar with the eggs and the remaining 35 grams (¼ cup) of flour. Stir in the lemon juice, cream, and limoncello.

6. Remove the lightly browned crust from the oven. Mix the filling again and pour the filling gently onto the hot crust (through a mesh strainer if you wish to remove the zest). Bake for 25 to 35 minutes, or just until the filling is set.

7. Let cool completely in the pan for at least 3 to 4 hours. Loosen the edges of the crust with a knife. Using the parchment paper, lift out carefully onto a cutting board. Cut into squares. Top with additional sifted confectioners' sugar when ready to serve. Refrigerate leftovers.

nonstick spray, for greasing

Nosh AP GF flour (page 4)
230 grams | 1¾ cups

confectioners' sugar, plus more for sprinkling
60 grams | ½ cup

kosher salt
½ teaspoon

cold unsalted butter
180 grams | 12 tablespoons or ¾ cup

granulated sugar
250 grams | 1¼ cups

lemon zest, freshly grated
10 grams | 2 tablespoons

eggs
300 grams | 5 extra-large

fresh lemon juice
134 grams | ⅔ cup

heavy cream
60 grams | ¼ cup

limoncello or lemon extract
1 teaspoon

CAKES *and*
CUPCAKES

While we were growing up, cakes and cupcakes were baked only for special occasions and holidays in our house. Mom's Marble Chiffon and angel cakes were the usual suspects, both of which she made with potato starch for Passover. The Jewish New Year always began with honey cake followed by an apple upside-down cake, if we were lucky. Layer cakes were reserved for birthdays well after she gave up on decades of birthday pies. These days in our house, even minor occasions warrant cake. Because who doesn't love cake? Cupcakes are never going out of style, no matter what anyone says. Why? Just hand a beautiful cupcake to someone and watch that person's face. That's why.

SPECIAL EQUIPMENT

Silicone spatulas; 8- or 9-inch layer cake pans; cupcake pans; heatproof bowls, double boiler (see page 10); greaseproof cupcake liners; plenty of toothpicks; offset spatulas; piping bags and tips (Wilton 2D, star tips, ½-inch plain tips; see page 10)

TIPS

- Unless otherwise specified, all ingredients should be at room temperature.
- If a recipe says to "grease" the pan, feel free to use nonstick spray (without flour), butter, or shortening.
- A pan for yellow cake is best dusted with flour; a pan for chocolate cake is best dusted with cocoa powder.
- Count on GF cakes and cupcakes to shrink slightly in height, so slightly overfilling the pan is necessary, like buying longer jeans knowing that they will shrink in the wash.
- Trust the toothpick: Remove the cake from the oven as soon as a toothpick comes out with dry crumbs.

- Chocolate baked goods will always be better the next day.
- Greaseproof liners help keep cupcakes fresher longer and they look great, too.
- To get a nice dome on the cupcake, fill each liner a very generous two-thirds full.
- Overbaking GF cupcakes is the kiss of cupcake death because the bottom of the cake will not be edible and instead could patch a tire on your car, should the event arise.
- Count on there being a generous amount of icing for each cupcake. Leftovers can be saved in the refrigerator: Swiss buttercream, 2 days; buttercream with butter, 4 days; and buttercream with shortening, 8 days.

HONEY CAKE

MAKES 8 TO 10 SERVINGS

BAKING TIME: 38 to 44 minutes
(plus resting overnight)

DAIRY-FREE

Inspired by *Joan Nathan's Jewish Holiday Cookbook*, our gluten-free honey cake is an ideal Rosh Hashanah dessert. Instant espresso powder and unsweetened cocoa add punch to the flavors and moderate the sweetness. Honey cake is only as good as the honey you use. For this occasion, try blackberry sage or orange blossom honey. Don't leave out the rum or rum flavoring. After all, can it be a Jewish holiday without a little sip of something spirited? Bake this ahead and let it age slightly–24 hours for best flavor.

1. Preheat the oven to 350°F. Grease one 8½ × 4½-inch loaf pan or one 10-cup Bundt pan with nonstick spray.

2. Using an electric mixer on medium-high speed, beat the shortening and sugar together until light and fluffy. Scrape down the sides as needed. Add the eggs and mix well. In a small bowl, whisk the honey, zests, vanilla, and rum. Add to the batter and mix thoroughly.

3. In a large bowl, whisk to combine the flour with espresso powder, cocoa, salt, baking soda, cinnamon, and cloves. Add the flour mixture to the wet ingredients and mix for a minute or two. Scrape down the sides with a spatula and continue to mix until all the dry ingredients are incorporated. Scrape the batter into the prepared pan.

4. Bake the cake for 20 minutes and rotate the pan for even baking. Bake for 18 to 24 minutes more; remove from the oven once a toothpick comes out with a few clingy crumbs and it is golden brown and beginning to shrink away from the edges of the pan. Let cool for 2 minutes in the pan and then turn out onto a rack to cool completely (being very careful because the cake is fragile while warm). Wrap the cooled cake in foil and let the flavors fuse together at room temperature for at least 24 hours before serving, for best flavor.

nonstick spray, for greasing

shortening
60 grams | 5 tablespoons

sugar
100 grams | ½ cup

eggs
180 grams | 3 extra-large

honey
325 grams | 1 cup

lemon zest, freshly grated
5 grams | 1 tablespoon

orange zest, freshly grated
5 grams | 1 tablespoon

vanilla extract
½ teaspoon

dark rum
1 tablespoon
    or
rum flavoring
1 teaspoon

Nosh AP GF flour (page 4)
300 grams | 2⅓ cups

instant espresso powder
(decaf is fine)
1 tablespoon

unsweetened cocoa powder, sifted
1 tablespoon

kosher salt
½ teaspoon

baking soda
½ teaspoon

ground cinnamon
¼ teaspoon

ground cloves
¼ teaspoon

nonstick spray, for greasing

tart apples: Pippin, Gala, McIntosh, or Granny Smith
2 medium

fresh lemon juice
1 to 2 teaspoons

brown sugar
40 grams | 3 tablespoons

honey
42 grams | 2 tablespoons

pomegranate concentrate
(see page 251) | 2 teaspoons

Nosh AP GF flour (page 4)
200 grams | 1½ cups

baking powder
1 teaspoon

baking soda
¼ teaspoon

kosher salt
¼ teaspoon

unsalted butter, slightly softened
130 grams | 9 tablespoons or ½ cup
plus 1 tablespoon
or
shortening
96 grams | 8 tablespoons or ½ cup

granulated sugar
200 grams | 1 cup

eggs
120 grams | 2 extra-large

vanilla extract
1 teaspoon

water or milk
115 grams | ½ cup

lemon zest, freshly grated
5 grams | 1 tablespoon

HONEY POMEGRANATE SYRUP

honey, orange blossom preferred
100 grams | ⅓ cup

pomegranate concentrate
(see page 251)
3 tablespoons

dark rum or rum flavoring
1 teaspoon

APPLE UPSIDE-DOWN CAKE WITH HONEY POMEGRANATE SYRUP

One of the strongest symbolic traditions celebrating Rosh Hashanah is dipping apples in honey. It symbolizes hope and optimism for the coming Jewish New Year. Apple upside-down cake made with honey is a wonderful way to honor that tradition. Adding pomegranate syrup to the cake makes it a perfect dessert for the second night of the holiday, when tradition says to introduce another new fruit in celebration of the upcoming year. Be sure to use pomegranate concentrate (100 percent pomegranate) and not pomegranate molasses, which contains additional ingredients. Flip the cake out of the pan when it is piping hot, because that is how you get the apples to stay with the cake and not the pan. Don't forget to use those pot holders.

1. Preheat the oven to 350°F. Generously grease one 8-inch round pan with nonstick spray.

2. Peel and core the apples. Cut the apples in half. With the cut side down, slice several ½-inch-wide wedges—enough to form a ring in the bottom of the pan. Cut the remaining apples into ¼-inch cubes. Sprinkle 1 teaspoon of the lemon juice over the cubed apples and set them aside. Place the apple wedges in a concentric circle in the bottom of the prepared pan with the points facing upward (remember— it's an upside-down cake). Sprinkle with the brown sugar, honey, and pomegranate concentrate.

3. In a small bowl, stir the flour, baking powder, baking soda, and salt just until combined. In a larger bowl, using an electric mixer on medium-high speed, combine the butter with the granulated sugar until fluffy. Add the eggs, vanilla, water, and lemon zest and beat to combine. Stir into the dry ingredients and beat for a minute until the batter is shiny and smooth. Add the apple cubes and fold gently with a spatula to combine. Pour or scoop the batter over the apple wedges. Rap the pan on the countertop to remove any air bubbles.

4. Bake the cake for 25 minutes and rotate the pan for even baking. Bake for 15 to 20 minutes more, until a toothpick

comes out clean and the cake is golden brown. Immediately run a knife around the edge of the cake and get your serving plate ready. Using pot holders (unless you have fingers of steel), place the cake plate over the pan and in one smooth motion flip it over. Wait until you hear the sound of the cake plop onto the plate and then tap the top of the inverted pan with a butter knife. Carefully lift the pan and if any apple bits are stuck in the pan, you can place them back on the cake while it is hot. This only works while it is hot. Let the cake cool completely before serving. Store, covered loosely, at room temperature.

HONEY POMEGRANATE SYRUP

Simmer the honey and pomegranate concentrate in a small saucepan over medium-low heat for a few minutes, until beginning to boil. Remove the saucepan from the heat, carefully add the rum, and give it a minute to thicken. Pour over the cake and serve, or slice the cake and pour over each serving.

PUMPKIN CUPCAKES WITH HONEY BUTTERCREAM

These pumpkin cupcakes with honey buttercream are a nontraditional nod to both the Jewish New Year and autumn. Mixed with chopped toasted walnuts and dried apples and topped with a whipped nondairy honey buttercream, these cupcakes are a superbly tasty way to welcome a new season.

1. Preheat the oven to 350°F. Place liners in a cupcake pan.
2. In a medium bowl, using an electric mixer on medium-high speed, cream the shortening with the granulated sugar until fluffy. Add the eggs and mix until light and fluffy. Add the pumpkin, zest, vanilla, and lemon extract and mix until fully incorporated. In a medium bowl, whisk together the flour, baking powder, salt, cinnamon, baking soda, cloves, and nutmeg. Add to the wet ingredients and beat until fully mixed and the batter is thick but smooth. Fold in the diced dried apples and walnuts with a silicone spatula.
3. Fill each liner two-thirds full. Bake for 18 to 24 minutes, or until a toothpick comes out with almost dry crumbs. Let cool in the pan for a minute. Carefully transfer the cupcakes to a rack and let cool completely before frosting.

HONEY BUTTERCREAM

Using an electric mixer on medium-high speed, whip the shortening and honey until fully combined and slightly fluffy. Add the sifted confectioners' sugar and mix on low speed until almost combined. Add the almond milk 1 tablespoon at a time and whip on high speed until the frosting is soft enough to be piped. Add the vanilla and whip on high speed for a few seconds. Pipe or spoon on top of the cooled cupcakes.

TOPPING

Sprinkle on the nuts immediately—before the frosting sets. The cupcakes are best served the same day.

shortening
120 grams | 10 tablespoons or ½ cup plus 2 tablespoons

granulated sugar
175 grams | heaping ¾ cup

eggs
180 grams | 3 extra-large

canned pure pumpkin puree
160 grams | ¾ cup

lemon or orange zest, freshly grated
5 grams | 1 tablespoon

vanilla extract | 1 teaspoon

lemon or orange extract | ½ teaspoon

Nosh AP GF flour (page 4)
175 grams | 1⅓ cups

baking powder | 1 heaping teaspoon

kosher salt | ½ teaspoon

ground cinnamon | ½ teaspoon

baking soda | ¼ teaspoon

ground cloves | ¼ teaspoon

nutmeg, freshly ground preferred
¼ teaspoon

dried apples, finely diced
35 grams | ⅓ cup

walnuts or pecans, toasted (see page 251) and roughly chopped
40 grams | ⅓ cup

HONEY BUTTERCREAM

shortening
110 grams | 9 tablespoons or ½ cup plus 1 tablespoon

honey, orange blossom preferred
30 grams | 1½ tablespoons

confectioners' sugar, sifted
220 grams | 2 cups

almond milk | 2 to 3 tablespoons

vanilla extract | ½ teaspoon

TOPPING

walnuts or pecans, toasted (see page 251) and roughly chopped
40 grams | ⅓ cup

GOLDIE'S POUND CAKE

My mother could never remember to preheat the oven and it turns out there is not only economy in that, but you'll be rewarded with a pound cake that has an intense vanilla-butter flavor and a lemon, almond back note as well as a tender crumb. Pound cake is named aptly: A pound of the four major ingredients—butter, sugar, eggs, and flour—goes into the cake. Fortunately, the recipe feeds the entire neighborhood, so you aren't required to eat it all.

1. Generously grease two 8½ × 4½-inch loaf pans.
2. Using an electric mixer on medium-high speed, beat the butter with the sugar until light and fluffy. The mixture should look thick and pale yellow.
3. Beat in the eggs one at a time until fully incorporated. Add the lemon zest, vanilla, almond extract, and limoncello. Mix well. In a medium bowl, whisk the flour with the baking powder, salt, and mace. Add the flour mixture to the wet ingredients and beat just until incorporated. Fold one more time from the bottom to mix in any rogue dry matter remaining in the bottom of the bowl.
4. Fill the prepared baking pans evenly, a bit more than half full. Rap the pans on the countertop to settle the batter and remove any air bubbles. Place the pans in a cold oven. Turn the oven temperature to 325°F and bake for 50 to 60 minutes. At 50 minutes, begin checking the loaves with a toothpick. When the cake is golden and starting to crack on top and the toothpick comes out with dry crumbs, transfer the pans to a rack to cool for 5 minutes. Remove the cakes from the pans and continue to cool on the rack.
5. Serve plain or with fresh berries and whipped cream.

nonstick spray or butter, for greasing

unsalted butter, slightly softened
460 grams | 32 tablespoons or 2 cups

sugar
500 grams | 2½ cups

eggs
480 grams | 8 extra-large

lemon zest, freshly grated
5 grams | 1 tablespoon

vanilla extract
1 teaspoon

almond extract
½ teaspoon

limoncello or fresh lemon juice
2 tablespoons

Nosh AP GF flour (page 4)
520 grams | 4 cups

baking powder
1 teaspoon

kosher salt
1 teaspoon

mace or nutmeg
¼ teaspoon

CHOCOLATE BABKA

Nosh AP GF flour (page 4), plus more
for dusting
325 grams | 2½ cups

tapioca starch
25 grams | ¼ cup

Expandex Modified Tapioca Starch
(see page 3) or additional tapioca
starch
50 grams | 5 tablespoons

granulated sugar
90 grams | 7 tablespoons or ¼ cup
plus 3 tablespoons

instant yeast, Red Star preferred
20 grams | 2 tablespoons

nonfat powdered milk
15 grams | 2 tablespoons

xanthan gum
2 teaspoons (3 teaspoons if not
using Expandex)

kosher salt
2 teaspoons

pectin
¼ teaspoon

guar gum
¼ teaspoon

unsalted butter, slightly softened
30 grams | 2 tablespoons

canola oil
75 grams | ⅓ cup

vanilla bean paste or vanilla extract
2 teaspoons

eggs
120 grams | 2 extra-large

egg yolks
50 grams | 2 extra-large

whole milk
170 grams | ⅔ cup

(INGREDIENTS CONTINUE)

I love the old New York City Jewish bakery babka and wanted one that reminded me of those big fat twisty loaves filled with chocolate and nuts. This loaf does just that. It is not hard to make, but it has a few components that take a bit of time. Freezing the chocolate chips overnight prior to making the recipe keeps them from clumping when mixing up the filling. Babka gets better with age and lasts for days if you cover it with foil, not plastic. A well-made babka is a nosh worth undertaking.

1. In a large bowl, combine the flour, tapioca starch, Expandex, sugar, yeast, powdered milk, xanthan gum, salt, pectin, and guar gum and whisk to mix. Add the butter and, using a fork, mix lightly to combine. In a separate bowl, whisk together the oil, vanilla bean paste, eggs, egg yolks, and milk. Add to the dry mixture and work the dough with a fork to make sure everything is well incorporated. Using a silicone spatula, scrape the sides and the bottom, turning the sticky dough until it is somewhat smooth. Cover with plastic wrap and let rise for 2 hours, or until it has doubled in size.

2. For the filling, in the bowl of a food processor or strong blender, pulse the frozen chocolate chips until they are almost powdered. Add the cinnamon and the butter cubes and process until the mixture starts to look like chocolate spread. Add the rum and mix in thoroughly.

TOPPING

In a small bowl, whisk together all the dry ingredients. Add the cubes of butter, and work the butter into the dry mixture just until it looks like coarse, ragged crumbs. Beat the egg in a small bowl and set aside for brushing the dough before baking.

ASSEMBLY

1. Generously butter a 9 × 5-inch loaf pan. Punch down the dough and place it on a parchment-lined floured surface. Add a little more flour to the top and keep your hands well

floured for best results. Knead the dough until it is smooth, shiny, and not quite sticky. Using more flour as needed, roll the dough into a small rectangle, using a piece of plastic wrap on top. Remove the plastic wrap. Fold the dough into thirds like a business letter. Turn the dough so the seam faces you, and roll and fold again like a business letter. Do that two more times. This helps work the dough so that it becomes pliable.

2. Roll the dough into a 16 × 14-inch rectangle. Spread the filling onto the dough all the way to the edges, leaving a ¼-inch border empty. Begin rolling the dough from the long side in jelly-roll fashion—snug but not tight enough to crack. Once the dough is rolled, give it a little stretch to get it to a 22-inch-long rope without breaking it. Coil the long rope gently, because it will want to crack as it bends. Pinch it together where it does try to crack. Once you have a coil, stand it up with the seam side down. Flatten it slightly. That helps eliminate air pockets. Place the coil seam side down in the center of the prepared loaf pan. Cover and let it rise in a draft-free area until it almost fills the pan, about 2 hours. Don't let it rise over the top.

3. Preheat the oven to 350°F. Place the loaf pan on a baking sheet. Brush the babka with the egg wash and scatter the streusel topping all over the top and even down the sides. Bake for 30 minutes and rotate the pan for even baking. Bake for 15 to 20 minutes more and remove the babka from the oven when it is between 185° and 190°F internally, golden brown, and even slightly overdone.

4. Let cool in the pan 15 to 20 minutes, then transfer the babka from the pan to a rack. Cool two hours to set the chocolate. Slice with a serrated knife. Store at room temperature wrapped tightly. Reheat slices on a baking sheet in a preheated 300°F oven for 5 minutes to refresh.

FILLING

semisweet chocolate chips, frozen
340 grams | 2 cups

bittersweet chocolate chips, frozen
60 grams | ⅓ cup

ground cinnamon
1 heaping teaspoon

cold unsalted butter, cubed
90 grams | 6 tablespoons or ¼ cup plus 2 tablespoons

dark rum
40 grams | 3 tablespoons
or
rum flavoring
1 teaspoon

STREUSEL TOPPING

Nosh AP GF flour (page 4)
65 grams | ½ cup

granulated sugar
50 grams | ¼ cup

brown sugar
50 grams | ¼ cup

salt
¼ teaspoon

ground cinnamon
½ teaspoon

cold unsalted butter, cubed
60 grams | 4 tablespoons or ¼ cup

egg
60 grams | 1 extra-large

Chocolate Babka (page 78)

Nosh AP GF flour (page 4)
140 grams | 1 heaping cup

superfine sugar
370 grams | scant 2 cups

kosher salt
½ teaspoon

unsweetened cocoa powder, sifted
3 tablespoons

instant espresso powder
(decaf is fine)
1 teaspoon

egg whites
245 grams | 7 extra-large

cream of tartar
½ teaspoon

vanilla extract
1 teaspoon

Boyajian orange oil (see page 7)
½ teaspoon
  or
pure orange extract
1 teaspoon

SERVING OPTIONS
- berries
- whipped cream or nondairy topping
- shaved chocolate curls

BLACK & WHITE ANGEL FOOD CAKE

An angel food cake is easier to make than you imagine. There are no magic tricks. It is more an effort in patience than any special skill. You are going to use all the bowls in the kitchen for this recipe, but it's worth it. Even if the cake is not perfect, the flavor of a cake wreck (page 211) will still be appreciated, and you can always dress it up with fresh berries.

1. Preheat the oven to 325°F. Get out your 10-inch angel food cake pan (the one with the tube in the center and a removable bottom). Do *not* grease it.

2. Place the flour in one bowl. Place the superfine sugar in another. Add half of the sugar and all of the salt to the flour. Whisk to combine. Transfer half of that mixture into a third bowl. To that third bowl, add the cocoa and espresso powder. Whisk to combine. You should have three containers at this point. One has half of the sugar, one has a flour mixture, and the other has some of the flour mixture combined with cocoa and espresso powder.

3. In a clean bowl, whip the egg whites and cream of tartar with an electric mixer on medium speed until combined. Turn up the mixer speed to medium-high and whip the whites until very soft peaks form. Add the vanilla extract and orange oil. Turn down the mixer to medium speed and very slowly pour in the remaining sugar. Stop the mixer when you see stiff peaks but the whites look smooth and silky. Don't overbeat them or they will become dry and separate.

4. Take one third to just under half of the whipped egg whites and place in yet another bowl. Using a mesh strainer, sift the flour mixture on top of the whites. Using a clean silicone spatula, fold in the flour mixture gently until fully combined with the whites. The whites will deflate a little bit, but don't worry about that. Just be gentle and make sure no dry ingredients remain.

5. Sift the remaining flour mixture (the one without cocoa) into the remaining whipped egg whites and use a clean

silicone spatula to gently fold in the flour mixture until no dry ingredients remain. Don't mingle the chocolate and the vanilla batter yet.

6. Scoop half of the vanilla batter mixture into the ungreased pan. Spread gently to create an even layer. Add all of the chocolate batter on top and smooth it gently. Top with the remaining vanilla batter and smooth with the spatula. As you add each layer, take care to make sure no pockets of air are formed or the cake will bake with giant holes. Use the spatula to press down lightly as you smooth the batter. You'll feel any air pockets if they exist. Press gently to fill them in.

7. Bake the cake for 40 to 45 minutes, or just until a toothpick comes out without crumbs. The top will be puffy and look golden. Invert the cake pan onto a rack, or, for a retro challenge, invert the cake pan onto a long-necked bottle inserted into the tube. Leave the cake upside down for at least an hour.

8. Once the cake is completely cool, run a sharp knife around the edge and release the removable bottom, bringing the cake out of the pan while still attached to the inside tube. Gently run a knife around the bottom edge of the cake and the inside tube and invert onto a serving plate. Even if the cake is perfect as you get it out of the pan, dropping it just a few inches onto the countertop may result in a slight imperfection called, say, a dent. If the top is not perfectly flat, then press it with the back of a spoon to even out the dent/channel around the circumference of the cake and fill with berries, a little shaved chocolate, whipped cream, or drizzled chocolate sauce—it'll look all dressed up. Store the plain cake, covered, at room temperature. Store in the refrigerator if the cake is covered with berries and/or whipped cream.

DARK CHOCOLATE CINNAMON CUPCAKES

MAKES 12 CUPCAKES

BAKING TIME: 18 to 20 minutes

DAIRY-FREE

A deep dark chocolate flavor with a hint of cinnamon is like a great cup of Mexican coffee all packaged in a small cake. Although the cupcake calls for ground chipotle pepper, it is not spicy. The smoky addition bridges the flavors of the chocolate and cinnamon in the cupcake. You may find yourself wanting to eat another cupcake just to taste that combination one more time.

1. Preheat the oven to 350°F. Place liners in a cupcake pan.
2. In a large bowl, whisk together the flour, granulated sugar, cocoa, baking powder, espresso powder, cinnamon, salt, and chipotle powder. Cut the shortening into four or five pieces. Add the shortening, eggs, almond milk, and vanilla to the dry mixture. Using an electric mixer, start on low speed and then increase the speed to beat the ingredients until the batter is smooth, lump-free, and a little bit fluffy, 2 to 3 minutes.
3. Fill each liner two-thirds full. Bake the cupcakes for 18 to 20 minutes, or just until a toothpick comes out without crumbs. Let cool in the pan for a few minutes. Transfer the cupcakes to a rack and let cool completely before frosting.

CINNAMON CHOCOLATE BUTTERCREAM

1. Using an electric mixer on low speed, mix the shortening, confectioners' sugar, cinnamon, vanilla, and 1 tablespoon of coffee. In a small bowl, whisk the cocoa with the hot water until the mixture is smooth. Add to the buttercream and whip on high speed until fully combined.
2. Whip the mixture until it is very light and fluffy. If it seems too stiff, add more coffee, up to 1 tablespoon at a time. Pipe or spoon onto each cupcake. Top each with a single chocolate-covered espresso bean.

Nosh AP GF flour (page 4)
130 grams | 1 cup

granulated sugar
200 grams | 1 cup

unsweetened cocoa powder, sifted
30 grams | ⅓ cup

baking powder | 1½ teaspoons

instant espresso powder
(decaf is fine) | 1 teaspoon

ground cinnamon
1 heaping teaspoon

kosher salt | ½ teaspoon

chipotle powder
½ teaspoon

shortening
96 grams | 8 tablespoons or ½ cup

eggs
180 grams | 3 extra-large

almond milk
150 grams | ⅔ cup minus
1 tablespoon

vanilla extract | 1 teaspoon

CINNAMON CHOCOLATE BUTTERCREAM

shortening
108 grams | 9 tablespoons or ½ cup
plus 1 tablespoon

confectioners' sugar, sifted
440 grams | 4 cups

ground cinnamon | ½ teaspoon

vanilla extract | 1 teaspoon

brewed coffee (decaf is fine)
1 to 3 tablespoons

unsweetened cocoa powder, sifted
20 grams | 3 tablespoons

hot tap water | 3 tablespoons

DECORATION

GF chocolate–covered espresso beans
12 beans

CHERRY CHOCOLATE CUPCAKES

These cupcakes taste even better the second day, so making them ahead is a great idea. However, plan to make the buttercream the same day you are serving the cupcakes, for best flavor. The liquid from the jar of maraschino cherries or cherry liqueur makes the buttercream turn a beautiful pale pink and gives it a great flavor. This is a stunning cupcake and easy to prepare—a fabulous dessert that makes everyone happy.

1. Preheat the oven to 350°F. Place liners in a cupcake pan.
2. In a large bowl, whisk together the flour, granulated sugar, cocoa, espresso powder, baking powder, salt, and baking soda. Add the hot water and stir. In a small bowl, combine the melted butter with the eggs and vanilla. Add to the large bowl and beat until the batter is smooth. Fold in the mini chocolate chips.
3. Scoop into the liners, filling each liner two-thirds full. Bake for 18 to 20 minutes, or until a toothpick comes out without crumbs. Let the cupcakes cool in the pan for a few minutes. Transfer the cupcakes to a rack to cool completely before frosting.

CHERRY BUTTERCREAM

Using an electric mixer on medium-high speed, whip the butter until slightly fluffy. Add the sifted confectioners' sugar and mix on low speed until incorporated. Add the vanilla and whip on high. Add the cherry liqueur 1 tablespoon at a time just until the buttercream is pale pink and rather thick but smooth enough to pipe. Pipe or spoon onto the cooled cupcakes and top each with a cherry.

Nosh AP GF flour (page 4)
110 grams | heaping ¾ cup

granulated sugar
150 grams | ¾ cup

unsweetened cocoa powder, sifted
50 grams | ½ cup

instant espresso powder
(decaf is fine)
1 teaspoon

baking powder
1 teaspoon

kosher salt
½ teaspoon

baking soda
¼ teaspoon

hot tap water
115 grams | ½ cup

unsalted butter, melted
135 grams | 9 tablespoons or ½ cup plus 1 tablespoon

eggs
180 grams | 3 extra-large

vanilla extract
1 teaspoon

semisweet mini chocolate chips
85 grams | ½ cup

CHERRY BUTTERCREAM

unsalted butter, slightly softened
115 grams | 8 tablespoons or ½ cup

confectioners' sugar, sifted
440 grams | 4 cups

vanilla extract
½ teaspoon

maraschino cherry liqueur or juice
(from cherry jar)
2 to 4 tablespoons

TOPPING

extra-large maraschino cherries with stems, drained and dried
12 cherries

MOM'S MARBLE CHIFFON CAKE

Nosh AP GF flour (page 4)
260 grams | 2 cups

superfine sugar
325 grams | 1½ cups plus 2 tablespoons

baking powder
1 tablespoon

kosher salt
½ teaspoon

unsweetened cocoa powder, sifted
50 grams | scant ½ cup

hot tap water
80 grams | ⅓ cup

canola oil
145 grams | ½ cup plus 2 tablespoons

vanilla extract
2 teaspoons

brewed coffee (decaf is fine)
1 tablespoon

warm water
160 grams | ⅔ cup

eggs, separated
360 grams | 6 extra-large

orange liqueur, Grand Marnier preferred
1 tablespoon
   or
fresh orange juice
1 teaspoon

cream of tartar
¼ teaspoon

There is something about marbling with chocolate and vanilla that made my mother happy. She liked to bake all kinds of things that could be swirled. It makes me happy that I was able to re-create this favorite so that the gluten-free cake tastes just as my brothers and I remember. Keep in mind that less swirling is better when it comes to marbling, and always try to drag the batter (using a butter knife) in a figure eight, for best results.

1. Preheat the oven to 325°F. Set aside a 10-inch angel food cake pan with a removable bottom. Do *not* grease the pan.

2. In a medium bowl, sift the flour with 150 grams (¾ cup) of the superfine sugar, and the baking powder and salt. Sift a second time. Yes, really.

3. In another medium bowl, sift the cocoa and add the hot water. Whisk until smooth. Add 25 grams (2 tablespoons) of the sugar, 30 grams (2 tablespoons) of the canola oil, 1 teaspoon of the vanilla, and the brewed coffee and whisk to combine.

4. To the flour mixture, add the warm water. Whisk in the remaining 115 grams (½ cup) of canola oil, all of the egg yolks, the remaining 1 teaspoon of vanilla, and the orange liqueur. Whisk to combine.

5. In a large bowl, using an electric mixer on high speed, whip all the egg whites and the cream of tartar until frothy and add the remaining 150 grams (¾ cup) of superfine sugar a little at a time, continuing to whip until soft peaks form.

6. Add the flour batter to the egg whites and fold in gently until fully combined. Take a third of that mixture and place in the bowl with the chocolate mixture. Fold gently to combine.

7. To layer the batter, place a small amount of the chocolate mixture in the bottom of the ungreased pan. Next, place half of the light-colored batter in the angel cake pan. Add half of the remaining chocolate mixture on top. Using a butter knife, marble that mixture just slightly. Add the remaining light-colored batter on top, followed

by the remaining chocolate batter. Marble the upper half of batter with a butter knife. Remember, less is more.

8. Bake the cake for 40 to 50 minutes, or just until a toothpick comes out without crumbs and the edges are beginning to look crusty golden. Invert the cake pan onto a rack, or for a retro challenge, invert the cake pan on a long-necked bottle. Leave the cake upside down to cool completely, an hour or so. Once the cake is completely cool, run a sharp knife around the edge and release the removable bottom, bringing the cake out of the pan while still attached to the inside tube. Gently run a knife around the bottom edge of the cake and the inside tube and invert onto a serving plate. Store, covered, at room temperature.

superfine sugar
400 grams | 2 cups

Nosh AP GF flour (page 4)
130 grams | 1 cup

kosher salt | ½ teaspoon

unsweetened cocoa powder, sifted
30 grams | 5 tablespoons

instant espresso powder (decaf is
fine)
1 teaspoon

cream of tartar
½ teaspoon

egg whites
280 grams | 8 extra-large

vanilla extract | 1 teaspoon

FILLING

marshmallows, homemade (page
242), or Paskesz kosher preferred
454 grams | 16 ounces

whole or nondairy milk, almond
preferred
245 grams | 1 cup

heavy cream or nondairy whipped
topping
485 grams | 2 cups

vanilla extract | 1 teaspoon

seedless raspberry or other fruit jam,
Bonne Maman preferred
370 grams | one 13-ounce jar

raspberry liqueur, Framboise
preferred | 2 tablespoons
  or
100% pure fruit juice | 1 tablespoon

TOPPINGS

unsweetened cocoa powder, sifted
50 grams plus 20 grams more for
dusting | ½ cup, plus 3 tablespoons
more for dusting

fresh berries, raspberries preferred
170 grams | 1 half-pint

CHOCOLATE ANGEL CAKE ROLL

This cake is best made the day before serving and refrigerated overnight to infuse the flavors, set the filling, and give you time to recover because while nothing about making the cake is complicated, it does take a number of steps. The trickiest part is rolling it up, but if you've prerolled the warm cake according to the directions, you should be just fine. That dusting of cocoa powder is not just for good looks; it covers all those tiny and inevitable little cracks. If possible, don't leave out the liqueur in the raspberry jam layer—it adds a great dimension to the flavors and by the end of a long seder, it won't hurt and might even help. Chocolate cake goes well with a variety of fruits, so feel to substitute your favorite fruit jam instead of raspberry.

1. Preheat the oven to 325°F. Line an ungreased baking sheet with parchment paper. Set aside an additional baking sheet–size piece of parchment paper and the same size cooling rack.

2. Place 200 grams (1 cup) of the superfine sugar in a large bowl. Sift in the flour, salt, cocoa, and espresso powder. Whisk to combine. Add the cream of tartar to the egg whites in a separate bowl. Whip the whites on high speed until soft peaks start to form. Add in the vanilla. Add the remaining 200 grams (1 cup) of superfine sugar to the whites a little at a time, until they form glossy peaks. Sift the flour mixture over the top of the whipped whites. Using a spatula, fold in gently until the mixture is combined. Scrape the batter onto the lined baking sheet and spread the batter to the edges as evenly as possible. Give it a gentle whack on the countertop to even it out and make sure no huge air bubbles remain, but don't slam it hard enough to sink the whole thing.

3. Bake the cake for 16 to 20 minutes, or just until a toothpick comes out with some gooey chocolate crumbs and the cake acts slightly springy when touched. Remove from the oven, and while it is warm, use a butter knife to loosen the cake from the edge of the pan. Place the baking

sheet–size piece of parchment paper on top of the cake. Next, place the baking sheet–size cooling rack upside down on the parchment so its feet are up in the air. Using pot holders, flip the whole thing over. The cake will fall onto the rack. Remove the baking sheet. Very carefully peel the parchment from the cake and then place it gently back on the cake. There should be a piece of parchment on the bottom and top of the cake at this point. Using both pieces of parchment, starting from the short side, roll the cake up tightly—the parchment will roll along with it. You are giving the cake a little idea of what you expect it to do once it is filled, and believe me, cake has memory. Leave it rolled for 10 minutes, or until it feels cool to the touch, then let it unroll gently. It should stay curved. Let it cool completely before filling and leave both sheets of parchment on the cake so it doesn't dry out.

FILLING

1. In a double boiler, melt the marshmallows with the milk. Stir to incorporate. Strain, if necessary, so that the mixture is completely smooth. While it cools, make the whipped cream. Don't dawdle, because the marshmallow will become solid if it cools too long.
2. Whip the cream just until soft peaks form (or scoop about 108 grams [2 cups] of nondairy whipped topping into the bowl). Fold in the vanilla. When the marshmallow mixture is cool, add to the cream and whip together until stiff peaks form. Do not overwhip or you will have marshmallow butter.
3. Heat the jam in the microwave for 20 seconds on high so that it is just slightly liquid and tepid. Mix in the liqueur and stir well.

ASSEMBLY AND TOPPINGS

1. Once the cake is fully cooled, have all your assembly ingredients together. Remove the parchment from the top of the cake. With the short side facing you, cover the entire cake with the raspberry mixture and use an offset spatula or the back of a spoon to apply the jam evenly. Next, with a clean spatula, apply an even but generous layer of the whipped filling, leaving a slight gap at the furthest end.
2. Taking the narrow edge closest to you, roll up the cake pretty tightly—apply some pressure but accommodate the filling and try not to crack the cake, if possible. As you are rolling, peel away the bottom layer of parchment. Keep it flat on the countertop under the cake, because you will need it to move the cake once it is rolled. Use the parchment to help transfer the cake, rolling it seam side down, to a serving platter or a smaller baking sheet. Sift the 50 grams (½ cup) of cocoa all over the cake, creating a thick coating.
3. Loosely cover the cake with plastic wrap and refrigerate overnight, for best flavor. Remove the cake from the refrigerator. Trim the edges and dust with the remaining 3 tablespoons of sifted cocoa to freshen up the coating. Cut the cake into generous slices and serve with fresh raspberries on the side and a dollop of whipped cream (or nondairy whipped topping), if you wish. Refrigerate any leftovers.

Chocolate Angel Cake Roll (page 90)

Coconut Snowflake Cake (page 94)

MAKES 8 SERVINGS

BAKING TIME: 27 to 30 minutes

unsalted butter, slightly softened,
plus more for greasing
  150 grams | 10 tablespoons or ½ cup
  plus 2 tablespoons

Nosh AP GF flour (page 4),
plus more for flouring pan
  260 grams | 2 cups

granulated sugar
  300 grams | 1½ cups

eggs
  240 grams | 4 extra-large

baking powder
  1½ teaspoons

baking soda
  ½ teaspoon

kosher salt
  ½ teaspoon

vanilla extract
  1 teaspoon

orange liqueur, Grand Marnier
preferred, or orange extract
  1 teaspoon

lemon extract
  ½ teaspoon

crème fraîche or sour cream
  110 grams | ½ cup

canned coconut milk
  120 grams | ½ cup

SIMPLE SPIRITED SYRUP

granulated sugar
  2 tablespoons

hot tap water
  115 grams | ½ cup

orange liqueur, Grand Marnier
preferred
  3 tablespoons
      or
orange extract
  2 teaspoons

(INGREDIENTS CONTINUE)

COCONUT SNOWFLAKE CAKE

Aside from a fabulous chocolate cake, there's nothing more show-stopping than an elegant coconut layer cake topped with a blizzard of beautiful snow-white coconut flakes. The cake is infused with coconut flavor aided by a little alcohol. The secret to this flavorful cake is the *liquid lunch*, as we call it around here. It's a simple sugar syrup infused with flavors that are brushed onto the cake layers before the icing is applied to keep the cake moist. But if the cake must be clear-headed, feel free to use a citrus extract instead of alcohol.

1. Preheat the oven to 350°F. Grease two 8-inch round layer cake pans with butter and line them with parchment rounds. Grease the parchment with butter. Dust with flour.

2. In a large bowl, using an electric mixer on medium-high speed, cream the butter with the granulated sugar. Add the eggs, one at a time, until incorporated. In a separate bowl whisk together the flour, baking powder, baking soda, and salt. Stir the vanilla, orange liqueur, and lemon extract into the butter mixture. Stir in the flour mixture. In a small bowl, stir together the crème fraîche and coconut milk. Add to the batter and beat until smooth.

3. Divide the batter evenly between the prepared cake pans. Bake the cake for 15 minutes and rotate the pans for even baking. Bake for 12 to 15 minutes more, or just until a toothpick comes out without crumbs and the cake is just starting to look golden brown. Let the cake cool in the pans for 5 minutes. Run a knife around the edges and invert the cake layers onto a rack to cool completely before adding the simple syrup and buttercream.

SIMPLE SPIRITED SYRUP

Dissolve the granulated sugar in the hot water. Add the liqueur. Let cool to room temperature. Brush on the top of the cooled cake layers. Brush on once more. There will be a little syrup left over. Let the layers dry for 30 to 60 minutes before applying the buttercream.

CITRUS COCONUT BUTTERCREAM

In a large bowl, using an electric mixer on medium-high speed, whip the butter. Add the confectioners' sugar and mix on low speed until incorporated. Add the vanilla, orange liqueur, and coconut milk, 1 tablespoon at a time. Whip on high speed until very light and fluffy. You want the mixture to be somewhat stiff and hold peaks, but soft enough to spread. Add more coconut milk as needed.

ASSEMBLY AND TOPPING

1. Using an offset spatula, coat the bottom layer of the cake with a thin layer of icing to secure the cake crumbs (this is called a crumb coat). Add a generous dollop of icing on top of the bottom layer before placing the other cake layer on top. Apply a crumb coat over the entire cake. Let the crumb coat set for 30 minutes. You can refrigerate or freeze the cake to shorten the time to 15 minutes. In the meantime, cover the remaining icing with plastic wrap so it doesn't dry out. When the crumb coat is set, apply the final layer of icing all over the cake in a consistent thickness.

2. With clean hands, press the coconut flakes gently all over the cake to make them adhere to the icing. You want a generous layer of coconut. Sprinkle extra flakes on top of the cake for a decorative touch. This cake is best served at room temperature.

CITRUS COCONUT BUTTERCREAM

unsalted butter, slightly softened
230 grams | 16 tablespoons or 1 cup

confectioners' sugar, sifted
440 grams | 4 cups

vanilla extract
1 teaspoon

orange liqueur, Grand Marnier preferred, or orange extract
1 teaspoon

canned coconut milk
2 to 4 tablespoons

TOPPING

unsweetened coconut flakes
400 grams | 7 cups

DARK CHOCOLATE RASPBERRY CREAM CAKE

This chocolate cake is dressed up in a cloud of raspberry liqueur–flavored whipped cream and decorated with a boatload of fresh raspberries. It is incredibly flexible: You could serve this cake at a dinner party and yet it would also be right at home at a backyard barbecue.

1. Preheat the oven to 350°F. Grease two 8-inch round layer cake pans and dust with unsweetened cocoa. Shake out the excess.

2. Cut the butter into two or three pieces. Place the cocoa, butter, and coffee in a medium saucepan. Simmer on low heat just until the butter is melted. Remove from the heat, add the superfine sugar, and mix thoroughly. Let the mixture cool until it is just warm to the touch. Whisk together the flour with the baking powder, baking soda, and salt in a small bowl. Add the flour mixture to the saucepan and mix thoroughly. Mix in the egg and stir in the sour cream, vanilla, and raspberry liqueur until combined. Cover the batter and let it sit for 20 minutes undisturbed.

3. Stir the batter once and divide evenly between the prepared cake pans. Bake the cake for 5 minutes, then turn down the temperature to 325°F. Bake for 25 to 30 minutes more, or until the cake is springy in the center and a toothpick comes out with some moist crumbs. Let cool in the pan for 15 minutes, then loosen the sides and invert the cakes onto a rack to cool completely.

4. To make the whipped cream topping, in a large bowl, using an electric mixer on high speed, whip the heavy cream until soft peaks form. Add the superfine sugar, jam, vanilla, and liqueur and whip on high speed until stiff peaks form.

5. Spread half of the cream on top of one cake layer. Place enough raspberries on the whipped cream, rather close together, fat side down, to cover the cream. Place the top cake layer gently on the first layer. Cover the top with the other half of the whipped cream and place the remaining raspberries close together in a decorative pattern. Serve immediately. Store leftovers in the refrigerator.

nonstick spray or butter, for greasing

unsweetened cocoa powder, sifted, plus more for dusting pan
  25 grams | 4 tablespoons or ¼ cup

cold unsalted butter
  135 grams | 9 tablespoons or ½ cup plus 1 tablespoon

brewed coffee (decaf is fine)
  155 grams | ⅔ cup

superfine sugar
  250 grams | 1¼ cups

Nosh AP GF flour (page 4)
  130 grams | 1 cup

baking powder | 1 teaspoon

baking soda | ½ teaspoon

kosher salt | ½ teaspoon

egg
  60 grams | 1 extra-large

full-fat sour cream
  115 grams | ½ cup

vanilla extract | 1 teaspoon

raspberry liqueur, Framboise preferred | 1 tablespoon
    or
raspberry flavoring | 1 teaspoon

WHIPPED CREAM TOPPING

heavy cream
  485 grams | 2 cups

superfine sugar
  100 grams | ½ cup

raspberry jam, Bonne Maman preferred | 2 to 4 tablespoons

vanilla extract | ½ teaspoon

raspberry liqueur, Framboise preferred | 1 tablespoon
    or
raspberry flavoring | 1 teaspoon

TOPPING

fresh raspberries
  340 to 510 grams | 2 to 3 half-pints

ANNIE'S CAKE

nonstick spray or butter, for greasing

Nosh AP GF flour (page 4), plus
more for flouring pan
    260 grams plus 1 teaspoon | 2 cups
    plus 1 teaspoon

baking powder
    1½ teaspoons

kosher salt
    ½ teaspoon

unsalted butter, slightly softened
    150 grams | 10 tablespoons |
    ½ cup plus 2 tablespoons

sugar
    200 grams | 1 cup

eggs
    120 grams | 2 extra-large

whole milk
    245 grams | 1 cup

vanilla extract
    1 teaspoon

fresh orange juice
    2 tablespoons

bittersweet bar chocolate, grated
    70 grams | one 3-ounce bar |
    ⅔ cup

GLAZE

semisweet bar chocolate, roughly
chopped
    285 grams | one 10-ounce bar |
    2½ cups

bittersweet bar chocolate, roughly
chopped
    285 grams | one 10-ounce bar |
    2½ cups

heavy cream
    245 grams | 1 cup

light corn syrup
    1 tablespoon

A dotted-Swiss cake with chocolate glaze was our daughter Annie's first birthday cake. Since then the cake has always been referred to as Annie's Cake. A rich chocolate glaze is a great way to dress up any simple cake and make it look elegant—even if your recipient is a one-year-old. We like to make the cake in heart-shaped tins, a family tradition more than a half-century old that started when my mother learned that birthday pies weren't going to make the cut any longer. No matter what shape pan you bake it in, this cake will be a classic. Mixing bittersweet with semisweet chocolate for the glaze gives the chocolate a rich, dark, not-too-sweet flavor.

1. Preheat the oven to 350°F. Grease and flour two 8-inch round layer cake pans.

2. In a small bowl, whisk together the 260 grams (2 cups) of flour, the baking powder, and the salt. In a large bowl, cream together the butter and sugar until well mixed and slightly fluffy. Add the eggs, one at a time. In a small bowl, combine the milk, vanilla, and orange juice.

3. Alternately add the flour mixture and the milk mixture to the butter mixture. Mix until the batter is smooth, 1 to 2 minutes. Toss the grated chocolate with the remaining 1 teaspoon of flour in a small bowl. Add to the cake batter and fold in gently just until combined. If you fold with enthusiasm there is a chance the batter will turn into a chocolate cake.

4. Divide the batter evenly between the two prepared pans. Rap the pans on the countertop to remove any air bubbles. Bake the cake for 20 minutes and rotate the pans for even baking. Bake for 8 to 10 minutes more, or until the cake starts to shrink away from the edges, the top is golden, and a toothpick comes out clean.

5. Let cool in the pans for 5 minutes and then invert each layer onto a rack and let cool completely before applying the glaze.

GLAZE

1. Place the chopped chocolate in a heatproof bowl. In a small saucepan, heat the cream and corn syrup until small bubbles appear—right before it simmers. Remove from the heat and pour over the chopped chocolate. Let the mixture sit undisturbed for 1 minute, then stir gently to avoid incorporating any air into the glaze, just until the chocolate is completely melted.

2. Let the glaze cool for 10 to 15 minutes, stirring occasionally. Pour over the cooled bottom layer of cake and let it drip down the sides. Add the top layer and repeat. Let the chocolate set at room temperature, about 30 minutes.

BERRY REDUCTION

fresh berries
170 grams | 1 half-pint

sugar
2 tablespoons

warm water
2 tablespoons

raspberry liqueur, Framboise
preferred, optional
1 tablespoon

freshly grated lemon zest
5 grams | 1 tablespoon

BERRY LEMON CUPCAKES

Nosh AP GF flour (page 4)
175 grams | 1⅓ cups

sugar
175 grams | ¾ cup plus 2
tablespoons

lemon zest, freshly grated
5 grams | 1 tablespoon

baking powder
1 teaspoon

kosher salt
¼ teaspoon

baking soda
¼ teaspoon

unsalted butter, melted
130 grams | 9 tablespoons or ½ cup
plus 1 tablespoon

vanilla extract
½ teaspoon

lemon extract
1 teaspoon

eggs
120 grams | 2 extra-large

fresh lemon juice
2 tablespoons

buttermilk (see page 250)
80 grams | ⅓ cup

Berry Reduction (above),
1 to 3 tablespoons, to taste

(INGREDIENTS CONTINUE)

BERRY LEMON CUPCAKES

A lemon cupcake swirled with a berry reduction and topped with berry-flavored Swiss buttercream (a meringue-based alternative to confectioners' sugar–based buttercream) is a cupcake that signals springtime. This is a nice change from the ubiquitous plain yellow cupcake, and with one bite you'll know it is special. The cupcake can be made with any seasonal berry you wish, making it as versatile as a little black dress that never goes out of style.

BERRY REDUCTION

1. In a small saucepan, place the berries, sugar, water, raspberry liqueur (if using), and lemon zest. Cook over medium heat until the mixture simmers. Lower the heat and simmer gently until the berriâes are mushy and the mixture thickens, 5 to 8 minutes, stirring often.
2. Strain into a container and let cool to room temperature. Set the reduction aside for swirling in the cupcake batter and the buttercream.

BERRY LEMON CUPCAKES

1. Preheat the oven to 350°F. Place liners in a cupcake pan.
2. Place the flour in a medium bowl. In a small bowl, using clean fingertips, mix the sugar and lemon zest together until the sugar turns pale yellow. Add to the flour. Add the baking powder, salt, and baking soda and whisk to combine. Stir together the butter, vanilla, lemon extract, eggs, lemon juice, and buttermilk. Add to the dry mixture and mix until the batter is smooth.
3. Place one quarter of the batter in a small bowl. Add 1 to 3 tablespoons of the Berry Reduction, as desired, and stir until thoroughly mixed (it should look pale purple). Add back to the batter and marble just slightly. It will continue to marble when you scoop—so don't overdo the marbling. Scoop into the prepared pan, filling each liner two-thirds full. Bake the cupcakes for 18 to 22 minutes, or just until a toothpick comes out clean. Let cool in the pan for a few minutes, then transfer to a rack and let the cupcakes cool completely before frosting.

BERRY SWISS BUTTERCREAM

1. Place the egg whites, sugar, salt, and cream of tartar in a double boiler and stir until the temperature reads 160°F, 4 to 5 minutes. Transfer the mixture to a large bowl. Using an electric mixer on high speed, whip until the whites have high glossy peaks and the bottom of the bowl is no longer warm when touched by your hand.

2. Switch to the paddle attachment if using a stand mixer (if using a hand mixer, just keep mixing). Turn the mixer speed to medium (and watch the whites deflate a little bit). Cut the butter into 1-inch cubes. Begin adding the butter, while continuing to beat, until it is all incorporated. Turn the mixer speed to high and beat until the buttercream comes together. It will go through a stage where it looks like a curdled wreck. Just keep going. It will eventually become a decent-looking buttercream. (It will happen within minutes in a stand mixer, but with a hand mixer it will take quite a bit longer, 10 to 12 minutes, depending on the power of your mixer. Don't give up—it will come together.)

3. Once the buttercream looks smooth and pulls away from the edges of the bowl, add the vanilla and 2 to 4 tablespoons of Berry Reduction, as desired, and beat on high speed until well mixed. The buttercream should be a nice pale shade of berry color. Pipe onto the cooled cupcakes, using your choice of tip, and top each with a fresh berry.

4. Refrigerate until 30 minutes before serving. Store leftovers in the refrigerator for up to two days, but serve at room temperature, for best flavor.

BERRY SWISS BUTTERCREAM

egg whites
  105 grams | 3 extra-large

sugar
  200 grams | 1 cup

kosher salt
  ¼ teaspoon

cream of tartar
  ¼ teaspoon

unsalted butter, slightly softened
  180 grams | 12 tablespoons or ¾ cup

vanilla extract
  1 teaspoon

Berry Reduction (page 100)
  2 to 4 tablespoons, to taste

fresh berries
  12 berries

COCONUT CUPCAKES

Vanilla and coconut are like favorite cousins who should clearly visit together more often. If you love coconut, this cupcake will become a favorite. Be sure to use a good-quality canned full-fat coconut milk and unsweetened coconut, for best flavor.

1. Preheat the oven to 350°F. Place liners in a cupcake pan.
2. In a large bowl, whisk together the flour, granulated sugar, baking powder, and salt. Cut the shortening into three or four pieces. Stir the coconut milk thoroughly. Add the shortening pieces, eggs, coconut milk, and vanilla to the dry mixture. Using an electric mixer on medium-low speed, mix the ingredients until the batter is smooth, lump-free, and a little bit fluffy, 2 to 3 minutes. Fold in the coconut. Fill each liner two-thirds full.
3. Bake the cupcakes for 18 to 22 minutes, or just until a toothpick comes out without crumbs. Let cool in the pan for a minute or two. Transfer the cupcakes to a rack and let cool completely before frosting with the buttercream.

COCONUT BUTTERCREAM

Using an electric mixer on low speed, whip together the shortening, confectioners' sugar, vanilla, and 1 tablespoon of the coconut milk. Whip the mixture on high speed until it is light and fluffy. Add more coconut milk if the mixture is too stiff to pipe. Pipe or spoon onto each cupcake. Sprinkle the coconut on the top of each cupcake.

Nosh AP GF flour (page 4)
175 grams | 1⅓ cups

granulated sugar
200 grams | 1 cup

baking powder
1 heaping teaspoon

kosher salt
½ teaspoon

shortening
96 grams | 8 tablespoons or ½ cup

canned coconut milk
160 grams | ⅔ cup

eggs
180 grams | 3 extra-large

vanilla extract
1 teaspoon

unsweetened shredded coconut, toasted (see page 251)
15 grams | ½ cup

COCONUT BUTTERCREAM

shortening
96 grams | 8 tablespoons or ½ cup

confectioners' sugar, sifted
330 grams | 3 cups

vanilla extract
1 teaspoon

canned coconut milk
1 to 3 tablespoons

unsweetened shredded coconut, toasted (see page 251)
15 grams | ½ cup

WHITE WEDDING CUPCAKES

unsalted butter, slightly softened
150 grams | 10 tablespoons or ½ cup plus 2 tablespoons

superfine sugar
175 grams | ¾ cup plus 2 tablespoons

vanilla extract
1 teaspoon

almond extract
½ teaspoon

orange extract
½ teaspoon

egg
60 grams | 1 extra-large

egg whites
70 grams | 2 extra-large

Nosh AP GF flour (page 4)
200 grams | 1½ cups

baking powder
1 heaping teaspoon

kosher salt
½ teaspoon

whole milk
120 grams | ½ cup

WHITE SWISS MERINGUE BUTTERCREAM

egg whites
140 grams | 4 extra-large

granulated sugar
200 grams | 1 cup

kosher salt
¼ teaspoon

cream of tartar
¼ teaspoon

unsalted butter, slightly softened
290 grams | 20 tablespoons or 1¼ cups

almond extract
½ teaspoon

orange extract
½ teaspoon

vanilla extract
¼ teaspoon

GF shiny sugar pearls, white decorative sugar, nonpareils, or sprinkles, for topping

White cupcakes are great for special events or parties. Be sure to find fancy greaseproof white cupcake liners (see page 252) to complete the look. When I serve these, we always feel as if we should get dressed up and use fancy dishes. Sometimes we do. Sometimes we eat leftovers for breakfast. What? You never ate a fancy cupcake for breakfast?

1. Preheat the oven to 325°F. Place fancy-schmancy liners in a cupcake pan.

2. Using an electric mixer, cream the butter with the superfine sugar on medium speed until light and fluffy—almost like frosting. Stir in the vanilla, almond, and orange extracts. Add the egg and egg whites, mixing until fully incorporated.

3. In a small bowl, whisk the flour with the baking powder and salt. Add to the butter mixture and mix on medium speed until just incorporated. Add the milk and mix just until incorporated. Remove the bowl from the stand and using a silicone spatula, fold the batter to make sure all the dry stuff is mixed in.

4. Fill each liner just one-half full. These should bake with a flat top just below the cupcake liner rim, to accommodate the buttercream. Bake for 17 to 19 minutes, or just until a toothpick comes out without crumbs. Don't let it get brown or golden—remember, you want a white cupcake. Let the cupcakes cool in the pan for a few minutes. Transfer the cupcakes to a rack to cool completely before frosting.

WHITE SWISS MERINGUE BUTTERCREAM

1. In a heatproof bowl, combine the egg whites, granulated sugar, salt, and cream of tartar. Place the bowl over a pan with simmering water (double boiler) and stir until the temperature reads 160°F, which should take 4 to 5 minutes. Using a stand or hand mixer on high speed, whip until the whites have high glossy peaks and the bottom of the bowl can be touched by your hand and it isn't terribly hot, less than 5 minutes.

2. Switch to the paddle attachment if using a stand mixer (if using a hand mixer, just keep mixing as you were). Turn the mixer speed to medium (and watch the whites deflate a little bit). Cut the butter into 1-inch cubes. Begin adding the pieces of butter until it is all incorporated. Turn the mixer speed to high and mix until the buttercream comes together. It will go through a stage where it looks curdled and like a wreck. Just keep going. You will hear the mixture go from slosh to thump right before it changes to a decent-looking buttercream. (It will happen within minutes in a stand mixer but with a hand mixer will take quite a bit longer, 10 to 12 minutes, depending on the power of your mixer. Don't give up—it will come together.)

3. Once the buttercream looks smooth and pulls away from the edge of the bowl, add the almond and orange extracts and vanilla. Pipe or spoon onto the cooled flat-top cupcakes. Sprinkle immediately with shiny sugar pearls or toppings of your choice.

4. Refrigerate until 30 minutes before serving. Store leftovers in the refrigerator but serve at room temperature, for best flavor.

PIES and TARTS

Long before I showed up as the *surprise* baby girl, my mother thought birthdays were celebrated with pie. My older brothers still talk about those pies at every family gathering. By the time I arrived, my mom had made the conversion to birthday cake, so I have no firsthand birthday pie experience, but if I were to pick one, I'd have apple, please. Or if I'd ever met a genuine fig during my childhood, I might want a fig tart. Maybe birthday pies will make a comeback.

Pies and tarts can be intimidating, and the gluten-free kind can seem downright impossible. But by the end of this chapter you will be able to make them anytime you wish. Included are picnic pies and small tart recipes that are not only easy to handle and less intimidating than a big pie, but also make everyone who gets one feel like he or she won the pie lottery—lots of flavor in small bites.

And last—there is absolutely nothing wrong with incorporating a store-bought GF piecrust into one of these recipes. There are some great premade crusts out there, and in the end, all anyone cares about is that the pie tastes good. A good pie is just good eating.

SPECIAL EQUIPMENT

Metal or ceramic pie and fluted metal tart pans and baking sheets, rolling pin, food processor or pastry blender, lots of plastic wrap

TIPS

- With practice you'll listen to the dough in the food processor and it will tell you when the ball is starting to form.
- Parchment and heavy-duty plastic wrap to encase the dough while rolling are a sanity saver.
- Chilling the pie or tart before baking ensures that the crust will be as flaky as possible.
- Brushing the dough with egg wash right before baking helps make it golden brown.
- To patch crust cracks in pies and tarts, always hold back a tablespoon-ish of raw dough—think spackle.
- To avoid a shrunken blind-baked crust, build up the sides slightly higher than necessary.

BUTTER CRUST

Nosh AP GF flour (page 4)
300 grams | 2⅓ cups

sugar
1 tablespoon

kosher salt
½ teaspoon

cold unsalted butter
115 grams | 8 tablespoons or ½ cup

shortening
85 grams | 7 tablespoons or ¼ cup
plus 3 tablespoons

ice water
80 to 100 grams | ⅓ to ½ cup

CREAM CHEESE CRUST

Nosh AP GF flour (page 4)
300 grams | 2⅓ cups

sugar
1 tablespoon

kosher salt
½ teaspoon

cold unsalted butter
115 grams | 8 tablespoons or ½ cup

shortening
25 grams | 2 tablespoons

cold full-fat cream cheese
60 grams | 4 tablespoons or ¼ cup

ice water
80 to 100 grams | ⅓ to ½ cup

JUST THE CRUSTS

Do not be intimidated by crusts. Gluten-free pie and tart crust is based on this sensible and proven baking ratio: 3 parts flour to 2 parts fat to 1 part liquid. The ratio is slightly adjusted to accommodate the properties of GF flour and starch. Each crust recipe makes one double-crust 9-inch pie or two single-crust 9-inch pies or tarts. Be brave and venture forward into the world of crusts.

The following four, interchangeable crust recipes are the only ones you'll ever need for any pie or tart in this chapter—or any pie filling you wish to make. The Savory Crust, however, is best saved for the Mushroom and Leek Quiche (page 232) and other savory recipes. The secret to great piecrust is taking advantage of the refrigerator and freezer to help handle the dough. The more you practice, the easier and quicker these crusts are to make.

DOUGH

1. Place the dry ingredients in a food processor and pulse to mix. If making the Savory Crust, add the mixed herbs at this point. Cut the butter (if using) into ½-inch cubes. Add the butter, shortening, and/or cream cheese and pulse until the mixture looks like coarse crumbs—ten good pulses will do it. Alternatively, use a pastry blender tool and mix together in a large bowl.

2. While the processor is running, slowly add about 50 grams (¼ cup) of the ice water. Keep adding water as needed. As soon as the dough merges into a ragged ball, stop adding water because it is perfect. Rarely will all the water be necessary. If mixing by hand, add the water in small amounts and mix with a fork just until the dough comes together in a ragged clump.

3. Turn out the dough onto a large piece of plastic wrap. Knead with the heel of your hand just until all the dough pieces come together. Divide the dough into two equal portions. Flatten into round disks, wrap in plastic, and refrigerate at minimum for 2 hours, or overnight, for best flavor.

4. Proceed with your preferred pie or tart recipe.

ASSEMBLY

1. Roll out one disk at a time, leaving the other to chill. Set aside a tablespoon-ish of dough to patch any cracks, which are inevitable. Raw dough equals sanity saver. Sandwich the remaining (chilled) dough between two large pieces of plastic wrap. Use the rolling pin to press down on the dough from the center out to warm it up slightly. Roll out the dough into a circle ⅛ inch thick and slightly larger than the pan's diameter. Remove the top piece of plastic. Using the bottom piece of plastic wrap to handle the dough, flip the dough into the pie or tart pan with the plastic wrap facing up. Gently settle the crust into the bottom without stressing the dough. Once in place, carefully peel away the plastic wrap. The dough may tear, but just pinch it back together. Settle the dough in place, and pinch or patch with extra dough where necessary. Using your fingers, build up the side wall just a bit taller than the pan, to accommodate any shrinkage when it bakes. Place the pie or tart pan on a baking sheet and chill in the freezer or refrigerator for 30 minutes.

2. If the pie requires a top crust, repeat step 1 for the second disk, rolling it out a bit larger and thinner than the first. Chill the crust, still encased in plastic wrap, on a baking sheet for 15 to 30 minutes.

3. At this point, the plastic-wrapped crust can remain chilled until you are ready to fill and bake a pie. It will keep in the refrigerator for 3 days or in the freezer for 3 months. Do not thaw before filling/blind baking. Add 5 minutes to all baking times for frozen piecrusts.

4. Let the top crust sit for 10 minutes at room temperature before trying to place it onto a filled pie. Once it starts to feel pliable, peel the top plastic sheet from the dough.

5. Flip the crust onto the center of the filling and peel off the remaining plastic wrap. Gently move the crust so that the edges meet and fold over to seal, while crimping the edge of the crust. Try to accommodate the filling and not stretch the top crust. Slice vent holes as needed.

6. Bake according to the recipe.

DAIRY-FREE CRUST

Nosh AP GF flour (page 4)
  300 grams | 2⅓ cups

sugar
  1 tablespoon

kosher salt
  ½ teaspoon

shortening
  195 grams | 16 tablespoons or 1 cup

ice water
  80 to 100 grams | ⅓ to ½ cup

SAVORY CRUST

To any of the crust recipes, add 1 tablespoon of mixed herbs to the dry mixture in the food processor. Combinations could include:
- thyme, sage, and parsley
- herbes de Provence
- oregano, basil, and parsley

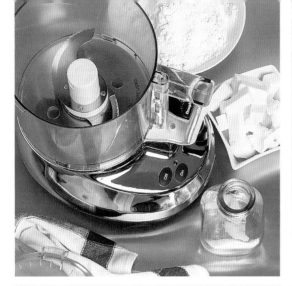

TOP LEFT:
The usual suspects, mise en place

TOP RIGHT:
What a ragged smeary dough ball should look like

MIDDLE LEFT:
The dough sandwich in plastic wrap

MIDDLE RIGHT:
Gently fitting the dough into a metal pie pan

BOTTOM RIGHT:
Crimped and ready to chill before filling or blind baking

MINI FRUIT TARTS

MAKES 8 TO 12 SMALL TARTS

BAKING TIME: 45 to 50 minutes

DAIRY-FREE OPTION AVAILABLE

These handheld fruit tarts are perfect desserts to serve to a crowd. Use whatever fruit is in season. You will want to pile as much fruit with as much variety of colors into the tart as possible for the best presentation. If you make the dairy version, a dollop of whipped cream added to the top before serving is a nice touch. They taste best slightly warm.

1. Roll out the crust dough on a parchment-lined surface dusted lightly with flour and covered with plastic wrap, until it is ⅛ inch thick. Using a 5-inch round cutter dipped in the GF flour, create as many circles as possible. Slide the parchment with the dough circles onto a baking sheet.
2. Beat the egg and brush each circle generously with the beaten egg. Sprinkle ½ teaspoon of sugar over the center of each circle.
3. Preheat the oven to 350°F. In the center of each circle over the sugar, mound your choice of fruit into a pyramid shape. Leave at least 1½ inches of margin around the edge of the dough. Pull up the edge around the fruit to make a cup, creating a wall by overlapping the dough and pinching as you go—the egg wash will help it stay in place. The wall should slope in toward the fruit. Add more fruit if it can be done without compromising the shape of the dough. Layer different color fruit on the top so when it bakes down, you get a view of the variety of fruits.
4. Sprinkle additional sugar into each fruit mound and splash a tiny amount of the liqueur into the center of the fruit mixtures.
5. Brush the outside of each tart crust with egg and sprinkle liberally with sugar. Bake for 20 minutes and rotate the pans for even baking. Bake for 25 to 30 minutes more, or until the fruit is bubbling and the crusts are dark golden brown. Let cool on the pan for 5 minutes. Transfer to a rack and serve slightly warm. Or if you are holding them for serving after they're cold, place the tarts on a freshly parchment-lined baking sheet and reheat in a preheated 300°F oven for 10 minutes.

Cream Cheese Crust (page 108) or Dairy-Free Crust (page 109)
  dough for 1 single crust

Nosh AP GF flour (page 4), for dusting

egg
  60 grams | 1 extra-large

sugar
  100 grams | ½ cup

seasonal berries: blackberries, blueberries, or raspberries
  510 g | 3 half-pints

ripe fresh or frozen peaches or apricots, sliced
  2 to 4 small

fruit liqueur or fruit juice
  1 to 2 tablespoons

APPLE POMEGRANATE TART

MAKES ONE 9- TO 10-INCH
TART; SERVES 6 TO 8

BAKING TIME: 75 minutes
(including blind-baking time)

DAIRY-FREE OPTION AVAILABLE

This tart contains figs, but it is bigger on the apple flavors. Be sure to cook this tart as long as it takes to get the juices to thicken—and they will. The apples should become browned around the edges. The final application of heated honey on the apples after the tart has baked gives it a nice shine.

1. Preheat the oven to 350°F. Roll out the crust dough between two sheets of plastic wrap. Place in the tart pan and smooth to fit. Freeze for 15 minutes. Bake the empty tart shell for 15 minutes. Patch any cracks with leftover raw tart dough as needed.

2. Mix the fig preserves, pomegranate concentrate, orange liqueur, salt, cloves, lemon juice, and zest together.

3. Spread 3 tablespoons of the fig mixture in a thin layer over the bottom of the partially baked tart crust. Peel, core, and slice the apples into thin slices. Cut one third of the apples into a small dice. Fill the tart crust with the diced apples and press flat. Spoon the remaining 3 table-spoons of the fig filling over the apples. Top with concentric circles of the thinly sliced apples.

4. Bake for 30 to 40 minutes and rotate the pan for even baking. Bake for 15 to 20 minutes more, until the crust is golden brown, the apples are soft and turning color and darkening on their edges, and the filling is bubbly hot and, most importantly, thick. Remove from the oven and, while the tart cools, prepare the topping.

5. To make the topping, heat the honey in a microwave-safe container on high for 15 seconds, or on low heat on the stove top just until it flows easily and is warm to the touch. Brush the top of the warm tart generously with the heated honey. Let the tart cool completely before serving.

Cream Cheese Crust (page 108) or
Dairy-Free Crust (page 109)
  dough for 1 single crust

fig preserves or jam, Bonne Maman
preferred
  128 grams | 6 tablespoons or ¼ cup
  plus 2 tablespoons

pomegranate concentrate
(see page 251)
  1 teaspoon

orange liqueur, Grand Marnier
preferred, or orange juice
  1 teaspoon

kosher salt
  ¼ teaspoon

ground cloves
  ¼ teaspoon

fresh lemon juice
  ½ teaspoon

lemon zest, freshly grated
  5 grams | 1 tablespoon

tart apples: Granny Smith, Gala, Fuji,
or McIntosh
  3 to 4 large

TOPPING

honey, orange blossom or
blackberry preferred
  2 tablespoons

FIG TART

When I was a kid, one honey cake was sufficient for Rosh Hasha-nah. If my mom was feeling really ambitious, an apple cake might follow the next night. But these days, with the generous abundance of the fall fruit harvest at the market, it makes sense to celebrate that bounty. This tart is gooey and a little juicy. Give it time to set up and cool before serving. The additional juice that runs out of the tart is intentional and provides a nice color contrast to the dark figs.

Cream Cheese Crust (page 108) or
Dairy-Free Crust (page 109)
  dough for 1 single crust

fig preserves or jam, Bonne Maman
preferred
  185 grams | half of a 13-ounce jar

tart apples: Granny Smith, Fuji,
McIntosh, or Gala
  2 to 3 large

lemon zest, freshly grated
  5 grams | 1 tablespoon

fresh lemon juice
  1 tablespoon

pomegranate concentrate
(see page 251)
  2 tablespoons

honey, blackberry or orange
blossom preferred
  80 grams | ¼ cup

fresh figs
  12 to 24 figs

TOPPING

honey
  1 to 2 tablespoons

pomegranate concentrate
(see page 251)
  1 to 2 teaspoons

1. Preheat the oven to 350°F. Roll the crust dough between sheets of plastic wrap. Place in the tart pan and smooth to fit. Freeze for 15 minutes. Bake the empty tart shell for 15 minutes. Patch any cracks with leftover raw tart dough as needed. Let cool for 15 minutes before filling.

2. Spread the fig preserves in a thin layer over the bottom of the partially baked tart crust. Peel, core, and cut the apples into ¼-inch cubes. In a small bowl, add the lemon zest and juice to the apples and stir gently.

3. In a small container, stir together the pomegranate concentrate and 40 grams (2 tablespoons) of the honey and add 1 tablespoon of the mixture to the apple mixture. Stir. Place the apples on top of the layer of fig preserves and gently press down to fit the apples snugly. Drizzle the remaining 40 grams (2 tablespoons) of honey over the apples. Trim off the stems from the figs and slice each fig in half. Lay in a circle on top of the apples, cut side down. Fill in the entire top of the tart with figs. Press gently. Drizzle the remaining pome-granate mixture over the top of the figs.

4. Place the tart pan on a baking sheet (to catch any drips). Bake for 35 minutes and rotate the pan for even baking. Bake for 15 to 20 minutes more, or until the crust is light-ly golden and the apples are soft when pierced with a knife. Let cool for 10 minutes.

5. To make the topping, combine the honey and pomegranate concentrate and heat in a microwave-safe container on high for 20 to 25 seconds or on low heat on the stove top until bub-bling. Immediately brush all over the warm tart. Let cool thoroughly before removing the tart from the pan.

MOM'S APPLE PIE

There is no such thing as too many apples in a pie. Be adventurous and pile those apples mile high. Mix up the apple varieties and punch up the flavor. They bake down considerably. Be generous with the cinnamon—apple pie is the better for it. Serve with very sharp Cheddar or a generous scoop of vanilla ice cream.

1. Place the bottom crust in a 9-inch pie pan. Place the pan on a baking sheet and chill in the refrigerator while preparing the filling.

2. Peel, core, and thinly slice the apples. Place the sliced apples in a large bowl. Sprinkle the lemon juice and zest over the apples and toss. This prevents them from turning brown and adds another layer of flavor. Add the brown sugar, granulated sugar, cinnamon, nutmeg, and salt. Fold in gently. Be sure to taste-test: This is a tart pie but you should notice a small hint of sweetness. Add the tapioca starch and fold until everything is well mixed.

3. Remove the pie pan from the refrigerator. Stir the apple pie filling one more time and place in the crust, pressing the apples down gently as you go for a snug fit. Keep the peak piled high in the center and slope toward the edges. Press firmly in place.

4. Preheat the oven to 375°F. Prepare the top crust per step 7 of the crust recipe. Beat the egg and brush on the top crust. Sprinkle with coarse sugar. Cut two vents in the center. Chill the pie in the refrigerator for 20 minutes before baking.

5. Place the pie on a baking sheet to catch drips and bake for 10 minutes. Rotate the pan for even baking and turn down the temperature to 350°F. Bake for 50 minutes more, or until the pie begins to brown and the apple filling juices start leaking. Turn down the temperature to 325°F and bake for 10 minutes more, or until the apples bubble in the middle and the crust looks nice and golden toasty.

6. Let cool until barely warm and serve with ice cream or Cheddar cheese. The apple filling will have cooked down and the top crust will probably collapse a bit as it cools, all part of the homemade apple pie charm.

Butter Crust (page 108), Dairy-Free Crust (page 109), or Cream Cheese Crust (page 108)
  dough for 2 single crusts

tart apples: Granny Smith, Gala, Pippin, McIntosh, or Fuji
  8 to 9 large

fresh lemon juice
  1 to 2 teaspoons

lemon zest, freshly grated
  5 grams | 1 tablespoon

brown sugar
  50 grams | ¼ cup, packed

granulated sugar
  40 grams | 3 tablespoons

ground cinnamon
  1 teaspoon

nutmeg, freshly grated preferred
  ¼ teaspoon

kosher salt
  ¼ teaspoon

tapioca starch or Nosh AP GF flour (page 4)
  25 grams | 3 tablespoons

egg
  60 grams | 1 extra-large

coarse sugar
  1 tablespoon

Cream Cheese Crust (page 108) or
Dairy-Free Crust (page 109)
  dough for 2 single crusts

Nosh AP GF flour (page 4)
  2 teaspoons

egg
  60 grams | 1 extra-large

coarse sugar | 2 tablespoons

APPLE BANANA FILLING (MAKES ENOUGH FOR 12 HAND PIES)

unsalted butter | 2 tablespoons
    or
shortening | 1 tablespoon

tart apples: Pippin, Gala, Granny
Smith, Fuji, or McIntosh, finely diced
  2 large

brown sugar | 1 heaping tablespoon

ground cinnamon | ½ teaspoon

nutmeg | ¼ teaspoon

gnarly (very ripe, blackened) banana
  1 medium, thinly sliced

dark rum | 2 tablespoons
    or
rum flavoring | 1 teaspoon

FIGGY FILLING (MAKES ENOUGH FOR 12 HAND PIES)

fig preserves, Bonne Maman
preferred
  185 grams | ½ cup

figs, fresh preferred, finely diced | 8

freshly grated lemon zest
  5 grams | 1 tablespoon

Nosh AP GF flour (page 4)
  1 teaspoon

mace or nutmeg
  ½ teaspoon

ground cinnamon
  ½ teaspoon

kosher salt | ½ teaspoon

PICNIC PIES

Picnic pies are hand pies, perfect for small hands, road trips, picnics, or just snacks. These pies are one of the most popular treats we make in our house. The variety of fillings for mini pies can be as diverse as your imagination. We have two favorites, apple banana and figgy filling. Pile a bunch of these pies in a tin and carry them with you on your next road trip. Watch out for envious stares when you open the tin and eat them at rest stops. We've been known to "make new friends" when that happens.

1. Roll out the chilled crust dough sandwiched between sheets of plastic wrap dusted with 2 teaspoons of flour until it is about ⅛ inch thick. Remove the top plastic wrap. Using a 5-inch round cutter dipped in the flour, create as many circles as possible. Reroll the scraps of dough and continue to make crust rounds until you have a total of twelve.

2. Place the dough circles on two parchment paper–lined baking sheets—six to each sheet—and refrigerate while preparing the filling.

APPLE BANANA FILLING

1. Melt the butter in a large sauté pan over high heat just until bubbly. Add the apples, brown sugar, cinnamon, and nutmeg. Stir to coat the apples. Cook over high heat, stirring frequently, until the apples are soft and begin to brown and caramelize.

2. Add the banana and cook, stirring, until just incorporated, about 1 minute more. Turn off the heat and add the rum to deglaze the pan. Let cool for 20 minutes, or until the mixture is no longer hot to the touch.

FIGGY FILLING

1. In a bowl, mix the fig preserves with the diced figs, lemon zest, flour, mace, cinnamon, and salt.

2. Let the mixture sit for 5 minutes. Stir before using.

ASSEMBLY

1. Preheat the oven to 350°F. Remove the crusts from the refrigerator and let them sit at room temperature until the dough is pliable, 5 minutes.

2. Divide your filling of choice into twelve equal portions. Beat the egg and brush each dough circle. Place the filling to one side of the circle and gently fold over the pastry to meet the other side. The dough should be warm enough to bend so it doesn't crack when you fold it over the filling.

3. Crimp the edges of each pie with a fork to seal. If the dough cracks, use a finger dipped in water to "paint" the dough until it seals. Use as little water as possible. Cut vents in the top. Brush each top with egg wash and sprinkle with coarse sugar. Bake for 5 minutes and turn down the temperature to 325°F. Bake for 25 to 30 minutes more, until the pastry is golden brown and the filling is bubbling though the vents. Let cool on the baking sheet for 5 minutes. Transfer to a rack and let cool completely. The hand pies are fragile when fresh from the oven but will become pretty sturdy as they cool.

SWEET POTATO PUMPKIN BUTTER PIE

This sweet potato pie is enhanced with pumpkin butter, giving it a layered flavor—the best of both. It's a nice twist on ordinary pumpkin pie that's perfect for Sukkot or Thanksgiving or just because you love sweet potato. Pumpkin butter can be found in many grocery stores year-round, but especially in the fall.

1. Preheat the oven to 375°F. Place the crust in a 9-inch pie pan. Place the pan on a baking sheet and freeze for 15 minutes. Remove from the freezer and bake for 10 minutes. Patch any cracks with leftover raw dough as needed.

2. Place all the filling ingredients in a food processor (preferred) or blender—or in a large bowl. Pulse to mix or blend or whisk by hand until the filling is frothy and looks pale orange. The crust is fragile at this point, so gently pour the filling into the warm crust until just full.

3. Bake for 20 minutes and rotate the pan for even baking. Bake for 20 minutes more, or until the pie filling is somewhat puffy and no longer jiggles in the middle. Let cool on a rack. Refrigerate but serve at room temperature, topped with toasted chopped pecans, if desired.

MAKES ONE 9-INCH SINGLE-CRUST PIE; SERVES 6 TO 8

BAKING TIME: 50 minutes (including blind-baking time)

DAIRY-FREE

Dairy-Free Crust (page 109)
dough for 1 single crust

canned sweet potato puree
425 grams | one 15-ounce can | 1¾ cups

sugar
100 grams | ½ cup

Nosh AP GF flour (page 4)
1 tablespoon

ground cinnamon
½ teaspoon

kosher salt
½ teaspoon

ground cloves
¼ teaspoon

vanilla extract
1 teaspoon

pumpkin butter (see page 255)
80 grams | 4 tablespoons

eggs
300 grams | 5 extra-large

full-fat canned coconut milk
240 grams | 1 cup

pecans, toasted (see page 251) and roughly chopped, optional
40 grams | ⅓ cup

CROSTATA FOR ALL SEASONS

MAKES ONE 9-INCH FREE-FORM TART; SERVES 6 TO 8

BAKING TIME: 45 to 50 minutes

DAIRY-FREE

A sweet crostata is a quick and rustic Italian dessert brought to us by way of the wandering Jews that were expelled from southern Italy to Rome during the reign of Ferdinand and Isabella. Savory crostata became a sweet once they were living near the Mediterranean and introduced to cane sugar and citrus, and we've never looked back. If you have a piecrust in the freezer or refrigerator, you're more than halfway done. All you need is enough seasonal fruit to cover the 9-inch crust to 1 inch in height. Add some sugar and zest and dessert is ready quickly.

1. Preheat the oven to 350°F. Line a rimmed baking sheet with parchment paper. The rim is necessary to catch the fruit juices.
2. Using the piece of parchment that was on the rimmed baking sheet and with plastic wrap on top, roll out the crust dough until it is a 10- to 11-inch circle or square. Remove the plastic wrap. Fold up the edge to make a generous lip of dough, making the crostata 8 or 9 inches in diameter. Slide the parchment back onto the rimmed pan.
3. If the fruit needs cutting, make sure the pieces are all the same size. Mix the fruit with the flour. Arrange the fruit evenly over the crust right up to the lip of dough. You will want to end up with fruit covering the entire crust to the lip, making it an inch deep. Manipulate the lip of the crostata dough to cover the edge of the fruit just slightly. Sprinkle the sugar over the entire crostata. Sprinkle with the zest. Beat the egg and use it to brush the edge of the dough.
4. Bake for 25 minutes and rotate the pan for even baking. Bake for 20 to 25 minutes more, or until the crust is dark golden brown and the fruit is bubbling in the middle. It's a rustic-looking free-form pie—it will look slightly browned and almost burned in some spots where the sugar caramelizes the fruit and crust.
5. Let cool in the pan until you can slide the parchment onto a rack. Let cool completely and serve at room temperature.

Dairy-Free Crust (page 109)
dough for 1 single crust

SEASONAL FRUIT
- berries
  340 to 510 grams | 2 to 3 half-pints
- apples or pears, cubed or sliced
  4 medium to large
- fresh figs, cubed
  2 pints | 680 grams

Nosh AP GF flour (page 4)
2 tablespoons

sugar
50 to 100 grams | ¼ to ½ cup

orange or lemon zest, freshly grated
5 grams | 1 tablespoon

egg
60 grams | 1 extra-large

MAKES TWELVE
2- TO 3-INCH TARTS

CHILLING TIME: 30 minutes
BAKING TIME: 25 to 30 minutes

ALMOND SCHMEAR

sugar
100 grams | ½ cup

GF almond flour
35 grams | ¼ cup

roasted, salted almonds
80 grams | ½ cup

Lyle's Golden Syrup (preferred) or
light corn syrup
40 grams | 3 tablespoons

almond milk
45 grams | 3 tablespoons

almond extract
½ teaspoon

TARTS

Cream Cheese Crust (page 108)
dough for 1 single crust

nonstick spray, for greasing

Almond Schmear (above)
150 grams | heaping ½ cup

roasted, salted almonds, roughly
chopped
140 grams | heaping 1 cup

unsweetened coconut flakes
60 grams | heaping 1 cup

sweetened condensed milk
80 grams | 4 tablespoons or ¼ cup

semisweet mini chocolate chips
85 grams | scant ½ cup

egg
60 grams | 1 extra-large

almond extract
1 teaspoon

CHOCOLATE NUT TWO-BITE TARTS

These bite-size layered tarts pack a big nosh. The bottom layer provides the big nutty flavor foundation, while the top layers give it a coconut, chocolate finish. The Almond Schmear recipe makes enough for two batches of tarts and keeps for a week in the refrigerator. Be sure to note that this recipe uses store-purchased roasted and salted nuts because they provide the best flavor. The schmear can also be used in the Frangelico Pear Tart (page 127).

ALMOND SCHMEAR

Place all the schmear ingredients in the bowl of a mini food processor or blender. Process until all the almonds are finely chopped and the mixture is well mixed and smooth. Place in a small covered container. Use immediately or refrigerate for up to 1 week.

TARTS

1. Divide the crust dough into twelve 30-gram pieces, reserving a teaspoon. Set aside the teaspoon of raw dough for patching, if needed. Roll the pieces into balls, using the palm of your hand. Flatten, slightly, into small disks and place on a platter. Cover with plastic wrap and chill for 30 minutes.

2. Preheat the oven to 350°F. Grease a 12-count muffin pan generously with nonstick spray. Cut 1 × 7-inch strips of parchment paper and set them in each muffin cup with the edges higher than the top of the pan, to act as a sling for the easy removal of the tarts. Remove the dough disks from the refrigerator. Arrange three or four at a time between sheets of plastic wrap, giving them plenty of space, and roll out to a little over 3 inches in diameter. Remove the top plastic. Using a 3-inch cutter with scalloped edges (preferred) cut out circles. Use the plastic wrap as an aid to lift the circles of dough, one at a time. Place each circle gently over a muffin cup opening. Use your fingertips to slide the dough in evenly without tearing. Press into the bottom and sides of the muffin pan. Use leftover raw dough to patch, if needed. Repeat the process

until all the muffin cups are filled. The dough should come up about one third of the way and be flat on the bottom. Place the pan in the freezer for 15 minutes while preparing the filling.

3. Alternatively (not as neat or pretty), place the refrigerated dough disks directly into the muffin cups. Using a shot glass covered in plastic wrap, press until the dough in each cup is flat on the bottom and expands up the sides of the muffin cup one third of the way. Place the pan in the freezer for 15 minutes while preparing the filling.

4. Place the almond schmear, 100 grams (⅔ cup) of the chopped almonds, 50 grams (1 scant cup) of the coconut, the condensed milk, and 70 grams (⅓ cup) of the mini chocolate chips in a medium bowl. Stir to combine. Stir in the egg and almond extract.

5. Remove the muffin pan from the freezer. Scoop 1 heaping tablespoon of filling into each tart, making sure each is filled to just below the edge of the crust.

6. Bake for 20 minutes and remove from the oven. Scatter the remaining chopped almonds, coconut flakes, and mini chocolate chips over the top of each tart. Bake for 5 to 10 minutes more, or until the top is bubbly and the coconut is starting to brown. Let cool in the muffin pan for 15 minutes. Remove each tart (using its parchment sling) to a rack to cool completely. Enjoy plain or with a scoop of vanilla ice cream or whipped cream, if desired.

FRANGELICO PEAR TART

MAKES ONE 9-INCH TART OR
FOUR 5-INCH TARTS;
SERVES 4 TO 8

BAKING TIME: 50 to 60 minutes
DAIRY-FREE OPTION AVAILABLE

This is the dessert that will make Aunt Hope wonder whether you bought it at that hip new kosher bakery because she won't believe you made it yourself. There are few ingredients in this tart, so be sure to find the best-tasting, ripe, yet firm pears you can. The variety doesn't matter as much as their flavor. Pears should not be soft, nor should they feel like a rock. The best way to pick a great pear is to smell it—if the perfume smells like a perfectly ripe pear, that's the one to take home. Sometimes the most elegant dessert is actually the simplest.

Cream Cheese Crust (page 108) or
Dairy-Free Crust (page 109)
  dough for 1 single crust

firm, ripe pears: Bosc or Anjou
  4 to 5 medium

fresh lemon juice
  1 teaspoon

Nosh AP GF flour (page 4)
  1 tablespoon

Almond Schmear (page 124)
  150 grams | heaping ½ cup |
  about ½ batch

lemon zest, freshly grated
  5 grams | 1 tablespoon

hazelnut liqueur, Frangelico
preferred, optional
  1 tablespoon

honey, orange blossom preferred
  60 grams | 3 tablespoons

1. Roll out the crust dough between two sheets of plastic wrap and then fit into one 9-inch or four 5-inch tart pans with removable bottom(s).

2. Peel, core, and slice the pears as thinly and evenly as possible. Reserve the more attractive slices and cut the remaining slices into small cubes. Drizzle the lemon juice over the reserved slices so they don't turn brown. Toss only the cubes with the flour. Remove the tart crust from the refrigerator. Spoon the almond filling evenly into the bottom of the crust. Evenly distribute all the cubed pear pieces over the almond filling. Sprinkle with the lemon zest. Place the reserved pear slices on top in an attractive pattern, covering the entire tart. Sprinkle the hazelnut liqueur over the sliced pears.

3. Preheat the oven to 325°F. Refrigerate the tart for 10 minutes. Place the tart pan on a baking sheet and bake for 50 to 60 minutes, rotating the pan halfway through for even baking. Bake until the crust is golden and the center of the tart is bubbling. The pear edges should start to brown. Remove from the oven and let cool on a rack for 10 minutes.

4. Heat the honey for 20 seconds in the microwave on high or on low heat on the stove top until it is liquid. Brush on top of the tart evenly but gently; the fruit is very fragile while warm and could tear. Let cool on a rack. Serve at room temperature or chilled; it tastes great both ways.

PASTRIES

When people hear the word *pastry*, they usually think of the person with the big white hat behind the counter at a fancy bakery or restaurant dessert station. Most people don't think *pastry* and the home kitchen. While pastry making is absolutely time-consuming, it should never be difficult. I like to break up the preparation. Chilling dough overnight gives the dough a chance to develop more flavor and makes the tasks manageable. Although electric gadgets, like food processors and mixers, will be the handiest tools, you can also mix the dough using a pastry blender tool (see page 10) or even just a fork and clean fingers. No need to run to the bakery for pastry. And never any need to do without pastry if you are gadget- or gluten-free.

SPECIAL EQUIPMENT

Food processor or pastry blender tool, stand or hand mixer, parchment paper and plastic wrap, pizza cutter, rolling pin, double boiler, Advil, and lots of coffee

TIPS

- Ingredients should be diced, cut, or cubed to about the same size, so they bake evenly.
- Fats like butter and cream cheese should be very cold when mixed into the flour.
- Egg whites separate best when cold, but whip best at room temperature.
- When removing dough from a food processor, always be careful when extracting the blade from the dough.
- Plastic wrap and parchment paper are the gluten-free baker's best friends. Use them to sandwich the pastry dough when rolling.
- Using a pizza wheel to slice pastry dough is better than using a knife, which can crush the edge.
- Tins are better for pastry storage—plastic containers may make them soggy.

Nosh AP GF flour (page 4)
300 grams | 2⅓ cups

xanthan gum
½ teaspoon

kosher salt
½ teaspoon

sugar
1 teaspoon

cold unsalted butter
180 grams | 12 tablespoons or ¾ cup

cold full-fat cream cheese
85 grams | 6 tablespoons or ⅓ cup

egg
60 grams | 1 extra-large

cold water
45 grams | 3 tablespoons

RUGELACH DOUGH

Basic rugelach dough can be paired with a variety of fillings. The dough contains cream cheese, which lends it a slightly tart flavor and also helps make dough handling much easier. Expect the dough to be sticky at first and resist the urge to add more flour. Be the boss of the dough. And chill that dough, because once it's ready, rugelach fillings await (see pages 131–135). When tackling the job of rolling out and filling the rugelach dough, it helps to imagine that you are making a pizza, with a couple of differences—slice first and then add the toppings. Each slice will get rolled from the outside edge toward the center point, becoming like a crescent roll in the process.

1. Place the flour, xanthan gum, salt, and sugar in the bowl of a food processor. If mixing by hand, place the ingredients in a large bowl. Cut the butter and cream cheese into 1-inch cubes and add to the bowl. Pulse two or three times to mix until you have coarse crumbs the size of peas. Add the egg and water. Pulse just until the dough forms a ragged, sticky ball. Alternatively, blend the ingredients together with a fork or a pastry blender tool.

2. Turn out the ball onto plastic wrap. Knead slightly. Divide into two equal balls. Flatten each dough ball into a flat disk. Wrap in plastic. Refrigerate for at least 4 hours or overnight, then proceed with the rugelach recipe of your choice.

RAISIN PECAN RUGELACH

I have a confession to make. The rugelach that inspired this recipe turned me into a bona fide rugelach cookie monster. Whenever a family friend brought these over to the house, they disappeared in a flash. Filled with raisins, pecans, and gooey brown sugar, these classic pastries are impossible to resist.

1. Preheat the oven to 350°F. Line two baking sheets with parchment paper.
2. Prepare one dough disk at a time while the other remains chilled. Roll out the disk sandwiched between two flour-dusted sheets of plastic wrap. Roll the disk into a 16-inch neat round as though you were making a thin-crust pizza. Remove the plastic wrap top. Using a pizza or pastry cutter, divide the circle into sixteen equal wedges—like cutting the pizza into sixteen slices. The easiest way to do this is to slice the dough into quarters. Slice those quarters in half, and then do that again.
3. Stir the filling ingredients together. Divide them in half and sprinkle over the dough. Cover with the plastic wrap and press lightly just to adhere the filling.
4. To roll up each rugelach, begin from the outside edge of the "slice." Lift the edge, using an offset spatula, and roll toward the center point, like a crescent roll, ending with the point. Gently pick up the rolled rugelach and place on a prepared baking sheet. Repeat steps 2 through 4 until there are thirty-two rolled crescents on the two baking sheets—sixteen to each sheet.
5. Set the filled baking sheets in the refrigerator for 15 minutes before baking.
6. To make the topping, stir the melted butter with the sugar and cinnamon. Just before baking, brush the tops of the rugelach with the mixture. Bake for 15 minutes and rotate the pans for even baking. Bake for 16 to 20 minutes more, or just until they are toasty, golden brown. Let cool on the baking sheet for a few minutes, then transfer to a rack to cool completely.

Rugelach Dough (page 130)
1 batch
Nosh AP GF flour (page 4), for dusting

FILLING
brown sugar
200 grams | 1 cup
raisins
150 grams | 1 cup
pecans, toasted (see page 251) and roughly chopped
120 grams | 1 cup
ground cinnamon
1 teaspoon
nutmeg, freshly grated preferred
½ teaspoon
lemon zest, freshly grated
5 grams | 1 tablespoon
kosher salt
¼ teaspoon

TOPPING
unsalted butter, melted
30 grams | 2 tablespoons
granulated sugar
2 teaspoons
ground cinnamon
½ teaspoon

Rugelach Dough (page 130)
1 batch

Nosh AP GF flour (page 4), for dusting

FILLING

semisweet chocolate chips, frozen
225 grams | 1⅓ cups

bittersweet chocolate chips, frozen
60 grams | ⅓ cup

ground cinnamon
1 heaping teaspoon

cold unsalted butter
85 grams | 6 tablespoons or ¼ cup
plus 2 tablespoons

dark rum
3 tablespoons
or
rum flavoring
1 teaspoon

orange zest, freshly grated
5 grams | 1 tablespoon

pecans, toasted (see page 251) and
roughly chopped
120 grams | 1 cup

TOPPING

unsalted butter, melted
30 grams | 2 tablespoons

sugar
2 teaspoons

ground cinnamon
½ teaspoon

CHOCOLATE PECAN RUGELACH

It would be easy to eat Chocolate Pecan Rugelach every day. The filling gets better with age and the rum flavor mellows. Although these taste best on the second day, they will last for four days. Freezing the chocolate chips in advance helps keep them from melting and clumping together when chopped. If you don't have a food processor or a strong blender, use mini chocolate chips or a finely chopped chocolate bar instead and mix the filling by hand in a bowl.

1. Preheat the oven to 350°F. Line two baking sheets with parchment paper.

2. Prepare one dough disk at a time while the other remains chilled. Roll out the disk sandwiched between two flour-dusted sheets of plastic wrap. Roll the disk into a 16-inch neat round as though you were making a thin-crust pizza. Remove the plastic wrap top. Using a pizza or pastry cutter, divide the circle into sixteen equal wedges—like cutting the pizza into sixteen slices. The easiest way to do this is to slice the dough into quarters. Slice those quarters in half, and then do that again.

3. To make the filling, in the bowl of a mini food processor or a blender, pulse the frozen chocolate chips until they are almost a powder. Add the cinnamon and pulse again a few times. Make sure the chocolate is fully ground. Cut the butter into several pieces, add to the processor, and pulse until fully incorporated and the mixture starts to look like chocolate spread. Add the rum and orange zest and pulse until thoroughly mixed. If mixing by hand, use a fork to stir the mini chocolate chips with the remaining filling ingredients in a bowl until the mixture is well mixed.

4. Divide the filling and chopped pecans into two equal portions. Sprinkle one portion of the filling and one of the pecans over the dough. Cover with plastic wrap and press lightly with the rolling pin just to adhere the filling.

5. To roll up each rugelach, remove the plastic wrap, then begin from the outside edge of the "slice." Lift the edge,

using an offset spatula, and roll toward the center point, like a crescent roll, ending with the point. Gently pick up the rolled rugelach and place on a prepared baking sheet. Repeat steps 2 through 4 until there are thirty-two rolled crescents on the two baking sheets—sixteen to each sheet.

6. Set the filled baking sheets in the refrigerator for 15 minutes before baking.

7. To make the topping, stir the melted butter with the sugar and cinnamon. Just before baking, brush the tops of rugelach with the cinnamon mixture. Bake for 15 minutes and rotate the pans for even baking. Bake for 16 to 20 minutes more, or just until they are toasty, golden brown. Let cool on the baking sheet for a few minutes, then transfer to a rack to cool completely.

Rugelach Dough (page 130)
  1 batch
Nosh AP GF flour (page 4), for dusting

FILLING

apricot jam
  85 grams | 4 tablespoons

semisweet mini chocolate chips
  255 grams | 1½ cups

dried apricots, finely chopped
  100 grams | ½ cup

ground cinnamon
  1 heaping teaspoon

orange zest, freshly grated
  5 grams | 1 tablespoon

TOPPING

unsalted butter, melted
  30 grams | 2 tablespoons

sugar
  2 teaspoons

ground cinnamon
  ½ teaspoon

DARK CHOCOLATE APRICOT RUGELACH

This variety of rugelach is a nod to my Sephardic ancestors from the Mediterranean who enjoyed a wide variety of fruits and nuts. Apricot and chocolate together is a combination I came to enjoy later on as an adult. I had no idea fruit, let alone dried fruit, could have a relationship with chocolate that was as good as, say, nuts and chocolate. Once you try apricot combined with chocolate, there is no going back.

1. Preheat the oven to 350°F. Line two baking sheets with parchment paper.

2. Prepare one dough disk at a time while the other remains chilled. Roll out the disk sandwiched between two flour-dusted sheets of plastic wrap. Roll the disk into a 16-inch neat round as though you were making a thin-crust pizza. Remove the plastic wrap top. Using a pizza or pastry cutter, divide the circle into sixteen equal wedges—like cutting the pizza into sixteen slices. The easiest way to do this is to slice the dough into quarters. Slice those quarters in half, and then do that again.

3. To make the filling, divide the jam in half. Stir the remaining filling ingredients together and divide in half. Spread one portion of the jam over the dough. Sprinkle one portion of the filling mixture over the dough. Cover with the plastic wrap and press lightly with the rolling pin just to adhere the filling.

4. To roll up each rugelach, remove the plastic wrap, then begin from the outside edge of the "slice." Lift the edge, using an offset spatula, and roll toward the center point, like a crescent roll, ending with the point. Gently pick up the rolled rugelach and place on a prepared baking sheet. Repeat steps 2 through 4 until there are thirty-two rolled crescents on the two baking sheets—sixteen to each sheet.

5. Set the filled baking sheets in the refrigerator for 15 minutes before baking.

6. To make the topping, stir the melted butter with the sugar and cinnamon. Just before baking, brush the tops of the rugelach with the cinnamon mixture. Bake for 15 minutes and rotate the pans for even baking. Bake for 16 to 20 minutes more, or just until they are toasty, golden brown. Let cool on the baking sheet for a few minutes, then transfer to a rack to cool completely.

DOUGH

Nosh AP GF flour (page 4), plus more
for dusting
  260 grams | 2 cups

Expandex Modified Tapioca Starch
(see page 3) or superfine sweet white
rice flour
  40 grams | 4 tablespoons or ¼ cup

pectin | ¼ teaspoon

xanthan gum | ½ teaspoon

kosher salt | ½ teaspoon

granulated sugar | 1 teaspoon

cold unsalted butter
  175 grams | 12 tablespoons or ¾ cup

full-fat sour cream
  200 grams | 1 cup minus 1
  tablespoon

FILLING

brown sugar
  100 grams | ½ cup

raisins
  75 grams | ½ cup

pecans, toasted (see page 251) and
roughly chopped
  120 grams | 1 cup

ground cinnamon | 1 teaspoon

honey
  20 grams | 1 tablespoon

TOPPING

unsalted butter, melted
  30 grams | 2 tablespoons

granulated sugar | 2 teaspoons

ground cinnamon | ½ teaspoon

RAISIN NUT STRUDEL BITES

This is not the kind of strudel dough that gets rolled thin enough
to read a newspaper through it, but it works out to be just as tasty.
Anyway, you're eating it, not reading it. Feel free to use your favorite
dried fruits and nuts, and don't forget to toast the nuts first, for best
flavor. Strudel bites are how I remember them from my childhood,
but this recipe will also make an attractive single strudel pastry that
can be cut into servings after baking.

1. To make the dough, place the flour, Expandex, pectin, xan-
    than gum, salt, and granulated sugar in the bowl of a food
    processor. Pulse to mix. Cut the butter into 1-inch cubes.
    Add to the processor and pulse until the mixture looks
    like coarse crumbs the size of peas. Add the sour cream
    and pulse until the dough just barely comes together in a
    very ragged, sticky ball. Turn out onto plastic wrap and
    remove the blade carefully. Knead with the heel of your
    hand to bring the dough together. It will be sticky. Flatten
    into a disk. Refrigerate for at least 4 hours or overnight.

2. Preheat the oven to 350°F. Line a baking sheet with parch-
    ment paper.

3. Let the dough sit at room temperature for 30 minutes
    before rolling so it doesn't crack. Meanwhile, stir together
    all the filling ingredients, except the honey, and set aside.

4. Roll out the dough on a sheet of parchment paper dusted
    lightly with flour. Top the dough with another dusting of
    flour and cover with plastic wrap. Roll into an 18 × 10-inch
    rectangle. Sprinkle the filling mixture over the dough,
    leaving a slight margin at the edges. Drizzle the honey
    over the filling.

5. Fold ½ inch of the dough from each edge toward the inside,
    over the filling. Begin rolling the dough from the long side,
    in jelly-roll fashion, being careful to keep it snug but not
    tight enough to crack. Finish seam side down. Give it a pat
    to make sure it is snug, and using a pizza cutter, cut into
    1-inch slices. If the dough is too soft to slice without crush-

ing it, set it on a pan in the refrigerator for 15 minutes. Place the cut pieces standing up on the prepared baking sheet.

6. Alternatively, chill the roll for 15 minutes, then make diagonal cuts only ½ inch deep every 1½ inches along the log. Set the log on the prepared pan on a diagonal so it will fit without bending.

7. To make the topping, stir the melted butter with the granulated sugar and cinnamon. Brush the top(s) of the strudel with the cinnamon mixture. Bake for 15 minutes and rotate the pan for even baking. Bake the individual strudels for 15 to 20 minutes more, or just until they are golden brown, or bake the whole log for 20 to 25 minutes longer, until the center is bubbly and the crust is golden brown. Let cool on the baking sheet for a few minutes, then transfer to a rack to cool completely.

Nosh AP GF flour (page 4)
160 grams | 1¼ cups

kosher salt
1 teaspoon

sugar
1 tablespoon

cold unsalted butter
75 grams | 5 tablespoons

whole milk
245 grams | 1 cup

eggs
240 grams | 4 extra-large

honey, blackberry sage preferred
100 grams | 5 tablespoons

nuts: pecans, walnuts or almonds, toasted (see page 251) and roughly chopped
60 grams | ½ cup

BAKED HONEY BITES

Teighlach have never been appealing to me, probably because of that pesky broken tooth incident, when I grabbed one that my Aunt Hope had made and tried to take a bite. But these are not that and so much more friendly to the teeth. Small-bite choux pastry is a great vehicle for drizzled honey covered in toasted nuts. They look attractive and taste great. Surprise Great-Aunt Millie and serve her this version of *teighlach*, honey bites, and see whether she doesn't ask you for the recipe.

1. Preheat the oven to 400°F. Line two baking sheets with parchment paper. Prepare a piping bag with a ½-inch tip or have ready a 2-tablespoon scoop.

2. In a small bowl, mix the flour with the salt and sugar. In a deep saucepan over medium heat, melt the butter with the milk and bring to a low simmer. With a wooden spoon, stir in the flour mixture all at once. The dough will almost immediately form a ball. Turn down the heat to the lowest setting and push the dough around as well as you can with the spoon for 2 minutes. Mostly you will be slapping the dough ball around the bottom of the pan, but keep going. At the 2-minute point, transfer the dough ball to a bowl.

3. Using an electric mixer on medium-low speed, mix the eggs into the dough, one at a time. Make sure each egg is fully worked into the dough before adding the next. At first, the egg will look like it is just slimy and sticking to the outside of the dough, but once it is incorporated, the dough gathers a little color and will become more yellow as the other eggs are mixed in. Make sure that last egg is really well incorporated. Using a spatula, fold the dough to make sure the egg is mixed in really well.

4. Place the dough in the piping bag. Pipe teaspoon-size domes onto the parchment, leaving about ½ inch in between each dome. They will look ridiculously small, but they expand like crazy. Keep going. You will get a lot on each sheet. Alternatively, hand scoop the mixture to form teaspoon-size domes.

5. Using your fingertips, sprinkle a few drops of cold water over the choux before placing the pan in the oven. Don't open the oven door at all during the baking because you risk the puffs falling flat. After 10 minutes, turn down the temperature to 350°F. Give them another 5 to 10 minutes; when they look puffed up and toasty brown, remove them from the oven. Transfer the puffs to a rack to cool completely.

6. Once the puffs are cool, set the rack over a baking sheet to catch drips. Warm the honey in the microwave on high for 30 seconds or on the stove top over low heat for just a few minutes. Drizzle the honey over the puffs. Drop the toasted chopped nuts on top while the honey is still warm, so they adhere. Wait for the honey to set, then enjoy.

HAMANTASHEN

In the old family slides there's a photo of my mother baking in the kitchen—making hamantashen, from the look of the dough. Those photos were taken before I was born, but those hamantashen sure look good. Purim is the Jewish holiday that celebrates the victory of Queen Esther and her Uncle Mordecai over that of bully, Haman; thus, we eat a replica of his hat filled with anything from poppy seeds to chocolate.

confectioners' sugar, sifted
   140 grams | 1¼ cups

Nosh AP GF flour (page 4)
   260 grams | 2 cups

kosher salt
   ½ teaspoon

cold unsalted butter
   60 grams | 4 tablespoons or ¼ cup

cold cream cheese
   58 grams | 4 tablespoons or ¼ cup

egg
   60 grams | 1 extra-large

lemon zest, freshly grated
   5 grams | 1 tablespoon

tapioca starch
   32 grams | ¼ cup

egg, for brushing
   60 grams | 1 extra-large

FILLING OPTIONS

GF poppy-seed filling, Love'n Bake preferred
   312 grams | 11 ounces

Nutella
   750 grams | one 26½-ounce jar | 2½ cups

caramel butterscotch sauce, Mrs. Richardson's preferred
   480 grams | one 17-ounce jar

fig preserves, Bonne Maman preferred
   370 grams | one 13-ounce jar

blueberry preserves, Bonne Maman preferred
   370 grams | one 13-ounce jar

1. In the bowl of a food processor, mix together 110 grams (1 cup) of the confectioners' sugar and the flour and salt. Cut the butter and cream cheese into 1-inch cubes. Add to the processor bowl. Pulse until the mixture looks like coarse crumbs. Add one egg and the lemon zest. Pulse until the dough forms a ragged ball.

2. Transfer the dough ball to plastic wrap. Knead the dough with the heel of your hand until it comes together and is smooth. Divide into two balls and wrap in plastic wrap. Refrigerate for 4 hours or overnight.

3. When ready to bake, preheat the oven to 350°F. Line two baking sheets with parchment paper.

4. Mix the tapioca starch and remaining 30 grams (¼ cup) of sifted confectioners' sugar in a small bowl. Sandwich one dough ball between two sheets of plastic wrap dusted with the tapioca starch mixture. Roll out the dough until it is between ⅛ and ¼ inch thick. Remove the top piece of plastic wrap, place the bottom piece with the dough on a baking sheet, and refrigerate or freeze for 10 minutes. Using a round 2½-inch cookie cutter, cut as many circles as possible and place them on the prepared baking sheets.

5. Repeat steps 2 through 4 with the other ball of dough.

6. Beat the remaining egg. Brush each circle with beaten egg. Place a teaspoon of the filling of your choice in the center of each cutout.

7. Pinch the edges of the circles up to form a triangle. Think of the circles as a clock. Pinch the dough between your thumb and index finger at three points: twelve o'clock,

four o'clock, and eight o'clock. It should look like a little pirate hat with the filling in the center of the hat.

8. Brush the whole thing with more egg wash. Refrigerate the pans for 15 minutes.
9. Bake for 10 minutes and rotate the pans for even baking. Bake for 5 to 8 minutes more, or until the hats are just golden brown and look set—the filling should be bubbling. Let cool on the baking sheet for a few minutes, then transfer to a rack to cool completely. They are exceptionally fragile while hot and warm. Using an offset spatula to move them to the rack is helpful.

instant yeast, Red Star preferred
10 grams | 1 tablespoon

nonfat dry milk powder
20 grams | 2 tablespoons

xanthan gum
1 teaspoon

kosher salt
1 teaspoon

guar gum
¼ teaspoon

pectin
¼ teaspoon

superfine sugar
80 grams | ⅓ cup

Nosh AP GF flour (page 4)
390 grams | 3 cups

unsalted butter, slightly softened
60 grams | 4 tablespoons or ¼ cup

eggs
120 grams | 2 extra-large

egg white
35 grams | 1 extra-large

fresh lemon juice
1 teaspoon

fresh lemon zest
5 grams | 1 tablespoon

vanilla extract
½ teaspoon

lemon extract
½ teaspoon

whole milk, scalded and cooled
245 grams | 1 cup

BUTTER LAYER

Nosh AP GF flour (page 4)
2 teaspoons

cold unsalted butter
115 grams | 8 tablespoons or ½ cup

(INGREDIENTS CONTINUE)

FLO'S DANISH

Florence was my Jewish deli pastry guru. That I knew Flo my entire life was my good fortune. As the end of her life came barreling forward the only thing she wanted to talk about with me were the finer points of her recipe for Danish and that there is no good reason for not wearing a good shade of lip coloring, even when housebound. Three days after she was gone, the Danish recipe arrived in the mail. Whenever I bake this gluten-free version, inspired by Flo, I make certain to wear a fabulous shade of lip gloss, in her honor.

1. In a large bowl, whisk together the yeast, milk powder, xanthan gum, salt, guar gum, pectin, superfine sugar, and flour. Mix in the butter with a fork just until it looks like coarse, uneven crumbs. In a small bowl, whisk together the eggs and egg white, lemon juice, lemon zest, vanilla, and lemon extract. Stir the egg mixture into the flour mixture. Add the milk and mix until it is well combined. Using a silicone spatula, scrape the dough down the sides. Fold from the bottom to make sure all the dry matter is mixed in. Cover the bowl with plastic wrap and place in the refrigerator for at least 2 to 3 hours or overnight.

2. To make the butter layer, place 1 teaspoon of the flour on a large sheet of plastic wrap. Place the butter on top of the flour. Cover the butter with the remaining teaspoon of flour. Fold the plastic wrap over the top and, using a rolling pin, pound the butter into a rough 4-inch square. Refrigerate the butter layer until needed.

3. Remove the dough from the refrigerator and place it on a flour-dusted sheet of plastic wrap or parchment paper. Form the dough into a 12 × 5-inch rectangle. Remove the prepared butter layer from the refrigerator, place it in the center of the rectangle, and fold the dough over the packet to seal it in.

4. Turn the dough so that the fold now faces you. Using the sides of your hand (think karate chopping) hit the dough until it is a rectangle that again measures 12 × 5 inches. Fold the dough like a business letter in thirds the long way and turn it so that the fold faces you. Repeat this four

more times so that you've folded the dough a total of six times.

5. Wrap the folded dough in plastic and place it in the refrigerator for at least an hour or overnight if you want to make the Danish the next morning.

6. Line three baking sheets with parchment paper.

7. Remove the dough from the refrigerator and divide it into three equal-size portions. Roll out each piece of dough into a 12 × 6-inch rectangle. Square up the edges as neatly as possible. Using a pizza cutter, slice the dough lengthwise into six 12-inch-long lengths. Roll up each strand and tuck the ends underneath. Flatten the rolled dough in the palm of your hand until it is about ½ inch thick and place on the prepared baking sheet. Repeat until you have 6 Danishes on each baking sheet. Cover with plastic wrap and let them rise until doubled in size, about an hour. You can also place them in the refrigerator overnight to rise.

8. To make the cheese filling, in the bowl of a food processor or blender combine the cheese, egg yolks, confectioners' sugar, vanilla, lemon extract, and zest. Pulse until the mixture is smooth. Transfer the filling to a small container with a lid and store in the refrigerator until needed.

9. Preheat the oven to 425°F. Using the back of a spoon or a clean thumb, press into the center of each Danish to create the crater that will hold the filling. Make the crater as wide as you wish but be sure it is surrounded by a raised rim of dough to keep the filling from spilling as it bakes. Fill each crater to the top with about 1 tablespoon of the filling of your choice. Brush each pastry with the beaten egg, taking care not to brush over the filling. As the Danishes bake, the filling will bubble up and look as though it will spill over (and some might), but it will settle back down once they finish baking.

10. Place two baking sheets at a time into the oven. Bake for 5 minutes. Reduce the oven temperature to 350°F and continue to bake the Danishes for 12 to 15 minutes more until the pastry is golden brown. An instant-read digital thermometer should read 200°F when they are finished baking. Cool the Danishes on the pan for 5 minutes, then transfer them to a rack to cool completely before adding the icing.

CHEESE FILLING

mascarpone cheese or cream cheese, at room temperature
225 grams | 8 ounces

egg yolks
50 grams | 2 extra-large

confectioners' sugar, sifted
25 grams | ¼ cup

vanilla extract
½ teaspoon

lemon extract
¼ teaspoon

fresh lemon zest
5 grams | 1 tablespoon

BERRY FILLING

fruit jam or preserves, Bonne Maman preferred
370 grams | one 13-ounce jar

egg, for brushing
60 grams | 1 extra-large

ICING

confectioners' sugar, sifted
110 grams | 1 cup

hot tap water
2 to 3 tablespoons

vanilla extract
¼ teaspoon

11. To make the icing, stir together the confectioners' sugar, 2 tablespoons of hot water, and the vanilla in a small bowl. Add the remaining tablespoon of water if needed so that the icing drips from a spoon in a long ribbon back into the bowl. Drizzle the icing onto the cooled Danishes. Let the icing set for 10 minutes, then serve the Danishes.

PASTRY CREAM–FILLED ÉCLAIRS

MAKES 10 TO 12 ÉCLAIRS

BAKING TIME: 20 to 22 minutes
(plus cooling and filling time)

Éclairs are a long-standing favorite treat around here. They are easy to make once you have the method down, and all it takes is a little practice. *Choux* is French and literally means "cabbage," but informally means "sweetheart." A little round pastry made from eggs, butter, flour, and milk, it uses steam from the oven to puff up into that familiar little shape. Be sure to make the dough exactly as directed and you will be surprised at how easy and inexpensive it is to make this seemingly complicated pastry at home. This recipe uses homemade vanilla pudding for the filling, but you can use whatever GF pudding or pastry cream you like. Be sure to share. Okay. Try to save some to share.

ÉCLAIR PASTRY

ÉCLAIR PASTRY

Nosh AP GF flour (page 4)
160 grams | 1¼ cups

kosher salt
1 teaspoon

sugar
1 tablespoon

cold unsalted butter
75 grams | 5 tablespoons

whole milk
245 grams | 1 cup

eggs, at room temperature
240 grams | 4 extra-large

VANILLA PUDDING

egg yolks
75 grams | 3 extra-large

cornstarch
25 grams | 3 tablespoons

whole milk
735 grams | 3 cups

sugar
2 tablespoons

kosher salt
¼ teaspoon

vanilla bean paste or extract
1½ teaspoons

CHOCOLATE GANACHE

heavy cream
120 grams | ½ cup

semisweet and bittersweet chocolate chips, mixed (half and half)
340 grams | 2 cups

1. Preheat the oven to 400°F. Line two baking sheets with parchment paper. Prepare a piping bag with a ½-inch plain tip or a resealable plastic bag with a scant ½-inch corner cut off.

2. In a small bowl, whisk the flour with the salt and sugar. In a deep saucepan over medium heat, melt the butter with the milk and bring to a low simmer. With a clean wooden spoon, stir in the flour mixture all at once. The dough will immediately form a ball. Turn down the heat to the lowest setting and stir as well as you can for 2 minutes. Mostly you will be slapping the dough ball around the bottom of the pan, but keep going because you are actually cooking the starch and flour. At the 2-minute point, transfer the dough ball to the bowl of a stand mixer or a large bowl for use with a hand mixer. Set aside for 2 minutes while you get the eggs ready. Crack the eggs into a small bowl.

3. With the mixer running on medium speed, add the eggs to the dough, one at a time. Make sure each egg is fully worked into the dough before adding the next—this is the key to choux success. Take your time. You'll know the dough is well combined when it is pale yellow and looks like batter rather than a slimy science project. Keep mixing until it looks like a thick yellow batter.

4. Place the dough in the piping bag. Pipe scant 3-inch-long ropes onto the parchment, five or six per sheet, spaced well apart from one another. They will look small, but they grow like the Hulk as they bake.

5. Using your fingertips, sprinkle a few drops of cold water over the choux before placing in the oven. Don't open the oven door at all during the baking because you risk the puffs falling flat. After 10 minutes, turn down the temperature to 350°F. Give them another 10 to 12 minutes and when they look puffed up and toasty brown, remove them from the oven.

6. Carefully poke each choux with a toothpick to release the steam and place on a rack to cool completely before filling.

VANILLA PUDDING

1. Whisk the egg yolks until smooth. Add the cornstarch and 110 grams (½ cup) of the milk to the yolks and whisk to combine. Set aside for 2 minutes.

2. Whisk the egg mixture again and strain into a medium saucepan. Add the remaining 625 grams (2½ cups) of milk and the sugar and salt to the saucepan. Stir over medium heat just until the mixture thickens and starts to simmer. Remove from the heat immediately or the cornstarch may break down. Add the vanilla bean paste and stir. Cover with plastic wrap and chill.

3. Using a long filling tip, pipe the vanilla pudding into each éclair. The other option is to slice off the top of each éclair (like a cap) and spoon in the filling, then replace the cap.

CHOCOLATE GANACHE

Heat the cream in a microwave-safe container on high until simmering, 25 to 40 seconds. Place the chocolate chips in a heatproof bowl. Pour the simmering cream over the chocolate and let it sit for a minute. Stir gently to combine.

ASSEMBLY

1. Place the rack over a baking sheet to catch any drips. For piped éclairs, dip the top side into the chocolate, letting the excess drip back into the bowl. Place back on the rack, right side up, to set. If you've cut off the tops and filled the éclairs, use a small spoon to drizzle chocolate over the top of each éclair while it sits on its rack.

2. Keep the filled éclairs refrigerated until you are ready to serve them. They are best served the same day.

LINZER BERRY TORTE

CHILLING TIME: 4 hours or overnight

BAKING TIME: 55 to 60 minutes

confectioners' sugar, sifted
140 grams | 1¼ cups

Nosh AP GF flour (page 4)
195 grams | 1½ cups

GF almond or hazelnut flour
200 grams | 2 cups

kosher salt
½ teaspoon

unsweetened cocoa powder, sifted
1 teaspoon

ground cloves
¼ teaspoon

ground cinnamon
¼ teaspoon

cold unsalted butter
115 grams | 8 tablespoons or ½ cup

eggs, beaten
120 grams | 2 extra-large

raspberry jam, Bonne Maman
preferred
370 grams | one 13-ounce jar

raspberry liqueur, Framboise
preferred, optional
1 tablespoon
    or
raspberry flavoring, optional
1 teaspoon

egg, beaten separately, for brushing
60 grams | 1 extra-large

The Linzer torte is rumored to be the oldest cake in the world, according to Austrian and German Linzer scholars. Just a guess, but I'm thinking that Linzer torte is less cake and more tart. No matter. It's a wonderful pastry, whatever the origin. Some think hazelnut is the traditional flour, but others prefer almond. Use either. Find the best-quality raspberry jam you can. The Framboise is optional but really adds dimension to the flavor and cuts the sweetness.

1. In the bowl of a food processor, pulse together 110 grams (1 cup) of the confectioners' sugar and the flour, almond flour, salt, cocoa, cloves, and cinnamon. Cut the butter into 1-inch cubes and add to the processor. Pulse until the mixture looks like coarse crumbs. Add the two beaten eggs all at once and pulse until the dough forms a ragged ball. Transfer the ball to plastic wrap. Knead the dough with the heel of your hand until it comes together. It will be very soft and sticky. Divide in two pieces, one slightly larger than the other. Wrap in plastic wrap and refrigerate for 4 hours or overnight.

2. Remove the larger piece of dough from the refrigerator and bring almost to room temperature. Press the dough evenly into a 9-inch tart pan with a removable bottom so that once it is baked and cooled, the pan collar can be removed and the tart can be placed on a serving plate, for easier serving and a pretty display. Chill in the freezer for 15 minutes. Flatten the remaining dough between two sheets of plastic wrap into a 10 × 8-inch rectangle. Slide onto a baking sheet and freeze for 30 minutes. Slice into equally wide lengths to create lattice strips. Place the pan back in the freezer.

3. After removing the pan from freezer, mix the preserves with the raspberry liqueur, if using. Spoon into the chilled crust. Remove the lattice lengths from the freezer and peel off the plastic wrap. Place the lattice pieces on top of the torte in a crosshatch, overlapping pattern. Let the dough warm up slightly and pinch the lattice pieces together at the edges so they look neat. Trim the edges

where necessary. Brush with the remaining beaten egg. Place the pan on a baking sheet (to catch drips while baking) and chill in the refrigerator while the oven preheats.

4. Preheat the oven to 325°F. Bake for 35 minutes. Rotate the tart pan for even baking and bake for 20 to 25 minutes more, or until the crust is a dark golden brown and darker on the edges and the filling is bubbling and leaking a bit. Depending on how thick the dough is, it might take a little longer to brown. Let cool completely in the pan on a rack. Right before serving, loosen the edges of the crust with a sharp paring knife. Carefully remove the tart pan bottom from the sides and place the torte on a serving plate. Dust with the remaining 30 grams (¼ cup) of sifted confectioners' sugar.

BAKING TIME: 25 to 28 minutes

DAIRY-FREE OPTION AVAILABLE

nonstick spray, for greasing

Nosh AP GF flour (page 4)
130 grams | 1 cup

sugar
200 grams | 1 cup

unsweetened cocoa powder, sifted
35 grams | ⅓ cup

baking powder
1 teaspoon

instant espresso powder (decaf is fine)
½ teaspoon

kosher salt
½ teaspoon

shortening
95 grams | 8 tablespoons or ½ cup

eggs
180 grams | 3 extra-large

almond milk
165 grams | ⅔ cup

vanilla extract
1 teaspoon

orange extract
½ teaspoon

raspberry jam, Bonne Maman
preferred
170 grams | ½ cup

raspberry liqueur, Framboise
preferred, optional
2 tablespoons
or
raspberry flavoring, optional
1 teaspoon

semisweet bar chocolate, roughly
chopped
450 grams | 16 ounces | 4 cups

cold unsalted butter
230 grams | 16 tablespoons or 1 cup
or
shortening
144 grams | 12 tablespoons or ¾ cup

light corn syrup
1 tablespoon

fresh raspberries, for serving, optional
170 grams | 1 half-pint

DARK CHOCOLATE RASPBERRY SACHERTORTE

If one day you want to follow a real-life soap opera, look up the history of the beleaguered Sachertorte. It began as a novel dessert baked by a young baker's apprentice for a king's fancy-schmancy dessert, then went on to inspire a wrangled lawsuit for ownership of the name generations later. By any other name, this is a chocolate cake extraordinaire. No kitchen should be without a recipe for this elegant dessert. These are usually up front and center in any bakery worth its bagels. A little slice goes a long way, so one cake will serve a village.

1. Preheat the oven to 350°F. Grease two 8-inch round layer cake pans with nonstick spray. Line the pan bottoms with parchment paper rounds and spray those, too.

2. Whisk together the flour, sugar, cocoa, baking powder, espresso powder, and salt. Add the shortening, eggs, almond milk, vanilla, and orange extract. Beat until smooth.

3. Divide the batter evenly between the prepared pans and bake for 25 to 28 minutes, or until a toothpick comes out with dry crumbs. Let cool completely in the pan on a rack. Once cool, loosen the sides with a sharp paring knife and turn out the cakes onto racks to cool completely.

4. Place one cake layer on a serving plate—this is now the bottom layer. Place parchment under the edges to catch chocolate glaze drips and keep the edges clean. Mix the raspberry jam with the raspberry liqueur, if using. Spread on the bottom layer to within ½ inch of the edge. Let that sit while preparing the chocolate glaze.

5. In a double boiler over low heat, melt the chocolate with the butter and corn syrup until fully combined. (A chocolate "pour" can be made with shortening instead of butter if you prefer to bake dairy-free.) Let cool for 30 minutes, stirring frequently. When the mixture starts to thicken, it is ready to pour. As it thickens, the faster it will set, so work quickly at this point.

6. Pour the glaze over the bottom layer. Spread with an offset spatula so that the chocolate pours over the edge and down the sides. Run the spatula over the sides to completely cover the bottom layer without disturbing the raspberry jam. Place the second cake layer on top and press gently to help it adhere but not enough to squish out the filling. Pour the remaining glaze over the top and repeat, using the offset spatula trick, getting the chocolate to run down the sides and spreading it around the edges of the cake. Use the spatula to bring the chocolate that dripped to the bottom of the plate back up the sides. Pour whatever remaining chocolate there is in the bowl on top and quickly spread into an attractive finish, using the offset spatula. Remove the parchment from the bottom, using the offset spatula, to help keep the chocolate in place on the bottom edge. Top and serve with fresh raspberries, if desired.

egg whites, at room temperature
  210 grams | 6 extra-large

cream of tartar
  ¼ teaspoon

kosher salt
  ½ teaspoon

superfine sugar
  200 grams | 1 cup

almond extract
  1 teaspoon

shaved or grated bittersweet
chocolate, optional
  70 grams | 10 tablespoons

mixed fresh berries: raspberries,
strawberries, blueberries, and
blackberries
  510 to 850 grams | 3 to 5 half-pints

whipped cream or nondairy whipped
topping, slightly sweetened
  10 tablespoons

mint sprigs, for garnish, optional

PASSOVER MINI BERRY PAVLOVAS

No matter what story you read about the origin of the pavlova dessert, it always ends up being about a ballerina. I like to think of these as a pirouette of lofty meringue twirled into a little bowl that is filled with fresh berries and, hidden underneath, dark, bittersweet chocolate. Save some effort on serving day by baking the pavlova bowls ahead of time. Store overnight on a baking sheet lined with fresh parchment paper—in a cold oven. Don't stack them or you'll risk their sticking together. If they get soggy, just refresh them in a low oven (175°F) for a few minutes. Let cool before filling.

1. Preheat the oven to 300°F. Line two baking sheets with parchment paper. Trace five 3½- to 4-inch circles in pencil on each sheet of parchment. Flip over the parchment so the pencil side is facing down. Prepare a piping bag with a ½-inch decorative tip, or have ready a large spoon and an offset spatula.

2. Place the egg whites in a stand mixer (or a large bowl if using a hand mixer) and add the cream of tartar and salt. Whip on medium-high speed until frothy. Turn the mixer speed to high and when the whites start to turn fluffy white, add the sugar in a slow, steady stream down the side of the bowl, making sure it all gets incorporated as it whips. Whip just until the whites are glossy and the peaks look shiny. Add the almond extract and whip for a few seconds, just to incorporate.

3. Transfer the meringue to the piping bag. Following the pencil outlines, pipe the meringue onto the parchment to form shallow bowls. Alternatively, use a large spoon to place a large dollop of meringue in the center of each circle and use an offset spatula to spread the meringue into a bowl shape just to the edge of each outline.

4. Bake for 10 minutes. Rotate the baking sheets and turn down the temperature to 225°F. Bake for an additional 30 to 40 minutes. After 30 minutes, watch them carefully— open the oven door, rotate the baking sheets, and as soon

as they start to turn color, remove them from the oven. You might think they are still too spongy, but they will become crisper as they cool.

5. Let the meringue bowls cool completely on the parchment. They will not come off easily when they are warm. When room temperature, peel the parchment from the bottom of each bowl very carefully.

6. Assemble the pavlovas right before serving. Place the shaved chocolate, if using, in the bottom of each bowl. Top with an attractive arrangement of fresh berries, slicing any that are larger than bite size. Add the whipped cream. Garnish each with a mint sprig, if desired. Serve immediately.

Passover Mini Berry Pavlovas (page 152)

DONUTS

batter with another outline. Repeat again with the remaining outline. Bake for 13 to 15 minutes, or just until the edges are slightly golden. Remove the pan from the oven and immediately slide the thin disks onto a rack, using a very large spatula. Let them rest until cool enough to handle and each disk feels sturdy. They will have to be trimmed to fit into the springform pan.

FILLING

1. In a double boiler, whisk the egg yolks, superfine sugar, liqueur, and salt. Simmer and stir over medium heat until the mixture thickens. Cool rapidly by placing it in the freezer for about 10 minutes and stirring it once in a while. Keep an eye on it and keep stirring so that it chills but does not freeze.

2. Meantime, whip up the cold mascarpone and cream, using an electric mixer. It should look like soft peaked whipped cream. Add the almond extract. Once the custard is chilled, fold the mascarpone mixture into it gently until combined. Keep the filling mixture chilled in the refrigerator.

ASSEMBLY

1. Line the 6- or 8-inch springform pan with a piece of parchment paper. Trim the cake layers to fit the pan. Place one disk on the bottom of the pan. Prepare the soaking liquid by mixing the brewed coffee, coffee liqueur, and almond extract. Brush the first layer with one third of the coffee mixture. You may find that poking toothpick holes in the layer helps it absorb the liquid, which takes just a moment to soak into the cake. Use the entire one third of the coffee mixture, though it may seem like too much liquid at this point—it won't be soggy once it is fully assembled, chilled, and rested overnight.

2. Top with a generous layer (a little more than one third) of the mascarpone filling. Top with one third of the grated bittersweet chocolate. You should not see the filling layer at all. Top with one more cake layer, trimmed to fit. Push down slightly so there are no gaps. Brush this layer with one third of the coffee mixture as you did in the bottom layer. Top with another generous layer of the mascarpone filling, leaving just a little bit for the top layer. Top with another layer of the grated bittersweet chocolate until you cannot see the filling. Top with the last cake layer and brush as instructed above with the remaining coffee mixture. Top with the remaining mascarpone filling. Pile a generous layer of grated chocolate on top. Cover the cake with foil and refrigerate for at least 5 hours; overnight is better. To serve, run a knife around the inside edge of the cake pan and release the latch. Carefully remove the springform collar, and because you've lined the pan with parchment, you can use a big spatula to slide the tiramisu onto a cake plate, if you wish. Or plate it directly from the pan to pretty little dishes.

MAKES ONE 6- OR 8-INCH
LAYERED TIRAMISU;
SERVES 6 TO 8

BAKING TIME: 13 to 15 minutes
(plus cooling, filling, and chilling,
5 to 24 hours)

CAKE

cold unsalted butter
115 grams | 8 tablespoons or ½ cup

Nosh AP GF flour (page 4)
130 grams | 1 cup

granulated sugar
100 grams | ½ cup

eggs
120 grams | 2 extra-large

kosher salt | ¼ teaspoon

vanilla extract | 1 teaspoon

coffee liqueur, Kahlúa preferred, or
mocha-flavored espresso drink
1 teaspoon

FILLING

egg yolks
125 grams | 5 extra-large

superfine sugar
65 grams| ⅓ cup

coffee liqueur, Kahlúa preferred, or
mocha-flavored espresso drink
60 grams | ¼ cup

kosher salt | ¼ teaspoon

cold mascarpone cheese
225 grams | 1 cup

cold heavy cream
120 grams | ½ cup

almond extract
½ teaspoon

bittersweet bar chocolate, grated
85 grams | 3 ounces | ¾ cup

SOAKING LIQUID

brewed coffee (decaf is fine), at room
temperature
235 grams | 1 cup

coffee liqueur, Kahlúa preferred, or
mocha-flavored espresso drink
2 tablespoons

almond extract | 1 teaspoon

TIRAMISU

Tiramisu is best served after sitting overnight in the refrigerator, making this a perfect and impressive dessert to prepare ahead for a special occasion. The sponge layer for this tiramisu has a texture similar to that of a madeleine and will soak up all the flavored liquid that makes the dessert special. Each layer is infused with such flavors as coffee and mocha or Kahlúa, and finished with plenty of grated bittersweet chocolate. Although it takes a little time to pre-pare and assemble, it is a swoon-worthy dessert memorable long after it is eaten.

CAKE

1. Line three baking sheets with parchment paper. Using a 6- or 8- inch springform pan, make three pencil outlines of the bottom circumference of the pan on each sheet of parchment paper. Turn over the parchment paper so the pencil marking is facing down and place back on the bak-ing sheets. The batter will need at least an hour to chill in the refrigerator, so plan ahead.

2. Cut the butter into three or four pieces and brown in a small saucepan over medium-low heat until nutty brown and fragrant, about 5 minutes. Set aside to cool slightly.

3. In a medium bowl, whisk together the flour and granu-lated sugar. Beat the eggs in a small bowl and mix into the flour mixture, stirring vigorously until the batter goes from clumpy to something like thick pancake batter. You'll see it start to happen rather quickly. Stir in the slightly cooled (but still liquid) brown butter. You'll have to mix vigorously for a minute and do a dance between folding and beating to get it all mixed in. Add the salt, vanilla, and coffee liqueur and mix again to incorporate. Cover the bowl with plastic wrap and refrigerate for at least an hour—2 hours is even better.

4. Preheat the oven to 375°F. Drop one third of the batter into the center of one pencil outline. Using an offset spatula or the back of a spoon, slightly flatten the batter within the circle but not all the way to the edge, because it will spread while baking. Repeat, using one third more of the

Tiramisu (page 156)

Any day that begins with a donut is a good one. We aren't big fans of frying anything in an apartment the size of a postage stamp, so baked donuts are a great solution and never a compromise. Anyone lucky enough to eat one will be surprised that they didn't actually come from your favorite donut shop. Keep in mind that a house of nosh cannot *ever* have too many donut pans. Freshly baked donuts ought to be eaten pretty quickly—but with these recipes, that won't be a problem.

SPECIAL EQUIPMENT

Six-count donut pan (two is best), English muffin rings (twelve), plenty of nonstick spray

TIPS

- Be generous with nonstick spray, even if you are using a nonstick pan.
- When filling the donut pan with batter, be sure to overlap scoops of batter around the stem so you don't mistakenly bake several donut holes in one donut cavity.
- To make sure the donut comes out looking like a donut with a hole in the center, make certain the center stem in the donut pan is never covered with batter, unless directed otherwise, of course.
- Always rap filled donut pans on the countertop to get rid of air bubbles and even out the batter.
- Donuts release from the pan more easily when they are hot. Place a rack gently on top of the hot donuts and using pot holders, flip it over in one smooth motion.
- To ensure quick cleanup, set the donuts on a rack over a baking sheet or parchment paper before adding the glazes or toppings.
- Glazes are best applied while the donut is warm, icing while the donut is cool.
- Donuts are best enjoyed when freshly baked, but let them cool a bit before handling because they are extra fragile while piping hot.

DONUTS

nonstick spray, for greasing

Nosh AP GF flour (page 4)
  300 grams | 2⅓ cups

GF almond flour
  50 grams | ½ cup

unsweetened cocoa powder
  1 tablespoon

baking powder | 2 teaspoons

baking soda | ½ teaspoon

kosher salt | ½ teaspoon

mace or nutmeg | ¼ teaspoon

ground cardamom | ¼ teaspoon

ground cinnamon | ¼ teaspoon

freshly ground black pepper
  ¼ teaspoon or 2 turns of the grinder

very ripe banana, peeled and pureed
  150 to 160 grams | 2 small

sour cream or full-fat plain Greek
yogurt
  115 grams | ½ cup

pure maple syrup
  60 grams | 3 tablespoons

eggs
  120 grams | 2 extra-large

unsalted butter, melted
  135 grams | 9 tablespoons or ½ cup
  plus 1 tablespoon

granulated sugar
  100 grams | ½ cup

brewed coffee (decaf is fine)
  1 tablespoon

vanilla extract | 1 teaspoon

GLAZE

confectioners' sugar, sifted
  110 grams | 1 cup

pure maple syrup
  40 grams | 2 tablespoons

hot tap water | 1 to 2 tablespoons

vanilla extract | ¼ teaspoon

pecans, toasted (see page 251) and
roughly chopped
  40 grams | ⅓ cup

BANANA MAPLE PECAN GLAZED DONUTS

Got gnarly old bananas that are ready for the compost heap? Got a little maple syrup and pecans in the pantry? Then you have the makings of a fabulous donut. Be sure to toast the raw pecans for best flavor.

DONUTS

1. Preheat the oven to 350°F. Grease two 6-count donut pans generously with nonstick spray.

2. In a medium bowl, whisk together the flour, almond flour, cocoa, baking powder, baking soda, salt, mace, cardamom, cinnamon, and black pepper. In a large bowl, beat together the banana, sour cream, maple syrup, eggs, butter, granulated sugar, coffee, and vanilla. Add the dry mixture and mix until fully incorporated.

3. Scoop the batter into the prepared pans, filling each donut cup a scant half-full. Rap the pan on the countertop to smooth the batter.

4. Bake the donuts for 16 to 18 minutes, or until a toothpick comes out with a few crumbs. Carefully transfer the hot, fragile donuts to a rack and let cool completely before adding the glaze.

GLAZE

1. In a small bowl, combine the sifted confectioners' sugar with the maple syrup and stir. Add the hot water, 1 tablespoon at a time, and continue stirring until the mixture is thoroughly mixed, no lumps remain, and it drizzles off the spoon slowly. Add the vanilla and stir again.

2. Spoon the glaze over the top side of the donuts until fully covered. Immediately sprinkle the chopped pecans on top of the glaze on each donut. Let the glaze set, about 10 minutes. Serve while still warm, for best flavor.

nonstick spray, for greasing

Nosh AP GF flour (page 4)
  260 grams | 2 cups

granulated sugar
  200 grams | 1 cup

baking powder | 1½ teaspoons

unsweetened cocoa powder
  1 teaspoon

ground cinnamon | ½ teaspoon

baking soda | ¼ teaspoon

ground cloves | ¼ teaspoon

kosher salt | ¼ teaspoon

apple butter (no sugar added)
  100 grams | 5 tablespoons

buttermilk (see page 250)
  60 grams | ¼ cup

pure maple syrup
  60 grams | 3 tablespoons

canola oil | 2 tablespoons

eggs
  120 grams | 2 extra-large

TOPPING

superfine sugar
  200 grams | 1 cup

ground cinnamon
  2 teaspoons

APPLE BUTTER DONUTS

The cocoa is not a misprint—don't leave it out. It doesn't make the donut taste like chocolate, but it makes the apple butter flavor pop, leaving you wanting another bite just to chase the cloves and cinnamon flavor. Use the best apple butter available and make sure it has no added sugar. These are an autumn favorite and at other times of year will remind you of those crisp fall apple-picking days.

1. Preheat the oven to 350°F. Generously grease two 6-count donut pans with nonstick spray.

2. In a large bowl, whisk together the flour, granulated sugar, baking powder, cocoa, cinnamon, baking soda, cloves, and salt. In a small bowl, whisk together the apple butter, buttermilk, maple syrup, canola oil, and eggs. Add the wet ingredients all at once to the dry mixture and fold gently just until combined. Let the batter sit for a minute or two and stir again. Fill the donut cups a generous half-full. Rap the pan on the countertop to smooth the batter.

3. Bake for 14 to 16 minutes, or just until a toothpick comes out clean. Carefully transfer the hot, fragile donuts to a rack and let cool until just barely warm to the touch.

TOPPING

Gently stir the superfine sugar and cinnamon together in a deep bowl that fits a donut. Place each cooled donut in the bowl and spoon the sugar mixture over it, gently shaking off the excess.

SWEET CORN BREAD HONEY DONUTS

Cornmeal and honey are flavorful partners in this unusual donut. Drizzle extra honey over the top of the warm donut, or dust it with confectioners' sugar. Serve with a steaming cup of coffee or tea for the perfect breakfast or midmorning snack.

1. Preheat the oven to 350°F. Grease two 6-count donut pans with nonstick spray.
2. In a large bowl, whisk together the flour, cornmeal, granulated sugar, baking powder, salt, baking soda, cinnamon, and nutmeg. In a smaller bowl, whisk together the butter, 40 grams (2 tablespoons) of honey, eggs, buttermilk, and vanilla. Add the wet ingredients all at once to the dry mixture and fold gently until just combined. Let the batter sit for a minute or two and stir again. Fill the donut cups a generous half-full. Rap the pan on the countertop to smooth the batter.
3. Bake the donuts for 14 to 16 minutes, or just until a toothpick comes out clean. Carefully transfer the hot, fragile donuts to a rack and let cool until just warm to the touch. Using a mesh strainer, dust with confectioners' sugar or drizzle with the remaining 40 grams (2 tablespoons) of honey, if desired.

Nosh AP GF flour (page 4)
195 grams | 1½ cups

GF cornmeal
35 grams | ¼ cup

granulated sugar
100 grams | ½ cup

baking powder | 1 teaspoon

kosher salt | ½ teaspoon

baking soda | ¼ teaspoon

ground cinnamon | ½ teaspoon

nutmeg, freshly grated preferred
¼ teaspoon

unsalted butter, melted
85 grams | 6 tablespoons or ¼ cup
plus 2 tablespoons

honey, orange blossom preferred
40 grams | 2 tablespoons

eggs
120 grams | 2 extra-large

buttermilk (see page 250)
185 grams | ¾ cup

vanilla extract | ½ teaspoon

confectioners' sugar, sifted, optional
30 grams | ¼ cup

honey, additional for drizzling, optional
40 grams | 2 tablespoons

MAKES 12 DONUTS

BAKING TIME: 13 to 16 minutes
(plus rising time for dough and
overnight for sponge)

SPONGE

water, heated to 90° to 100°F
235 grams | 1 cup

instant yeast
1 teaspoon

Nosh AP GF flour (page 4)
130 grams | 1 cup

DONUTS

nonstick spray, for greasing

Nosh AP GF flour (page 4)
195 grams | 1½ cups

tapioca starch
155 grams | 1¼ cups

cultured dry buttermilk powder or
milk powder
2 tablespoons

kosher salt
2 teaspoons

instant yeast
1 tablespoon

granulated sugar
1 teaspoon

cold unsalted butter
60 grams | 4 tablespoons or ¼ cup

water, heated to 90° to 100°F
115 grams | ½ cup

eggs
120 grams | 2 extra-large

egg yolk
25 grams | 1 extra-large

vanilla extract
2 teaspoons

TOPPING

superfine sugar
200 grams | 1 cup

ground cinnamon
2 teaspoons

unsalted butter, melted
45 grams | 3 tablespoons

FILLING

fruit preserves, Bonne Maman
preferred, strained
370 grams | one 13-ounce jar

BIG FAT BAKED SUFGANIYAH JELLY DONUTS

These raised jelly donuts are an authentic Hanukkah treat without the messy frying part. It's not a complicated recipe but it does require a little advance planning (and the water temperature really is important). You will want to make the simple sponge the night before so it has time to age properly for just the right yeast donut flavor. If you don't already have English muffin rings, now's a great time to get them because they are useful in making all kinds of GF batter breads and sweet dough. Also, if you don't add the cinnamon-sugar topping or jelly filling to this donut, it makes a fine, delicate sliced sandwich roll.

SPONGE

The evening before making the donuts, mix the water, yeast, and flour in a small bowl until smooth. Cover loosely with plastic wrap and refrigerate overnight. Remove the sponge from the refrigerator 30 minutes before mixing the donut dough.

DONUTS

1. Line two baking sheets with parchment paper. Generously grease twelve English muffin rings with nonstick spray. Place six rings on each prepared baking sheet, leaving about an inch of space between them. Give the rings one more spray once they are in place on the baking sheets.

2. Whisk together the flour, tapioca starch, dried buttermilk powder, salt, yeast, and granulated sugar in a large bowl. Cut the butter into ½-inch cubes. Make a well in the center of the bowl and add the butter pieces, warm water, eggs, egg yolk, and vanilla. Add the sponge. Using a fork, stir the ingredients together until they form a lumpy batter-like paste. Using an electric mixer on medium-high speed, beat the mixture for 5 minutes, until it is well mixed, smooth, and somewhat stretchy and elastic looking.

3. Grease a ⅓-cup scoop. Scoop the dough into the center of each ring. Grease a large piece of plastic wrap and place loosely on top of the donuts. Place the baking sheets in a

warm place for 45 minutes so that the dough rises to fill the rings to just below the top of but not over each ring.

4. Preheat the oven to 375°F. Remove the plastic wrap. Bake the donuts for 13 to 15 minutes, or until the internal temperature is 200°F on an instant-read digital thermometer. The donuts will not have much color and should look pale with a touch of golden brown on the edges. Remove from the oven and let cool for 1 minute in the pans. Using large tongs, remove the rings and place the donuts on a rack. Let cool for another 3 to 5 minutes.

5. To make the topping, mix the superfine sugar and cinnamon together in a bowl deep enough to hold a donut. Brush one donut with the melted butter on all exposed sides. Place the donut in the cinnamon mixture. Flip the donut all around so that all sides are thoroughly covered in the cinnamon mixture. Shake off any excess. Place the donut back on the rack to cool completely. Repeat with all the donuts.

6. Place the strained jam in a piping bag with a Bismarck piping tip (see page 252). Using a small paring knife, slice an X on the side of each donut and push the knife carefully into the donut to the center without piercing the outside of the donut on the top or bottom. Move the knife around a little bit to disturb the inside crumb so there is room for the jam. Remove the knife, insert the piping tube, and fill until you feel the donut start to expand slightly. Remove the piping tube and the jam should bubble up slightly out the opening. For best flavor, eat the donuts immediately after filling.

nonstick spray, for greasing

Nosh AP GF flour (page 4)
260 grams | 2 cups

GF almond flour
100 grams | 1 cup

granulated sugar
150 grams | ¾ cup

baking powder
2 teaspoons

kosher salt
½ teaspoon

almond milk
230 grams | 1 cup minus 1
tablespoon

canola oil
110 grams | ½ cup

eggs
180 grams | 3 extra-large

vanilla extract
1 teaspoon

lemon zest, freshly grated
5 grams | 1 tablespoon

confectioners' sugar, sifted
220 grams | 2 cups

jam, Bonne Maman preferred
240 grams | 12 tablespoons or ¾ cup

LEMON JAMMER DONUTS

These lemon jammer donuts are perfect for a Hanukkah gathering. They are quick to make and bake without much fuss. Unlike our other donut recipes, where you don't want to cover the stem of the pan, this donut requires that the stem be covered with batter to create the perfect jammer-holder.

1. Preheat the oven to 350°F. Generously grease two 6-count donut pans with nonstick spray.

2. Whisk together the flour, almond flour, granulated sugar, baking powder, and salt in a large bowl. In a medium bowl, whisk together the almond milk, oil, eggs, vanilla, and lemon zest. Add to the dry mixture and mix with a spatula until incorporated.

3. Scoop the batter into the donut pans until the donut cups are a generous two-thirds full, covering their stems. Bake for 14 to 16 minutes, until the donuts are starting to gain color and the edges are golden. A toothpick should come out without crumbs. Transfer the hot, fragile donuts to a rack, taking care to be gentle so that the dough covering the stem remains intact with its donut and doesn't break away and stay in the pan. Let cool completely.

4. Place the sifted confectioners' sugar in a deep bowl big enough to hold a donut. Place a donut in the bowl of sugar and cover the donut completely with the sugar. Cover the donut at least twice so that no cake shows through. Place back on the rack and repeat with the remaining donuts.

5. Using a tablespoon-size scoop, fill the center of each donut with jam until it reaches the top of the center hole. Only fill the donuts that have a dough bottom on one end to hold the jam. These are best served immediately once filled with jam.

OLD-FASHIONED COFFEE-DIPPING DONUTS

These old-fashioned donuts are made for dipping in a cup of coffee. They have a similar flavor and texture to their fried counterparts. This gluten-free donut might become an all-time favorite plain donut.

1. Preheat the oven to 375°F. Grease two 6-count donut pans with nonstick spray.

2. In a large bowl, whisk together the flour, sugar, baking powder, cocoa, baking soda, cinnamon, cloves, and salt. In a small bowl, mix together the buttermilk, brewed coffee, butter, eggs, vinegar, and vanilla. Add the wet ingredients all at once to the dry mixture and fold until just combined. Let the batter sit for a minute or two and stir again. Fill the donut cups a generous half-full. Rap the pan on the countertop to smooth the batter.

3. Bake for 8 minutes. Turn down the temperature to 350°F and bake for 6 to 8 minutes more, or until a toothpick comes out without crumbs. Carefully transfer the hot, fragile donuts to a rack and let cool until just warm. Serve warm.

Nosh AP GF flour (page 4)
260 grams | 2 cups

sugar
200 grams | 1 cup

baking powder
1 teaspoon

unsweetened cocoa powder
1 teaspoon

baking soda
½ teaspoon

ground cinnamon
½ teaspoon

ground cloves
¼ teaspoon

kosher salt
½ teaspoon

buttermilk (see page 250)
120 grams | ½ cup

brewed coffee (decaf is fine)
120 grams | ½ cup

unsalted butter, melted
130 grams | 9 tablespoons or ½ cup plus 1 tablespoon

eggs
120 grams | 2 extra-large

cider vinegar
1 teaspoon

vanilla extract
1 teaspoon

DONUTS

nonstick spray, for greasing

Nosh AP GF flour (page 4)
  195 grams | 1½ cups

granulated sugar
  200 grams | 1 cup

unsweetened cocoa powder, sifted
  50 grams | ½ cup

baking powder | 1½ teaspoons

instant espresso powder
(decaf is fine)
  ½ teaspoon

kosher salt | ½ teaspoon

canola oil
  110 grams | ½ cup

eggs
  180 grams | 3 extra-large

almond milk
  165 grams | ⅔ cup

vanilla extract | 1 teaspoon

semisweet mini chocolate chips
  85 grams | ½ cup

VANILLA GLAZE

confectioners' sugar, sifted
  220 grams | 2 cups

hot tap water
  2 to 3 tablespoons

vanilla extract | ½ teaspoon

DARK CHOCOLATE GLAZE

almond milk or canned coconut milk
  60 grams | ¼ cup

semisweet mini chocolate chips
  170 grams | 1 cup

TOPPING OPTIONS

- chopped nuts | ½ cup
- GF sprinkles | ½ cup
- colored sugar | ½ cup
- dried chopped fruit | ½ cup
- flaked coconut, toasted
  (see page 251) | ½ cup

GLAZED CHOCOLATE DONUTS

Dunkin' Donuts was the go-to donut shop for the first half of my life. Even today, if I spy a glazed chocolate donut with sprinkles, it brings a wave of nostalgia and the desire to bake some donuts. Now that I live on the West Coast, Portland's Voodoo Doughnut has proven to me that almost any ingredient can be a fun topping. Add your favorite sprinkles, nuts, dried fruit, GF cereal, or colored sugar and say hello to Dunkin'-at-home with a Voodoo twist.

DONUTS

1. Preheat the oven to 350°F. Grease two 6-count donut pans generously with nonstick spray.

2. In a large bowl, whisk together the flour, granulated sugar, cocoa, baking powder, espresso powder, and salt. Add the oil, eggs, almond milk, and vanilla. Using an electric mixer on medium speed, beat until the batter is smooth and lump-free, 1 minute. Using a silicone spatula, stir in the mini chocolate chips.

3. Fill the prepared donut cups a scant half-full and make sure all the stems remain free from any batter splatters. Rap the pan on the countertop to smooth the batter. Bake the donuts for 14 to 16 minutes. Remove from the oven when a toothpick comes out without crumbs. Carefully transfer the hot, fragile donuts to a rack and let cool completely before adding the glaze of your choice.

VANILLA GLAZE

1. In a bowl, stir the sifted confectioners' sugar with 1 tablespoon of hot water at a time until the glaze gently drizzles off the spoon. Stir in the vanilla. If the glaze becomes too thick, add more hot water 1 teaspoon at a time—a little goes a long way with glaze.

2. Using a spoon, drizzle as much glaze on each donut as you like. Add any topping options or combinations of options at this point before the glaze hardens. Let the glaze set, about 10 minutes.

DARK CHOCOLATE GLAZE

1. Heat the almond milk to a simmer over medium heat. Place the chopped chocolate in a heatproof bowl. Pour the hot milk over the chocolate and let it sit for a minute. Stir gently to combine. Let the mixture cool for a few minutes.
2. Dip the completely cooled donuts top down into the chocolate and flip back up. Place the donuts back on the rack. Sprinkle on your desired toppings before the chocolate sets. Let the glaze set, about 10 minutes.

BREADS, MUFFINS, MATZO, *and* CRACKERS

Anyone who has tried to buy tasty gluten-free bread knows frustration quite well. Homemade gluten-free bread has challenges, too, but the results can be rewarding. We have developed recipes for great-tasting quick and easy challah, and for traditional challah that can be braided or rolled into a round (contrary to general opinion, it *can* be done).

Don't be tempted to leave out the gluten-free helpers (see page 8) or the sparkling mineral water, which helps the bread rise and gives it a great crumb. Embrace the world of GF challah bread making—it sometimes feels like a science project, but it gets easier each time.

On the other hand, quick breads, muffins, matzo, and crackers mix together in such a flash, you'll wonder why you ever bought them from a store. The recipes make enough to keep you happy through a blizzard. And Puppy Pumpkin Crackers (page 183) will win you all kinds of four-pawed friends.

SPECIAL EQUIPMENT

9-inch square baking pans, 8½ × 4½-inch loaf pans, muffin pans, cupcake liners, baking sheets, parchment paper, pizza cutter, instant-read digital thermometer, plastic wrap

TIPS

■ It is worth the trouble to get Expandex (see page 3) because there is no substitute for how it helps keep the bread stretchy and bendy. When *not* using Expandex, use the substitutions indicated in the recipe: additional tapioca starch and xanthan gum.

■ Sweet white rice flour helps create the soft texture we expect in bread. It is not the same as white rice flour.

■ Don't add more flour to sticky dough, unless indicated in the recipe.

■ The trick to getting seeds to adhere is to place plastic wrap over the dough after sprinkling with the seeds and giving it a firm press with a rolling pin.

■ Docking (poking holes in the dough with a fork or rolling docking tool) is always useful and keeps crackers from puffing up too much while baking.

■ When baking at high temperatures, watch that the parchment paper doesn't burn.

FLUFFY BISCUITS

MAKES 9 BISCUITS

BAKING TIME: 16 to 20 minutes

Fluffy biscuits, warm from the oven—what could be better? The fluffiness in this biscuit is brought to you by a happy chemistry accident between too much baking powder and extra milk protein. When you cut in the fats, use a fork or your fingers and be sure to work it lightly—big lumps are fine. Don't overdo the mixing or the biscuit will be tough. There is no rolling required in this recipe. Just drop the dough, pat it square, and do a rough cut into small squares. They like to just touch one another on the baking sheet to get that pull-apart fluffiness. Use real buttermilk and not a substitute for this recipe, because the biscuits rely on the tang and fats from the buttermilk to make flavorful, flaky, fluffy biscuits.

Nosh AP GF flour (page 4), plus more for dusting
   260 grams | 2 cups

sweet dairy whey or milk powder (see page 254)
   25 grams | 3 tablespoons

baking powder
   15 grams | 4 teaspoons

kosher salt
   1 teaspoon

baking soda
   ¼ teaspoon

cold unsalted butter
   30 grams | 2 tablespoons

shortening
   25 grams | 2 tablespoons

cold buttermilk
   200 grams plus 30 grams for brushing | ¾ cup plus 1 tablespoon, plus another 2 tablespoons for brushing

1. Preheat the oven to 425°F. Line a baking sheet with parchment paper.
2. In a medium bowl, whisk together the flour, dairy whey powder, baking powder, salt, and baking soda. Cut the butter into three or four pieces. Using a fork, mix the butter and shortening with the dry mixture just until it looks like lumpy, coarse, uneven crumbs. Work quickly so the fats stay chilled. Make a well in the center. Pour in the 200 grams (¾ cup plus 1 tablespoon) buttermilk all at once. Using a fork, stir everything together quickly but thoroughly. Don't knead the dough because you'll chance losing the flaky layers.
3. Gather the dough onto a lightly floured surface, like a small cutting board. Using the sides of your hand, pat the mixture into a 9-inch square almost ½ inch thick. Cut nine biscuits, using a pizza cutter (cut into thirds in one direction, and into thirds in the other).
4. Place the biscuits on the prepared baking sheet, just barely touching one another. Brush the remaining 30 grams (2 tablespoons) of buttermilk on top. Bake the biscuits for 16 minutes and rotate the pan for even baking. Bake for 2 to 4 minutes more, until the tops turn golden brown. Serve warm with butter and jam.

PUMPKIN CORN BREAD STREUSEL MUFFINS

MAKES 12 TO 14 MUFFINS

BAKING TIME: 16 to 18 minutes
DAIRY-FREE OPTION AVAILABLE

Pumpkin is actually a fruit—a big giant berry. So it's just fine to think of this muffin as a berry muffin, just in case anyone asks. The addition of raisins and nuts only makes the muffin more interesting. Be generous with the streusel in this recipe because it provides a sweet and crunchy balance to the texture of the cornmeal and the good-for-you pumpkin.

1. Preheat the oven to 350°F. Place liners in a muffin pan.
2. In a large bowl, whisk together the flour, cornmeal, brown sugar, baking powder, salt, cinnamon, nutmeg, and cloves. In a small bowl, whisk together the pumpkin puree, orange juice, canola oil, eggs, and vanilla. Add the wet mixture to the dry and gently fold with a silicone spatula until just combined. Fold in the raisins and pecans.
3. Scoop the batter into the liners, filling a scant two-thirds full, leaving room for the streusel topping.
4. To make the streusel topping, in a small bowl, mix all the ingredients together with a fork or clean fingers just until the butter is incorporated and the mixture looks like coarse crumbs. Distribute evenly on top of the muffin batter.
5. Bake the muffins for 16 to 18 minutes, or just until a toothpick comes out without wet crumbs. Let cool in the pan for 1 minute, then transfer the muffins to a rack to cool. Serve barely warm.

Nosh AP GF flour (page 4)
175 grams | 1⅓ cups

GF cornmeal
70 grams | ½ cup

brown sugar
50 grams | 4 tablespoons or ¼ cup

baking powder | 1½ teaspoons

kosher salt | ½ teaspoon

ground cinnamon | ½ teaspoon

nutmeg, freshly grated preferred
¼ teaspoon

ground cloves | ¼ teaspoon

canned pure pumpkin puree
160 grams | ¾ cup

fresh orange juice
40 grams | 3 tablespoons

canola oil
110 grams | ½ cup

eggs
120 grams | 2 extra-large

vanilla extract | 1 teaspoon

raisins
75 grams | ½ cup

pecans, toasted (see page 251) and roughly chopped
40 grams | ⅓ cup

STREUSEL TOPPING

Nosh AP GF flour (page 4)
40 grams | scant ⅓ cup

unsalted butter
15 grams | 1 tablespoon
   or
shortening
12 grams | 1 tablespoon

brown sugar
25 grams | 2 tablespoons

ground cinnamon | ¼ teaspoon

CARAMEL BANANA BREAD WITH CRANBERRIES

MAKES FIVE MINI LOAVES
OR ONE LARGE LOAF;
SERVES 8 TO 10

BAKING TIME: 35 to 55 minutes

This is a great Rosh Hashanah or autumn dessert. If you are not a fan of cranberries, try substituting chocolate chips or dried fruits. Browning the butter gives the banana a deep caramel flavor. Be sure to use the bananas that are ready for the compost heap because they will provide the most intense, sweet flavor.

1. Grease five mini loaf pans or one 8½ × 4½-inch loaf pan lightly with nonstick spray. Place the pan(s) on a baking sheet.

2. In a large bowl, whisk together the 210 grams (1½ cups) of flour, sugar, baking powder, cocoa, salt, mace, cinnamon, cloves, and black pepper. In a small saucepan over low heat, brown the butter until it is nutty in color, 1 minute. Add the pureed banana to the browned butter and stir to incorporate. The mixture will bubble up slightly. Let it cook while stirring for 30 seconds. Remove from the heat and add the rum, stirring to incorporate. Set aside to cool for a few minutes.

3. Preheat the oven to 350°F. In a medium bowl, whisk together the canola oil, eggs, milk, vanilla, and orange extract. Add the cooled banana mixture and stir to combine. In a small bowl, toss the cranberries and chopped nuts with the remaining 1 teaspoon of flour to coat. Using a silicone spatula, add the wet ingredients to the dry, folding from the bottom of the bowl just until no dry material remains. Let the mixture sit for 2 minutes. Add the cranberries and pecans and fold to incorporate. Scrape the mixture into the prepared pan(s), filling evenly two-thirds full.

4. For mini loaf pans, bake for 20 minutes and rotate the pans for even baking. Turn down the temperature to 325°F and bake for 15 to 20 minutes more, or until a toothpick comes out with dry crumbs. For a larger loaf, bake at 350°F for 30 minutes and rotate the pan for even baking. Bake for 20 to 25 minutes more, until a toothpick comes out with fairly dry crumbs. Let cool in the pan(s) on a rack for 5 minutes. Remove the loaf or loaves from the pan(s) and transfer to a rack to cool completely.

nonstick spray, for greasing

Nosh AP GF flour (page 4)
210 grams plus 1 teaspoon | heaping 1½ cups plus 1 teaspoon

sugar
150 grams | ¾ cup

baking powder
1½ teaspoons

unsweetened cocoa powder
1 teaspoon

kosher salt
½ teaspoon

mace or nutmeg
¼ teaspoon

ground cinnamon
¼ teaspoon

ground cloves
¼ teaspoon

freshly ground black pepper
¼ teaspoon or 2 turns of the grinder

unsalted butter
30 grams | 2 tablespoons

banana (very ripe), pureed
200 grams | 2 to 3 medium

dark rum or rum flavoring
1 teaspoon

canola oil
110 grams | ½ cup

eggs, at room temperature
180 grams | 3 extra-large

milk or nondairy milk | 1 tablespoon

vanilla extract
1 teaspoon

orange extract
½ teaspoon

raw cranberries, roughly chopped
50 grams | ½ cup

pecans, toasted (see page 251) and roughly chopped
120 grams | 1 cup

PUMPKIN HONEY BREAD

MAKES 5 MINI LOAVES OR
ONE LARGE LOAF;
SERVES 8 TO 10

BAKING TIME: 35 to 55 minutes
DAIRY-FREE

Pumpkin is a popular Rosh Hashanah fruit in other parts of the world, particularly in northern Italy, and to honor that Sephardic tradition, this bread combines the best of both: honey and pumpkin. This recipe can be made as mini loaves that can be given as hostess gifts or as one large loaf that would also make a fantastic breakfast bread.

1. Preheat the oven to 350°F. Grease five mini loaf pans or one 8½ × 4½-inch loaf pan lightly with nonstick spray. Place the pan(s) on a baking sheet.
2. In a large bowl, whisk together the 260 grams (2 cups) of flour and the sugar, baking powder, salt, cinnamon, nutmeg, ginger, cloves, mace, and black pepper. In a medium bowl, whisk together the pumpkin puree, honey, canola oil, orange juice, eggs, orange zest, vanilla, and orange extract. Using a silicone spatula, add the wet ingredients to the dry, folding from the bottom just until no dry material remains. In a small bowl, mix the raisins and pecans, if using, with the remaining 1 teaspoon of flour and fold into the dough. Scrape the mixture into the prepared pan(s) filling evenly two-thirds full.
3. For mini loaf pans, bake for 20 minutes and rotate the pans for even baking. Turn down the temperature to 325°F and bake for 15 to 20 minutes more, or until a toothpick comes out with dry crumbs. For a larger loaf, bake at 350°F for 30 minutes and rotate the pan for even baking. Bake for 20 to 25 minutes more, until a toothpick comes out with fairly dry crumbs and the edges are dark brown and crispy. Cool in the pan(s) on a rack for 5 minutes. Transfer the loaf or loaves to a rack to cool completely.

nonstick spray, for greasing

Nosh AP GF flour (page 4)
  260 grams plus 1 optional teaspoon
  2 cups plus 1 optional teaspoon

sugar
  150 grams | ¾ cup

baking powder
  1½ teaspoons

kosher salt
  ½ teaspoon

ground cinnamon | ½ teaspoon

nutmeg, freshly grated preferred
  ¼ teaspoon

ground ginger | ¼ teaspoon

ground cloves
  ¼ teaspoon

ground mace
  ¼ teaspoon

freshly ground black pepper
  ¼ teaspoon or 2 turns of the grinder

canned pure pumpkin puree
  125 grams | ½ cup

honey, orange blossom or
blackberry sage preferred
  125 grams | 5 to 6 tablespoons

canola oil
  110 grams | ½ cup

orange juice
  50 grams | 3 tablespoons

eggs
  120 grams | 2 extra-large

orange, tangerine, or clementine
zest, freshly grated
  5 grams | 1 tablespoon

vanilla extract
  1 teaspoon

orange extract
  ½ teaspoon

raisins, optional
  75 grams | ½ cup

pecans, toasted (see page 251) and
roughly chopped, optional
  40 grams | ⅓ cup

QUICK CORN BREAD

Corn bread has been on our breakfast menu for what feels like centuries. On a cold winter morning we serve it with honey butter and jam, along with steaming cups of coffee. In the summer we serve it with honey butter and jam, along with iced coffee. But in the fall we also use this recipe as part of the Challah Corn Bread Stuffing recipe (page 230) for holidays. We call that a win-win.

nonstick spray, for greasing

GF cornmeal
150 grams | 1 cup

Nosh AP GF flour (page 4)
130 grams | 1 cup

granulated sugar
50 grams | ¼ cup

brown sugar
25 grams | 2 tablespoons

baking powder
1½ teaspoons

kosher salt
1 teaspoon

extra virgin olive oil, cold-pressed preferred
70 grams | ⅓ cup

almond milk
185 grams | ¾ cup

eggs
120 grams | 2 extra-large

1. Preheat the oven to 375°F. Grease a 9-inch square pan or pie pan with nonstick spray.
2. In a medium bowl, whisk together the cornmeal, flour, granulated and brown sugars, baking powder, and salt. In a small bowl, whisk the olive oil, almond milk, and eggs until mixed. Add to the dry mixture and stir with a wooden spoon just until combined.
3. Let the batter sit for 2 minutes without stirring. Stir once more and scrape into the prepared pan. Bake for 18 to 22 minutes, or until a toothpick comes out clean. Let cool in the pan on a rack until just warm. Serve with jam and honey butter.

RUSTIC FLAT CRACKERS WITH SEEDS

MAKES 90 TO 120 SMALL
RECTANGULAR CRACKERS

BAKING TIME: 15 to 18 minutes per
baking sheet

DAIRY-FREE

These crackers look great because of the wide variety of seeds on top. Be sure to use a large crystal sea salt like Esprit du Sel as a topping to accent those chunky seeds. Roll the crackers as thinly as possible for the best crunch.

Nosh AP GF flour (page 4)
260 grams | 2 cups

kosher salt
1 teaspoon

hot tap water
175 grams | ¾ cup

extra virgin olive oil
40 grams | 3 tablespoons

TOPPINGS
- sea salt | 3 tablespoons
- sesame seeds | 3 tablespoons
- poppy seeds | 3 tablespoons
- caraway seeds | 3 tablespoons
- dried minced garlic | 3 tablespoons
- dried minced onion, freshly ground | 3 tablespoons
- freshly ground black pepper | 3 tablespoons

1. In a large bowl, whisk the flour with the salt. Add 150 grams (⅔ cup) of the hot water and the oil. Stir with a fork until the mixture is well mixed. Add more of the remaining 25 grams (about 1 tablespoon) of hot water as needed—the dough should look crumbly until it is kneaded. Turn out the dough onto a board and knead for at least 5 minutes, until it is smooth and not sticky. Time it: 5 minutes, no less.

2. Preheat the oven to 400°F. Divide the dough into thirds. Wrap two portions in plastic wrap and set on the counter.

3. Place one portion of the dough on a piece of parchment the same size as the baking sheet. Cover with plastic wrap. Roll out the dough to the edges of the parchment paper, completely filling it. Roll the dough as thinly as possible without tearing it.

4. Remove the plastic wrap. Sprinkle one third of each of the toppings all over the dough, adding one topping at a time for a layered effect. Cover again with plastic wrap. Give the dough a firm roll to press the toppings into the top of the dough. Carefully remove the top plastic. Using a docking tool or a fork, poke holes in the dough.

5. Use a pizza cutter to run small vertical and horizontal cuts throughout the dough, making rows of 1 × 5-inch crackers, thirty to forty per sheet. Carefully drag the parchment onto the baking sheet. Bake for 9 minutes and rotate the pan for even baking. Bake for 6 to 9 minutes more, or just until the edge pieces look almost black and the center is golden brown. Let cool on the baking sheet. When the crackers are completely cool, break them apart where you cut them.

6. Repeat steps 3 through 5 with the remaining dough.

PUPPY PUMPKIN CRACKERS

MAKES 40 TO 400
(YIELD DEPENDS UPON
CRACKER SIZE)

CHILLING TIME: 1 hour
BAKING TIME: 20 to 35 minutes
(plus drying time)
DAIRY-FREE

Every good dog deserves a treat. These are gluten-free and good for their digestive system. Use pure pumpkin (not a pie mix).

nonstick spray, for greasing

brown rice flour
   400 grams | 3¼ cups

canned pure pumpkin puree, organic preferred
   115 grams | ½ cup

eggs
   120 grams | 2 extra-large

olive oil
   30 grams | 2 tablespoons

1. Place 350 grams (2¾ cups) of the brown rice flour in a large bowl and make a well in the center. Add the pumpkin puree, eggs, and 15 grams (1 tablespoon) of the olive oil. Using a fork, mix the dough together by pushing the flour into the center. Mix until the dough comes together. Add more flour and oil as needed, but mix thoroughly first. You can always add more, but you can't take it out. On a board, knead the dough, adding small amounts of flour to get the dough ball smooth and not sticky.

2. Cut the dough into two or three pieces and wrap in plastic wrap. Let the dough rest for an hour in the refrigerator.

3. Preheat the oven to 325°F. Line two baking sheets with parchment paper. Remove one piece of dough at a time while the others remain in the refrigerator. Sandwich the dough between sheets of plastic wrap and roll out into a rectangle ¼ inch thick. Cut out small round disks or other cutouts, depending on the size cracker you want to make for your dog. Roll out the scraps and repeat. Making larger cutouts will go faster. I make little button-size crackers, which takes what sometimes feels like 4 hours (but is worth it).

4. Bake for 20 minutes and rotate the pan for even baking. Bake for 15 minutes more, or until crisp but not burned. Once all the crackers are baked, turn off the oven and wait for it to cool down slightly. Place all the crackers back into the warm oven for 30 to 60 minutes to dry completely. Make sure the oven is warm but not hot enough to brown the crackers—you want them to dry out, not continue to bake. I also like to leave them uncovered on the counter to dry overnight. Store in an airtight container for up to a week on the shelf or a month in the refrigerator, and share with as many friends—and pups—as you can find.

QUICK CHALLAH

MAKES ONE 2-POUND
ROUND OR LOAF CHALLAH

BAKING TIME: 32 to 35 minutes
(plus rising time for dough)
DAIRY-FREE

This challah can be made in just a few hours from start to finish. It has a lighter flavor than the version with the poolish (page 186), but it still tastes like a great challah. It can be baked in the round or in a loaf pan. Expandex is a big helper in this recipe, getting the bread to stretch easily, but if you are not using it, please add extra xanthan gum as indicated in the recipe. Traditionally, a round challah is served to celebrate the Jewish New Year, representing the circle of life and the ending of one year and the beginning of another. The baked bread has a great crumb. The loaf makes excellent sandwich bread and leftovers can be used for Challah Corn Bread Stuffing (page 230).

1. In a large bowl, combine both flours and the tapioca starch, Expandex, sugar, yeast, xanthan gum, salt, pectin, and guar gum and whisk. In a medium bowl, whisk four of the eggs, the egg yolks, and the honey and canola oil.

2. Add 110 grams (½ cup) of the sparkling mineral water to the dry mixture. Add the egg mixture to the dry mixture. Using a fork, work the flour mixture into the wet mixture until it is thoroughly combined. If the dough looks very sticky and tough, work in up to 30 grams (2 tablespoons) of additional sparkling water.

3. Grease a tube pan or an 8½ × 4½-inch loaf pan with non-stick spray. Place the dough all around the bottom of the pan, using a silicone spatula. Wet the spatula with water and smooth the dough. Cover loosely with greased plastic wrap and let the dough rise in a draft-free area until doubled in size, but not higher than the top of the pan, 1½ to 2 hours.

4. Preheat the oven to 350°F. Beat the remaining egg and brush it gently over the top of the bread. Sprinkle the top with the seeds. Bake for 15 minute and rotate the pan for even baking. Bake for another 17 to 20 minutes and remove when the internal temperature is 185° to 190°F on an instant-read digital thermometer and the top is pale golden brown. Don't overbake the bread or it will be a little tough. Let cool in the pan for a couple of minutes and then transfer the bread to a rack to cool completely.

Nosh AP GF flour (page 4)
300 grams | 2⅓ cups

superfine sweet white rice flour
60 grams | 7 tablespoons

tapioca starch
50 grams | 5 tablespoons

Expandex Modified Tapioca Starch (see page 3) or additional tapioca starch
50 grams | 5 tablespoons

sugar
50 grams | 4 tablespoons or ¼ cup

instant yeast, Red Star preferred
20 grams | 2 tablespoons

xanthan gum
2 teaspoons (2½ teaspoons if not using Expandex)

kosher salt
2½ teaspoons

pectin
¼ teaspoon

guar gum
¼ teaspoon

eggs
240 grams | 4 extra-large

egg yolks
75 grams | 3 extra-large

honey or Lyle's Golden Syrup
40 grams | 2 tablespoons

canola oil
75 grams | ⅓ cup

sparkling mineral water, Pellegrino preferred
110 to 140 grams | ½ cup plus 2 optional tablespoons

nonstick spray, for greasing

egg, for brushing
60 grams | 1 extra-large

poppy or white sesame seeds
2 tablespoons

BAKING TIME: 32 to 35 minutes
(plus rising time for dough and
3 to 4 days for poolish)

DAIRY-FREE

POOLISH

Nosh AP GF flour (page 4)
  140 grams | 1 cup plus 1 tablespoon

lukewarm water
  175 grams | ¾ cup

instant yeast, Red Star preferred
  ¼ teaspoon

CHALLAH

Nosh AP GF flour (page 4)
  150 grams | 1 cup plus 2
  tablespoons

superfine sweet white rice flour
  60 grams | 7 tablespoons

tapioca starch
  50 grams | 5 tablespoons

Expandex Modified Tapioca Starch
(see page 3) or additional tapioca starch
  50 grams | 5 tablespoons

sugar
  50 grams | 4 tablespoons or ¼ cup

instant yeast, Red Star preferred
  14 grams | 1 tablespoon

xanthan gum
  2 teaspoons (2½ teaspoons if not
  using Expandex)

kosher salt | 2½ teaspoons

pectin | ¼ teaspoon

guar gum | ¼ teaspoon

eggs | 240 grams | 4 extra-large

egg yolks | 75 grams | 3 extra-large

honey or Lyle's Golden Syrup
  40 grams | 2 tablespoons

canola oil
  75 grams | ⅓ cup

sparkling mineral water, Pellegrino
preferred
  35 to 50 grams | 2 to 3 tablespoons

nonstick spray, for greasing

egg, for brushing
  60 grams | 1 extra-large

poppy or white sesame seeds
  2 tablespoons

QUICK CHALLAH IN THE ROUND WITH POOLISH

This challah requires some advance planning, but very little actual hands-on work. It's pretty much a no-fail recipe. If you have the time to create the poolish—a starter that begins the fermentation process—the final bread flavor is incredibly worth the extra effort. The Expandex Modified Tapioca Starch makes all the difference in the bread, taking it from being just okay to being bendy and chewy, as you expect from bread. Your reward will be a challah that everyone will look forward to noshing.

POOLISH

Three to five days before baking the challah, combine the flour, water, and yeast in a small container. Whisk until smooth. Cover loosely with plastic wrap and leave out for 4 hours. Keep covered and refrigerate for 3 days, for best flavor. The poolish will have small bubbles but will not rise much at all. It will have a slightly sweet, fermented flavor if you taste it after a couple of days—that's a good thing. Remove the poolish from the refrigerator on challah-baking day.

CHALLAH

1. In a large bowl, combine both flours and the tapioca starch, Expandex, sugar, yeast, xanthan gum, salt, pectin, and guar gum and whisk. In a medium bowl, whisk four of the eggs, the egg yolks, and the honey and canola oil.

2. Add 35 grams (2 tablespoons) of the sparkling mineral water to the dry mixture. Add the egg mixture to the dry mixture. Add the poolish. Using a fork, work the flour mixture into the wet mixture until it is just combined. Using the dough hook on an electric mixer on low speed, mix for 5 to 7 minutes, until the dough looks shiny and stretchy. If the dough looks very sticky and tough, add up to 15 grams (1 tablespoon) of additional sparkling water.

3. Grease a tube pan with nonstick spray. Place the dough all around the bottom of the pan, using a silicone spatula. Wet the spatula with water and smooth the dough. Cover

loosely with greased plastic wrap and let the dough rise in a draft-free area until doubled in size, but not higher than the top of the pan, 1½ to 2 hours.

4. Preheat the oven to 350°F. Beat the remaining egg and brush it gently over the top of the bread. Sprinkle the top with the seeds. Bake for 15 minutes and rotate the pan for even baking. Bake for 17 to 20 minutes and remove from the oven when the internal temperature is 185° to 190°F on an instant-read digital thermometer and the top is pale golden brown. Don't overbake the bread or it will be a little tough. Let cool in the pan for a couple of minutes and then transfer the bread to a rack to cool completely.

BRAIDED CHALLAH

Our braided challah can be made in one afternoon. The dough will be sticky, so be sure to keep those hands floured. This braided version is baked in a loaf pan and is perfect for sandwiches as well as Shabbat dinner.

Nosh AP GF flour (page 4)
  300 grams plus up to 40 grams more for kneading | 2⅓ cups, plus up to ⅓ cup for kneading

superfine sweet white rice flour
  60 grams | 7 tablespoons

tapioca starch
  50 grams | 5 tablespoons

Expandex Modified Tapioca Starch (see page 3) or additional tapioca starch
  50 grams | 5 tablespoons

sugar
  50 grams | 4 tablespoons or ¼ cup

instant yeast, Red Star preferred
  20 grams | 2 heaping tablespoons

xanthan gum
  2 teaspoons (2½ teaspoons if not using Expandex)

kosher salt
  2½ teaspoons

pectin | ¼ teaspoon

guar gum | ¼ teaspoon

eggs
  240 grams | 4 extra-large

egg yolks
  50 grams | 2 extra-large

honey or Lyle's Golden Syrup
  40 grams | 2 tablespoons

canola oil
  75 grams | ⅓ cup

sparkling mineral water, Pellegrino preferred
  110 grams | ½ cup

nonstick spray, for greasing

egg, for brushing
  60 grams | 1 extra-large

poppy or white sesame seeds
  2 tablespoons

1. In a large bowl, combine 300 grams (2⅓ cups) of the Nosh AP GF flour and the sweet rice flour, tapioca starch, Expandex, sugar, yeast, xanthan gum, salt, pectin, and guar gum and whisk. In a medium bowl, whisk four of the eggs, the egg yolks, and the honey and canola oil.

2. Add the sparkling mineral water to the dry mixture. Add the egg mixture to the dry mixture. Using a fork, work the flour mixture into the wet mixture until it is thoroughly combined. Line the countertop with parchment paper dusted with some of the remaining Nosh AP GF flour. Place the dough on the flour. Keep your hands floured, for best results. Knead lightly and work in only the amount of flour necessary to keep the dough from sticking to your hands. Less is more. Break the dough into three equal portions. Form each piece into a log 15 inches long.

3. Place the logs next to one another. Braid from the middle to the end, then reverse and repeat. The ends should be narrower than the center. Don't force the dough, because it is not all that elastic. If the dough breaks, you can still rework it by undoing the braid and starting over. Once the braid is formed, gently push the ends toward the center so the braid is fat in the center and narrow on the ends. It will be relatively short in length and no bigger than the loaf pan. Grease an 8½ × 4½-inch loaf pan with nonstick spray. Lift the braid carefully and place it in the loaf pan.

4. Smooth the top of the braid with wet hands. Cover the braid loosely with greased plastic wrap and let the dough rise in a draft-free area until it has doubled in size—an hour or so.

5. Preheat the oven to 350°F.

6. Beat the remaining egg and brush it gently over the top of the bread, making sure all the exposed dough is covered. Sprinkle the top with the seeds.

7. Bake for 20 minutes. Rotate the pan for even baking and bake for 15 to 20 minutes more. Remove from the oven when the internal temperature is 185° to 190°F on an instant-read digital thermometer and the top is pale golden brown. Don't overbake the bread or it will be a little tough. Let cool in the pan for a couple of minutes and then transfer the bread to a rack to cool completely.

Nosh AP GF flour (page 4)
130 grams plus 40 grams more for
kneading | 1 cup plus ⅓ cup more
for kneading

superfine sweet white rice flour
75 grams | ½ cup

tapioca starch
60 grams | ½ cup

Expandex Modified Tapioca Starch
(see page 3) or additional tapioca
starch
50 grams | 5 tablespoons

sugar
50 grams | 4 tablespoons or ¼ cup

instant yeast, Red Star preferred
20 grams | 2 tablespoons

xanthan gum
2 teaspoons (3 teaspoons if not
using Expandex)

kosher salt | 2½ teaspoons

pectin
¼ teaspoon

guar gum
¼ teaspoon

eggs
240 grams | 4 extra-large

egg yolks
50 grams | 2 extra-large

honey or Lyle's Golden Syrup
40 grams | 2 tablespoons

canola oil
40 grams | 3 tablespoons

sparkling mineral water, Pellegrino
preferred
110 grams | ½ cup

egg, for brushing
60 grams | 1 extra-large

poppy or white sesame seeds
1 to 2 tablespoons

BRAIDED CHALLAH IN THE ROUND

A braided challah round is a familiar sight on the Rosh Hashanah table. This recipe is similar to the Turban Challah with Raisins (page 192) but takes a little more patience to make the braids and create the spiral.

1. In a large bowl, combine 130 grams (1 cup) of the Nosh AP GF flour with the sweet white rice flour, tapioca starch, Expandex, sugar, yeast, xanthan gum, salt, pectin, and guar gum and whisk. In a medium bowl, whisk four of the eggs, the egg yolks, and the honey and canola oil.

2. Add the sparkling mineral water to the dry mixture. Add the egg mixture to the dry mixture. Using a fork, work the flour mixture into the wet mixture until it is just combined. Using the dough hook on an electric mixer on low speed, mix for 8 minutes, or until the dough looks shiny and stretchy.

3. Place the dough on a parchment-lined surface that has been dusted generously with some of the remaining Nosh AP GF flour. Add more flour on top of the dough and keep your hands floured, for best results. Knead until most of the flour is worked into the dough. When the dough starts to look smooth, begin rolling it into a fat log. When it is a smooth log (smooth helps keep it from tearing or coming apart during braiding) cut into three equal portions. Continue rolling those into smaller logs until each is 15 inches long.

4. Place the logs next to one another, and where the center would be, cross the logs like a braid. Then beginning at that center point, braid in one direction and then move (yourself) and braid the other end. Tuck and pinch the ends together. Push the braided dough very gently into a long, skinny strand and start coiling it very gently without tearing it. Once it is a circle, tuck the end under and gently push it into a tight round.

5. Line a baking sheet, 9-inch pie dish, or round baking pan with parchment paper. Very gently slide your hands under the coiled braid or use a huge spatula and lift it into

the pan. Pat gently to fix the spiral shape. Smooth with wet hands. Cover the braid loosely with plastic wrap and let the dough rise in a draft-free area until it has doubled in size—an hour or so.

6. Preheat the oven to 350°F. Beat the remaining egg and brush it gently over the top of the bread, making sure all the exposed dough is covered. Sprinkle with the seeds. Turn down the temperature to 325°F. Bake for 20 minutes. Rotate the pan for even baking. Bake for 20 to 25 minutes more and remove from the oven when the internal temperature is 185° to 190°F on an instant-read digital thermometer and the top is pale golden brown. Let cool in the pan for a couple of minutes and then transfer the bread to a rack to cool completely.

TURBAN CHALLAH
WITH RAISINS

Another traditional shape for a Jewish New Year challah is the turban. Filled with sweet raisins, this is by far easier to shape than the braid. Leftovers make great French toast.

Nosh AP GF flour (page 4)
130 grams plus 40 grams more for kneading | 1 cup plus ⅓ cup more for kneading

superfine sweet white rice flour
75 grams | ½ cup

tapioca starch
60 grams | ½ cup

Expandex Modified Tapioca Starch (see page 3) or additional tapioca starch
50 grams | 5 tablespoons

sugar
50 grams | 4 tablespoons or ¼ cup

instant yeast, Red Star preferred
20 grams | 2 tablespoons

xanthan gum
2 teaspoons (3 tablespoons if not using Expandex)

kosher salt | 2½ teaspoons

pectin
¼ teaspoon

guar gum
¼ teaspoon

eggs
240 grams | 4 extra-large

egg yolks
50 grams | 2 extra-large

honey or Lyle's Golden Syrup
40 grams | 2 tablespoons

canola oil
40 grams | 3 tablespoons

sparkling mineral water, Pellegrino preferred
110 grams | ½ cup

raisins
150 grams | 1 cup

egg, for brushing
60 grams | 1 extra-large

poppy or white sesame seeds, optional | 1 to 2 tablespoons

1. In a large bowl, combine 130 grams (1 cup) of the Nosh AP GF flour and the sweet white rice flour, tapioca starch, Expandex, sugar, yeast, xanthan gum, salt, pectin, and guar gum and whisk. In a medium bowl, whisk four of the eggs, the egg yolks, and the honey and canola oil.

2. Add the sparkling mineral water to the dry mixture. Add the egg mixture to the dry mixture. Using a fork, work the flour mixture into the wet mixture until it is just combined. Using the dough hook on an electric mixer on low speed, mix for 8 minutes, or until the dough looks shiny and stretchy.

3. Line the countertop with parchment paper and flour generously with some of the remaining Nosh AP GF flour. Place the dough on the floured surface and add more flour on top of the dough. Keep your hands well floured, for best results. Knead until most of the flour is worked into the dough. Form into a rough rectangle and flour the top. Cover with plastic wrap and roll out to a 25 × 7-inch rectangle. Sprinkle the dough with the raisins. Begin rolling the dough from the long side, in jelly-roll fashion. Pinch the roll so that it forms a long rope.

4. Line a baking sheet, 9-inch pie dish, or round baking pan with parchment paper. Roll the spiral gently from the outside in so that the last portion in the center is slightly stacked. Be sure to push the spiraled circle in toward the center and tuck the ends under.

5. Smooth with wet hands. Cover the turban loosely with plastic wrap and let the dough rise in a draft-free area until it has doubled in size—an hour or so.

6. Preheat the oven to 350°F. Beat the remaining egg and brush it gently over the top of the bread, making sure all the exposed dough is covered. Sprinkle with the seeds, if

using. Turn down the temperature to 325°F. Bake for 20 minutes and rotate the pan for even baking. Bake for 20 to 25 minutes more and remove from the oven when the internal temperature is 185° to 190°F on an instant-read digital thermometer and the top is pale golden brown. Don't overbake the bread or it will be a little tough. Let cool in the pan for a couple of minutes and then transfer the bread to a rack to cool completely.

CHALLAH ROLLS

Pull-apart challah rolls are an alternative to making an entire loaf. They will take the same amount of preparation work, except at the end where they will rise more quickly. Plus, they also make great sandwich rolls.

Nosh AP GF flour (page 4)
130 grams plus 40 grams more for kneading | 1 cup plus ⅓ cup more for kneading

superfine sweet white rice flour
75 grams | ½ cup

tapioca starch
60 grams | ½ cup

Expandex Modified Tapioca Starch (see page 3) or additional tapioca starch
50 grams | 5 tablespoons

sugar
50 grams | 4 tablespoons or ¼ cup

instant yeast, Red Star preferred
20 grams | 2 tablespoons

xanthan gum
2 teaspoons (2½ teaspoons if not using Expandex)

kosher salt | 2½ teaspoons

pectin
½ teaspoon

guar gum
¼ teaspoon

eggs
240 grams | 4 extra-large

egg yolks
50 grams | 2 extra-large

honey or Lyle's Golden Syrup
40 grams | 2 tablespoons

canola oil
40 grams | 3 tablespoons

sparkling mineral water, Pellegrino preferred
110 grams | ½ cup

nonstick spray, for greasing

egg, for brushing
60 grams | 1 extra-large

poppy or white sesame seeds
1 to 2 tablespoons

1. In a large bowl, combine 130 grams (1 cup) of the Nosh AP GF flour and the sweet white rice flour, tapioca starch, Expandex, sugar, yeast, xanthan gum, salt, pectin, and guar gum and whisk. In a medium bowl, whisk four of the eggs, the egg yolks, and the honey and canola oil.

2. Add the sparkling mineral water to the dry mixture. Add the egg mixture to the dry mixture. Using a fork, work the flour mixture into the wet mixture until it is just combined. Using a dough hook on an electric mixer on low speed, mix for 8 minutes, or until the dough looks shiny and stretchy.

3. Line the countertop with parchment paper. Flour generously with some of the remaining Nosh AP GF flour. Place the dough on the flour. Add more flour to the top of the dough and keep your hands floured, for best results. Knead until most of the flour is worked into the dough. When the dough starts to look smooth, begin hand rolling it into a fat log. Cut into sixteen equal portions. Roll each piece into a smooth ball in the palm of your hand.

4. Line a baking pan with parchment and grease the parchment and sides of the pan with nonstick spray. Place each ball an inch apart in the pan. Smooth the tops with wet hands. Cover loosely with plastic wrap and let the dough balls rise in a draft-free area until they have doubled in size to about 3-inch rolls—an hour or so. With about 15 minutes to go, preheat the oven to 350°F.

5. Right before baking, beat the remaining egg and brush gently over the top of each roll, making sure all the exposed dough is covered. Sprinkle with the seeds. Turn down the temperature to 325°F. Bake for 20 minutes and rotate the pan for even baking. Bake for 10 to 13 minutes more and remove from the oven when the internal temperature is 185° to 190°F on an instant-read digital thermometer and the top of the rolls are pale golden brown. Let cool in the pan for a couple of minutes and then transfer the rolls to a rack to cool almost completely.

mixed stinky hard cheeses: Cheddar,
Romano, Asiago, or Parmigiano-
Reggiano
   400 grams | 14 ounces

Nosh AP GF flour (page 4)
   200 grams | 1½ cups plus
   1 tablespoon

onion powder
   ½ teaspoon

garlic powder
   ½ teaspoon

cayenne pepper
   ¼ teaspoon

kosher salt
   ¼ teaspoon

cold unsalted butter
   45 grams | 3 tablespoons

milk, as needed
   45 to 75 grams | 3 to 5 tablespoons

CHEESY CRACKER BITES

Is there anyone who is gluten-free that does not miss those little cheesy snack crackers? Use whatever cookie cutter you want to make tiny shapes. I have a fish, as well as stars, cats, and even dog bones. The addition of cayenne in these crackers makes them way more interesting than the standard. This is a fabulous way to use up ends of hard cheeses that are lurking in the refrigerator. The crackers store for weeks in a tin and taste even better as they age.

1. Cut the cheese into 1-inch pieces. In a medium bowl, mix the cheese with 1 tablespoon of the flour. Place in a food processor and pulse until finely ground. Or finely grate the cheese by hand. Add the remaining flour, onion powder, garlic powder, cayenne, and salt to the cheese mixture and pulse (or stir) to mix. Add the butter and pulse until everything is mixed well and the dough starts to come together in a ragged ball. If the mixture is too dry, add the milk 1 tablespoon at a time while the processor is running. Depending on the cheese's moisture, you may or may not need the milk.

2. Transfer the dough to plastic wrap. Knead the dough together until it is fairly smooth. Divide the dough into four pieces. Flatten into disks and wrap them in plastic. Refrigerate the dough for at least 4 hours; overnight is even better because it allows the flavors to develop.

3. Preheat the oven to 350°F.

4. Remove one piece of dough at a time while the others remain in the refrigerator. Place the dough on 13 × 9-inch sheet of parchment. Cover with plastic wrap and roll out the dough into a rectangle ⅛ inch thick.

5. Place the parchment paper on the baking sheet and chill the rolled dough in the refrigerator for 15 minutes, which will make cutting out shapes much easier. Remove the plastic wrap and cut the crackers into whatever shape you want. Line a baking sheet with parchment. Place the crackers close together on the prepared baking sheet. Reroll the scraps and continue to fill the baking sheet. Refrigerate as needed to get the dough to cooperate.

6. Bake the crackers for 10 minutes and rotate the pan for even baking. Bake for 3 to 6 minutes more, until they are beginning to turn crispy and golden. The crackers will continue to crisp as they cool. Let the crackers cool on a rack.

7. Repeat steps 4 to 6 with the remaining dough. Store the completely cooled crackers in a tin for up to a week on the shelf or 2 to 3 weeks in the refrigerator.

Potato Matzo

Matzo Squares

MATZO

Matzo, in the spirit of Passover, should be made in less than 18 minutes from the moment the water hits the flour to finish. With a bit of preparation, it can be done. Leftover matzo is perfect for making matzo brie or matzo balls. The ingredients in this recipe can be purchased kosher for Passover (KFP) if ordered from a supplier that stocks KFP products (see page 255). If you are not concerned about kosher for Passover and just enjoy a flat potato cracker, these recipes are very quick and easy. The all-purpose matzo squares also make great crackers when topped with sesame or poppy seeds and extra kosher salt. Be careful to make certain the ingredients are all gluten-free.

1. Preheat the oven to 450°F. Line two baking sheets with parchment paper.
2. In a small bowl, whisk the dry ingredients together. When the oven is preheated and all your materials and ingredients are in place, set the timer for 18 minutes.
3. Immediately pour the hot water into the dry mixture and stir with a fork. Using clean hands, knead the dough quickly. Break into three or four pieces and roll into balls. Sandwich one dough ball between sheets of plastic wrap dusted with tapioca starch. Roll the dough into a thin round for potato matzo or into a thin square for matzo squares. Remove the top plastic and flip the matzo onto the prepared baking sheet. Sprinkle the seeds and salt, if using, onto the matzo squares.
4. Repeat the process and place two rounds or squares on each baking sheet. Using a docking tool or a fork, poke holes in the dough. Quickly place the baking sheets in the oven and bake for as much remaining time as possible if you are working within the 18-minute rule. Otherwise, bake the matzo for 6 minutes. Flip the matzos over and bake for 6 to 8 minutes more, or until they are very brown with some black spots. Let the matzo cool on a rack.

POTATO MATZO

potato flour
  30 grams | 3 tablespoons

potato starch
  60 grams | ⅓ cup

tapioca starch, plus 2 tablespoons for dusting
  140 grams | 1 cup

kosher salt
  1 teaspoon

hot tap water
  175 grams | ¾ cup

MATZO SQUARES

Nosh AP GF flour (page 4)
  260 grams | 2 cups

kosher salt
  1 teaspoon

hot tap water
  175 grams | ¾ cup

tapioca starch
  25 grams | 2 tablespoons

OPTIONAL MATZO SQUARES TOPPING

poppy or white sesame seeds
  2 to 3 teaspoons

kosher salt
  1 teaspoon

OUT OF A BOX

In our house, box mixes reside alongside all kinds of scratch ingredients. No need to segregate or sacrifice one for another. A mix can be a time-saver or just a way to eliminate gathering all those individual ingredients together to make a scratch cake or treat. These recipes are by no means ordinary when it comes to using a box mix. Think whimsy from a box.

SPECIAL EQUIPMENT

8-inch round baking pans, baking sheets, muffin pans, greaseproof cupcake liners, parchment paper, piping bags and tips

TIPS

- A 425-gram (15-ounce) box of GF cake mix (yielding 2 heaping cups of dry mix) works best for these recipes, but all GF mixes should perform adequately.
- These tested best with Betty Crocker GF cake mixes and Gluten Free Pantry brand, both 15 ounces.
- If you intend to make the dairy-free versions of the recipes, check the ingredients in the cake mix to make sure it is dairy-free (most are).

- For best layer cake loft, use an 8-inch round layer cake pan. Use no larger than a 9-inch pan.
- For recipes that require icing, a store-purchased GF frosting can be substituted.
- Count on GF cake mixes to yield about twelve cupcakes, one 8-inch layer cake, or twenty-four mini cupcakes.

GOLDIE'S QUICK APPLE CAKE

MAKES ONE BUNDT CAKE OR
ONE 9-INCH ROUND CAKE;
SERVES 6 TO 8

BAKING TIME: 35 to 40 minutes
DAIRY-FREE

I've been told by a relative who was there back in the day that my grandmother, Lina, liked to bake a frugal version of her mother's apple cake. She'd start by taking a baking pan and toss in chopped, almost fermented apples that were ready for a compost heap. This is a quick and easy, updated version using dried apples for that concentrated flavor. Although my grandmother served her version as dessert, this would also make a tasty brunch cake.

1. Preheat the oven to 350°F. Grease a Bundt or 9-inch round baking pan.
2. In a large bowl, whisk the cake mix with the cinnamon, mace, and cloves to combine the ingredients and remove any lumps. Add the shortening, eggs, and milk. Using an electric mixer on medium to high speed, blend until the batter is smooth and a little bit fluffy. Using a silicone spatula, carefully fold in the diced dried apples. Pour or scrape the batter into the prepared pan.
3. Rap the pan on the countertop to remove any air bubbles. Bake for 20 minutes and rotate the pan for even baking. Bake for 15 to 20 minutes more, or until a toothpick inserted into the center of the cake comes out with dry crumbs. Let cool in the pan for 5 minutes and then transfer the cake to a rack to cool completely. Place on a cake plate and sprinkle with a dusting of confectioners' sugar, if desired.

nonstick spray or butter, for greasing

GF yellow/vanilla cake mix
  425 grams | one 15-ounce box |
  2 heaping cups

ground cinnamon
  1 teaspoon

mace or nutmeg
  ¼ teaspoon

ground cloves
  ¼ teaspoon

shortening
  85 grams | 7 tablespoons or ¼ cup
  plus 3 tablespoons

eggs
  180 grams | 3 extra-large

nondairy milk, almond preferred
  165 grams | ⅔ cup

dried apples, diced
  100 grams | 1 cup

confectioners' sugar, sifted, optional
  30 grams | ¼ cup

BAKING TIME: 15 to 18 minutes
(standard), 12 to 14 minutes (mini)
DAIRY-FREE OPTION AVAILABLE

chocolate or yellow/vanilla GF cake
mix
　425 grams | one 15-ounce box |
　2 heaping cups

shortening
　70 grams | 6 tablespoons or ¼ cup
　plus 2 tablespoons
　　　　or
unsalted butter, slightly softened
　100 grams | 7 tablespoons or ¼ cup
　plus 3 tablespoons

eggs
　180 grams | 3 extra-large

nondairy milk, almond preferred
　165 grams | ⅔ cup

vanilla extract
　1 teaspoon

OPTIONAL BATTER ADDITIONS
- mini semisweet chocolate chips
　85 grams | ½ cup
- toasted nuts (see page 251),
　roughly chopped
　　70 grams | ½ cup
- dark or golden raisins
　75 grams | ½ cup
- unsweetened shredded coconut
　30 grams | ½ cup
- GF candy bar, crushed
　60 grams | ½ cup
- lemon or orange zest
　1 teaspoon
- jam, Nutella, or nut butter
　2 to 3 tablespoons
- orange, lemon, or peppermint
　extract
　　½ teaspoon
- instant espresso powder (decaf
　is fine)
　　1 teaspoon

(INGREDIENTS CONTINUE)

MIXED-UP CUPCAKES

Got a cupcake craving? Got a cake mix? Then you're a lucky duck
and this cupcake variety show can be yours in less than 30 minutes.
These are also fabulous when the notice comes the night before that
you're in charge of bringing cupcakes to a classroom or work party.
Not only will everyone love them, but also no one will even think to
ask whether they are gluten-free. My favorite version features mini
chocolate chips in the cake *and* frosting.

1. Preheat the oven to 350°F. Place liners in a cupcake pan.
2. In a large bowl, whisk the cake mix to combine the ingredients and remove any lumps. Add the shortening, eggs,
   milk, and vanilla. Using an electric mixer on low speed,
   combine the ingredients. As soon as the dry mixture is
   incorporated, turn up the mixer speed to medium-high
   and mix until the batter is smooth, lump-free, and somewhat fluffy. Using a silicone spatula, fold in any optional
   batter additions, if desired.
3. Fill each liner two-thirds full for a nice dome effect. Bake
   for 15 to 18 minutes for standard size and 12 to 14 minutes
   for mini cupcakes. Test with a toothpick. If it comes out
   without crumbs, remove the cupcakes from the oven. If it
   comes out with wet batter, give them a minute more—but
   no more than that. Let them cool in the pan for 2 minutes,
   then transfer to a rack to cool completely.

BUTTERCREAM

1. Place the confectioners' sugar in a large bowl and add the shortening. Mix on low speed until the sugar is combined with the shortening. Add the vanilla and 1 tablespoon of milk. Whip the buttercream until it is smooth and fluffy. If it is too stiff, add up to another tablespoon of milk and whip. Fold in any optional buttercream additions.
2. Pipe or spoon the buttercream onto the cupcakes. Place any optional toppings on the cupcakes, if desired.

BUTTERCREAM

confectioners' sugar, sifted
330 grams | 3 cups

shortening
72 grams | 6 tablespoons or ¼ cup plus 2 tablespoons

vanilla extract
1 teaspoon

nondairy milk, almond preferred, or water
1 to 2 tablespoons

OPTIONAL BUTTERCREAM ADDITIONS
- lemon or orange zest
   1 tablespoon
- maraschino cherry liquid, fruit liqueur, Nutella, nut butter, pureed and strained berries, or brewed coffee
   1 to 3 tablespoons
- powdered instant espresso; freshly grated nutmeg; ground cinnamon; or peppermint, almond, orange, or lemon extracts
   1 teaspoon

OPTIONAL CUPCAKE TOPPINGS
- crushed GF candy
- roughly chopped toasted (see page 251) nuts
- semisweet mini chocolate chips
- fresh berries
- chopped dried fruits: raisins, ginger, dates, cherries, or cranberries
- GF chocolate-covered coffee beans

NIAGARA FALLS LAYER CAKE

As college students with small kids we lived in a neighborhood where everyone gathered for coffee on a stoop. It didn't matter what time it was; there was always cake–a cake I made. Sometimes it was a frosted layer cake that we shared at breakfast time. A cake mix is the foundation for this favorite layer cake and reminds us of those days when we'd take wagers on whether the professor could hear any of us snoring through class in those giant lecture halls. Cake makes everything better.

nonstick spray or butter, for greasing

Nosh AP GF flour (page 4) or unsweetened cocoa powder, for dusting
    1 tablespoon

GF cake mix, chocolate preferred
    425 grams | one 15-ounce box |
    2 heaping cups

shortening
    70 grams | 6 tablespoons or ¼ cup plus 2 tablespoons
        or
    unsalted butter, slightly softened
    100 grams | 7 tablespoons

eggs
    180 grams | 3 extra-large

whole milk
    170 grams | ⅔ cup
        or
    nondairy milk, almond preferred
    165 grams | ⅔ cup

brewed coffee (decaf is fine)
    1 tablespoon

vanilla extract
    1 teaspoon

semisweet mini chocolate chips
    85 grams | ½ cup

seedless raspberry jam
    130 grams | 6 tablespoons or ¼ cup plus 2 tablespoons

Buttercream (page 205)
    1½ batches
        or
    GF fluffy white frosting
    2 containers | 680 grams |
    24 ounces

GF chocolate sprinkles, optional
    4 to 5 tablespoons

(INGREDIENTS CONTINUE)

1. Preheat the oven to 350°F. Grease two 8-inch layer cake pans and dust with flour for vanilla cake or unsweetened cocoa for chocolate cake.

2. In a large bowl, whisk the cake mix to combine the ingredients and remove any lumps. Add the shortening, eggs, milk, coffee, and vanilla. Using an electric mixer on low speed, combine the ingredients. As soon as the dry mix is incorporated, turn up the mixer speed to medium-high and mix until the batter is smooth, lump-free, and somewhat fluffy. Fold in the mini chocolate chips with a silicone spatula.

3. Divide the batter evenly between the prepared pans. Rap the pans on the countertop to remove any air bubbles. Bake for 5 minutes. Turn down the temperature to 325°F and bake for 20 minutes more. Remove the cakes from the oven as soon as a toothpick comes out clean. Let the cakes cool in the pans for 5 minutes. Turn them out onto a rack to cool completely before applying the frosting.

4. Place one cake layer on a serving plate. Place parchment paper pieces around the bottom edge of the cake to catch any sprinkles or chocolate spills. Spread the raspberry jam on top of the first layer. Next, apply a crumb coat of buttercream on the cake, taking care not to disturb the raspberry jam. Add the second cake layer and finish applying the buttercream until the whole cake is covered with a thick layer of buttercream. Using a medium to large star tip, pipe large flowers or stars on the top edge

of the cake, spaced evenly apart. If desired, carefully apply GF sprinkles to the bottom of the cake, using a small spoon or offset spatula. Refrigerate the cake to set the buttercream while making the chocolate glaze.

GLAZE

In a double boiler over low heat, melt the butter with the chocolate and corn syrup, stirring to completely combine. Let the mixture cool until it starts to slightly thicken, 20 to 30 minutes. Remove the cake from the refrigerator. Gently pour the glaze onto the center of the top of the cake, and using a small offset spatula, help it flow over the edges—think slow-moving Niagara Falls—in between the star or flowers. A little glaze goes a long way. You might have leftover chocolate glaze, which can be stored covered in the refrigerator for up to 2 weeks (and reheated in the microwave as an ice-cream topping). Let the chocolate set at room temperature. Remove the parchment before serving.

GLAZE

unsalted butter
  90 grams | 6 tablespoons
    or
  shortening
    60 grams | 5 tablespoons

semisweet bar chocolate, roughly chopped
  170 grams | 6-ounce bar | 1½ cups

light corn syrup
  40 grams | 2 tablespoons

GF chocolate cake mix
425 grams | one 15-ounce box |
2 heaping cups

instant espresso powder
(decaf is fine)
1 teaspoon

shortening
60 grams | 5 tablespoons

eggs
120 grams | 2 extra-large

nondairy milk, almond preferred
60 grams | ¼ cup

vanilla extract
1 teaspoon

FAST FILLING (MAKES ENOUGH FOR 6 WHOOPIE PIES)

GF fluffy white frosting
1 container | 340 grams | 12 ounces

Marshmallow Fluff or Creme
100 grams | ½ cup

vanilla extract
1 teaspoon

instant espresso powder
(decaf is fine)
1 teaspoon

STILL PRETTY QUICK FILLING (MAKES ENOUGH FOR 6 WHOOPIE PIES)

shortening
145 grams | 12 tablespoons or ¾ cup

confectioners' sugar, sifted
220 grams | 2 cups

Nosh AP GF flour (page 4)
2 tablespoons

canned coconut milk
80 grams | ⅓ cup

vanilla extract
1 teaspoon

instant espresso powder
(decaf is fine)
1 teaspoon

(INGREDIENTS CONTINUE)

FAST MOCHA WHOOPIE PIES

Whoopie pies are so popular they even have their own section in bookstores. This recipe is easy to prepare and we think one of the tastiest whoopie pies. These would make a great contribution to a Hanukkah party because they are like *gelt* on steroids. Of course, you can make them much smaller for little hands. These remind me (if only they were frozen) of Carvel Flying Saucers, which we can no longer eat in our gluten-free life. Wait—they *can* be filled with ice cream and frozen just like flying saucers. Oh, happy day.

1. Preheat the oven to 350°F. Line two baking sheets with parchment paper.
2. In a large bowl, whisk the cake mix and espresso powder to combine the ingredients and remove any lumps. Add the shortening, eggs, milk, and vanilla. Using an electric mixer on medium speed, beat the batter until it is smooth, fluffy, and very thick. Scoop the batter onto the prepared baking sheets in equal-size round mounds, six to a sheet. Smooth the tops with a clean wet finger, but don't flatten the batter.
3. Bake for 6 minutes and rotate the pans for even baking. Bake for 5 to 6 minutes more, or just until a toothpick comes out with dry crumbs. Let cool on the pans for a minute. Transfer the cookies to a rack and let cool completely before filling.

FAST FILLING

In a large bowl, whip together the frosting, Marshmallow Fluff, vanilla, and espresso powder.

STILL PRETTY QUICK FILLING

In a large bowl, combine the shortening, confectioners' sugar, flour, coconut milk, vanilla, and espresso powder. Using an electric mixer, mix on low speed until all the ingredients are combined. Scrape down the sides with a silicone spatula. Turn up the mixer speed to medium-high and keep mixing for 3 minutes. The filling will eventually turn smooth and fluffy.

WHOOPIE FLYING SAUCER FILLING

Soften the ice cream until it can be easily scooped.

ASSEMBLY

Scoop a generous dollop of whichever filling you are using onto the flat side of one cookie. Top with the flat side of the other. Wrap the ice-cream-filled flying saucers individually in plastic wrap and place in the freezer. The others are best served on the same day.

FLYING SAUCER FILLING (MAKES ENOUGH FOR 6 FLYING SAUCERS)

ice cream or nondairy ice cream
  900 grams | 2 pints

CAKE WRECK PARFAITS

MAKES 10 TO 12 SMALL
PARFAITS

DAIRY-FREE OPTION AVAILABLE

Everyone experiences a cake wreck now and then. Sometimes the cake doesn't do what you want it to—it might bake lopsided, burn a little, or even suffer a slight fall. I have an entire section of cake wrecks on my blog. The day our editor called to talk about this book, I had two perfect cake wrecks cooling in the kitchen. I might not have mentioned that fact. My first thought was to hide them before the publisher found out, but a good cake wreck is an opportunity to be creative. As long as it tastes good, you have something to work with to build a brand-new dessert. These are some of my favorite cake-rescue recipes.

1. Let the cake cool completely. If the edges are burned, cut those away. Slice the cake into 1-inch cubes.
2. Whip the cream with the sugar and vanilla until soft peaks form.
3. Place ten to twelve parfait or small drinking glasses, ramekins, or any other mixed glassware of similar sizes on a baking sheet (Weck or small Mason jars are great).
4. Place a shallow layer of cake in the bottom of each glass. Sprinkle a few berries or cherries on the cake layer. Top with a layer of whipped cream. Be careful to add each ingredient without touching the sides of the inside glass, for the best look. Continue to layer in the same order until you reach just below the rim of each glass or a designated height that looks appropriate. Add a dollop of the whipped cream and top with a berry or cherry.
5. Chill the baking sheet in the refrigerator until ready to serve. Be sure to mention you always intended to serve cake parfaits.

STRAWBERRY SHORTCAKE

baked yellow cake wreck
  1 cake

heavy cream or nondairy whipped topping
  485 grams | 1 pint

sugar | 1 tablespoon

vanilla extract | 1 teaspoon

fresh strawberries
  340 to 510 grams | 2 to 3 half-pints, reserving 12 berries for topping

BLACK FOREST

baked chocolate cake wreck
  1 cake

heavy cream or nondairy whipped topping
  485 grams | 1 pint

sugar | 1 tablespoon

vanilla extract | 1 teaspoon

fresh cherries, pitted
  340 to 510 grams | 2 to 3 half-pints

maraschino or fresh cherries, pitted for topping | 12 cherries

MIXED BERRY PARFAIT

baked yellow or chocolate cake wreck
  1 cake

heavy cream or nondairy whipped topping
  485 grams | 1 pint

sugar | 1 tablespoon

vanilla extract | 1 teaspoon

fresh mixed berries
  340 to 510 grams | 2 to 3 half-pints, reserving 12 whole berries for topping

BAKING TIME: 10 to 14 minutes
(canoe pan) or 18 to 20 minutes
(muffin pan)

DAIRY-FREE OPTION AVAILABLE

nonstick spray, for greasing

GF yellow cake mix
 425 grams | one 15-ounce box |
 2 heaping cups

unsalted butter, slightly softened
 90 grams | 6 tablespoons or ¼ cup
 plus 2 tablespoons
    or
 shortening
 60 grams | 5 tablespoons

eggs
 120 grams | 2 extra-large

milk or nondairy milk, almond milk
preferred
 165 grams | ⅔ cup

vanilla extract
 1 teaspoon

lemon extract
 ¼ teaspoon

GOOEY FILLING

shortening
 195 grams | 16 tablespoons or 1 cup

confectioners' sugar, sifted
 220 grams | 2 cups

Nosh AP GF flour (page 3)
 2 tablespoons

canned coconut milk
 80 grams | ⅓ cup

vanilla extract
 1 teaspoon

GOOEY FILLED VANILLA CAKES

It's really not a huge secret that almost everyone likes the idea of Twinkies. We may have fond memories of eating them as kids if we were lucky, but they certainly were not something I'd go out of my way to purchase as an adult. You might be more inclined to enjoy a gooey filled vanilla cake once again if you tasted one of these. To make these look like a clone, you will need canoe pan (see page 252) but they taste just as good when made in a muffin pan.

1. Preheat the oven to 350°F. Grease a 6-count canoe or 12-count muffin pan with nonstick spray. Place little strips of parchment in each canoe or muffin cup, like mini slings. It helps keep the cake from browning too much because we all remember that beige look.

2. In a large bowl, combine the cake mix, butter, eggs, milk, vanilla, and lemon extract. Using an electric mixer, beat on low speed until all the ingredients are incorporated. Turn the speed to high and beat until the batter is smooth.

3. Using a spatula, scrape down the sides of the bowl and fold up from the bottom to make sure all the dry stuff is mixed in. Fill the canoe pans slightly less than halfway—don't be tempted to fill them more or you will have battleships and not canoes. If using a muffin pan, fill half-full. There might be a little batter left over.

4. Bake for 10 minutes and rotate the pan for even baking. Bake for 2 to 4 minutes more, or just until a toothpick comes out clean. You want them to look very pale. Let cool in the pan for 1 minute. Use the parchment to help lift them out of the pan and let the cakes cool completely on a rack before filling. Repeat the process for filling and baking if using a canoe pan.

5. To make the gooey filling, combine all the ingredients in a medium bowl and, using an electric mixer, mix on low speed until combined. Scrape down the sides as needed. Turn the speed to medium-high and keep mixing for a few minutes, until the filling turns smooth and fluffy.

6. When the cakes are cool, use a chopstick or wooden skewer to poke a hole into the side of the canoe cakes from one end, and twist it around gently, to make room for the filling—taking care not to go all the way through the other end. Do this from the bottom for muffin cakes. This prepares the cake to have room for the filling.

7. Fill a piping bag fitted with a Bismarck piping tip (see page 252). Fill the cakes, being gentle to not pop them apart. A little goes a long way. Some filling may pop out, but just wipe it off so it's even with the cake. It usually takes one sacrificed cake to get the idea. Someone has to taste-test, right?

8. Alternatively, to fill the muffin cakes, core out a cap (neatly) from the top into the cupcake, excavate a little cake to make room, and spoon the filling into the cavity. Replace just the cake cap flush with the top and serve.

GF chocolate cake mix
425 grams | one 15-ounce box |
2 heaping cups

shortening
95 grams | 8 tablespoons or ½ cup

eggs
180 grams | 3 extra large

almond milk
120 grams | ½ cup

vanilla extract
1 teaspoon

GOOEY FILLING

shortening
195 grams | 16 tablespoons or 1 cup

confectioners' sugar, sifted
220 grams | 2 cups

Nosh AP GF flour (page 4)
2 tablespoons

canned coconut milk
80 grams | ⅓ cup

vanilla extract
1 teaspoon

CHOCOLATE GANACHE

semisweet chocolate chips
340 grams | 2 cups

heavy cream
120 grams | ½ cup

vanilla extract
1 teaspoon

GF fluffy white icing, optional
1 container | 340 grams | 12 ounces
or
GF white icing in a can with a piping tip
1 container | 180 grams | 6.4 ounces

GOOEY FILLED CHOCOLATE CUPCAKES

Those chocolate filled cupcakes with the squiggly icing on top were a childhood coveted favorite, mostly because we weren't allowed to eat them. When I finally saved enough money to buy a package I was terribly disappointed in the flavor, but intrigued about how the filling got in the cupcake. Now I know. This recipe yields twelve cupcakes that are nothing like the stuff from the cellophane package—these are a deep, rich, dark chocolate cake with a fresh-tasting gooey filling and topped with semisweet chocolate ganache.

1. Preheat the oven to 350°F. Place liners in a 12-count cupcake pan.

2. In a large bowl, whisk the mix to combine the ingredients and remove any lumps. Add the shortening, eggs, milk, and vanilla. Using an electric mixer on medium-low speed, combine until the batter is smooth, lump-free, and a little bit fluffy, 1 minute.

3. Fill each liner two-thirds full. Bake for 18 to 22 minutes and remove from the oven when a toothpick comes out without crumbs. Let cool in the pan for a few minutes. Transfer the cupcakes to a rack and let cool completely before adding the filling and dipping in ganache.

4. To make the gooey filling, combine all the ingredients in a medium bowl and, using an electric mixer, mix on low speed until combined. Scrape down the sides as needed. Turn the speed to medium-high and keep mixing for a few minutes, until the filling turns smooth and fluffy.

5. When the cupcakes are cool, use a chopstick or skewer to poke a hole through the top of the cupcake and rough up the insides a bit—taking care not to go all the way through the other end.

6. Prepare a piping bag with a Bismarck piping tip (see page 252). Fill the cake until it begins to come out the top. You'll get an idea of when to stop, though you may have to sacrifice one cupcake to know (one for the baker). Wipe off any extra filling so it's even with the edge of the cake.

7. Alternatively, cut out a cylindrical plug (cap) from the cupcake top. Excavate a little cake and spoon the filling into the cavity. Cover with a cupcake cap as neatly as possible so the cap is even with the top.

8. To make the chocolate ganache, place the chocolate chips in a heatproof bowl. Heat the cream until almost simmering and quite hot. Pour over the chocolate and let the mixture sit without touching it for a minute. Then stir gently—so that no air bubbles form—until all the chocolate is melted. Stir in the vanilla. Let the ganache sit while you set up the cupcakes for dipping.

9. Place the filled cupcakes on a rack over a baking sheet. Make sure all the cake caps are firmly in place or, if piped, that the filling is flush and flat. Stir the ganache once more. Taking one cupcake, dip it head first up to its liner into the ganache and gently twirl it so that all the edges of cake are covered in chocolate. Lift it up and let any excess drip back into the bowl. With one flip of the wrist, turn it right side up without dripping any chocolate down the sides of the cupcake. If the chocolate settles into any caverns created by the filling construction, do a double dip right away, if desired. Place on the rack so the ganache sets. Repeat with all the cupcakes.

10. As soon as the ganache starts to set, pipe or spoon an optional dollop of the fluffy white icing in the center, if desired. A tiny star pattern looks attractive.

BAKED SAVORIES

Who said baked stuff has to be sweet all the time? Some of the best Jewish food is actually not dessert, to the surprise of many. Although *kugel* means "pudding," it is more like a casserole. In our family, potato latke season (or as others call it, Hanukkah) began with the men gathering about a month before our annual ginormous Hanukkah party, to plan the latke invasion with a precision that would make a five-star general proud. Making latkes for fifty required an army of potato graters. Baked savories are all about making delicious meals from the traditional, like kugel, to the more modern, like kefir quiche and chèvre hand pies. Savory piecrusts, homemade egg noodles, and a fine challah corn bread stuffing find a home in this chapter. A baked savory is one tasty dish best served warm.

SPECIAL EQUIPMENT

A great cast-iron skillet, muffin pans, 9-inch square baking pan, 9-inch tart pan, pizza cutter for noodles, ramekins, a grater or two or three, plenty of clean kitchen towels, and a hearty appetite

TIPS

- Noodle kugels are best eaten fresh because GF noodles will soak up all the liquid, eventually making the dish seem dried out.
- Too low a temperature and the latkes soak up oil; too high and they burn and have raw centers.
- For latkes, use oils that are specifically labeled high-heat: safflower, canola, or peanut oil.
- The vegetable kugels taste best right from the oven.

BAKING TIME: 25 minutes (ramekins)
or 45 minutes (9-inch square pan)

DAIRY-FREE

nonstick spray, for greasing

sweet potatoes
4 medium | 1,130 grams | 2½ pounds

red onion
1 medium | 225 grams | ½ pound

extra virgin olive oil
50 grams | ¼ cup

kosher salt
2½ teaspoons

freshly ground black pepper, to taste
¼ to ½ teaspoon

baking powder
½ teaspoon

baking soda
¼ teaspoon

eggs
420 grams | 7 extra-large

Nosh AP GF flour (page 4)
130 grams | 1 cup

green onions, chopped, for garnish
1 to 2 green onions

SWEET POTATO KUGEL

Potato kugel is a regular at most Jewish holiday tables. Different from the usual dish, our Sweet Potato Kugel is dairy-free, bright with flavor, light, and full of good healthy vitamins and minerals. This is one kugel that might become a regular request. Be sure to eat this fresh from the oven.

1. Preheat the oven to 350°F. Grease a 9-inch square baking dish or eight to ten ramekins with nonstick spray.

2. Peel the sweet potatoes and cut to fit a food processor chute. Using the grater attachment, grate all the sweet potatoes and the onion together. Transfer the mixture to a large bowl. Place half of the mixture back in the food processor, and using the cutting blade, finely grind the potato mixture. If grating by hand, half of the mixture should be coarse, and the other half fine. Combine the two mixtures in a large bowl. Add the oil and stir. Stir in the salt, pepper, baking powder, and baking soda. Stir in the eggs. Fold in the flour, making sure everything is well mixed.

3. Scoop into the prepared baking dish(es) and smooth the top. For a 9-inch dish, bake for 45 minutes, or until the top is golden and the edges are browned. For ramekins, bake for 25 minutes, until a knife inserted into the center comes out clean. Let cool slightly. Top with the freshly chopped green onions. Serve immediately.

GLUTEN-FREE EGG NOODLES

MAKES 225 TO 255 GRAMS
(8 TO 9 OUNCES) FRESH
NOODLES OR 170 GRAMS
(6 OUNCES) DRY NOODLES

COOKING TIME: 1 to 3 minutes
DAIRY-FREE

The best gluten-free noodle kugels are made with homemade egg pasta. The dough is easy to make, and rolling them out as thin as necessary is worth every bicep ache. Nothing comes close to matching the flavor of homemade gluten-free egg noodles. Be sure to use both brown and white rice flours (without adding starch) when making the noodles. Brown rice flour is not only a whole grain but also makes the dough softer, while the white rice flour gives it structure and snap. Starch would only make the noodle doughy. Start to finish, you can have these noodles ready in under an hour, including the time it takes to rest the dough. It really is that easy.

superfine brown rice flour
100 grams | ¾ cup

superfine white rice flour
40 grams | ¼ cup

kosher salt
½ teaspoon

canola or extra virgin olive oil
1 teaspoon

egg
60 grams | 1 extra-large

egg yolks
50 grams | 2 extra-large

tapioca starch, for dusting
17 grams | ¼ cup

1. In a large bowl, whisk the flours with the salt. Make a well in the center and add the oil, eggs, and egg yolks. Mix with a fork until everything is combined. It will look more like coarse crumbs until you bring the dough together with your hands in the bowl. Knead into a ball in the bowl.

2. Transfer the dough ball to the countertop and knead by hand for a minimum of 10 minutes (20 minutes is even better) until the dough is shiny, smooth, and elastic. Wrap in plastic wrap and leave to rest on the countertop for 30 minutes.

3. Sandwich the dough between two very large sheets of parchment dusted with some tapioca starch and roll out very thinly so that it is almost transparent. Use only as much starch as you need to keep the dough from sticking—you may have leftover starch.

4. Using a pizza or pastry cutter, slice into ½-inch ribbons. Then slice those ribbons into 2-inch lengths. Transfer the noodles to a rack and let the dough dry for a few minutes while you bring a large pot of salted water to a boil over high heat.

5. Cook the pasta in the boiling water for 1 to 3 minutes, or until al dente, and then drain and rinse the noodles with cool water. Proceed with your pasta recipe as directed, or let the noodles sit out until fully dry, then store in an airtight container in the refrigerator and use within a week.

PINEAPPLE RAISIN NOODLE KUGEL

MAKES ONE 9-INCH SQUARE
KUGEL; SERVES 9

BAKING TIME: 45 to 50 minutes

Noodle kugel is a holiday comfort food. From Great-Grandma Goldie's kitchen all the way through the years to my mother's kitchen, kugel was there not only to break the Yom Kippur fast but also whenever someone needed a comforting casserole. Gluten-free kugel tastes best with Gluten-Free Egg Noodles (page 219), but it also tastes just fine with any decent gluten-free pasta or Thai wide rice noodles. It is best eaten the day it is made because no matter how we wish it were not so, GF noodles are fragile. Not to worry; there are rarely leftovers when this is served.

1. Preheat the oven to 350°F. Butter a 9-inch square baking dish. If using dried homemade or store-bought noodles, parboil, drain, and rinse them in cool water (following the instructions on page 219 or on the package).

2. Stir the rum and water together. Soak the raisins in the rum mixture for 15 minutes. In a large bowl, stir together the cottage cheese and sour cream. Add the pineapple, sugar, eggs, butter, salt, cinnamon, and nutmeg. Drain the raisins and add to the mixture. Fold in the noodles very gently, just until the mixture is combined. Pour into the prepared baking dish. Sprinkle with additional cinnamon.

3. Bake the kugel for 30 minutes and rotate the pan for even baking. Bake for 15 to 20 minutes more, or until a knife almost comes out cleanly. Let the kugel cool slightly to set and serve warm.

dark rum
25 grams | 2 tablespoons
or
rum flavoring
1 teaspoon

warm water
2 tablespoons

raisins
110 grams | ¾ cup

full-fat cottage cheese
450 grams | one 16-ounce container

full-fat sour cream
225 grams | one 8-ounce container

crushed canned pineapple
225 grams | one 8-ounce can packed in juice, drained

sugar
100 grams | ½ cup

eggs, beaten
300 grams | 5 extra-large

unsalted butter, melted
60 grams | 4 tablespoons or ¼ cup

salt
½ teaspoon

ground cinnamon, plus more for sprinkling
½ teaspoon

nutmeg, freshly grated preferred
¼ teaspoon

Gluten-Free Egg Noodles (page 219)
1 batch
or
store-bought GF pasta or Thai wide rice noodles
170 grams | 6 ounces

SPINACH NOODLE KUGEL

Used to be, the neighbors would get together during a Jewish holiday and share kugel. There would always be a variety of sweet kugels, but then there was the rare savory version. Only back then, *savory* meant merely not adding sugar to a cottage cheese kugel. There were always leftovers that no one would claim. This Spinach Noodle Kugel is savory but full of flavor and will not disappoint. The absence of sugar won't even cross your mind.

1. Preheat the oven to 350°F. Butter a 9-inch square pan. If using dried homemade or store-bought noodles, parboil, drain, and rinse them in cool water (following the instructions on page 219 or on the package).
2. Whisk together the sour cream and eggs. Heat the olive oil in sauté pan over medium-low heat. Add the mushrooms, leek, and garlic and sauté until caramelized. Add the white wine to deglaze the pan.
3. Place a layer of the noodles in the bottom of the buttered pan. Add half of the mushroom mixture. If using frozen and thawed spinach, be sure to wring it dry first. Top with half of the spinach. Top with half of the goat cheese. Pour half of the sour cream mixture over the goat cheese. Repeat the layers and end with the sour cream mixture.
4. Bake for 35 to 45 minutes, or just until the center is set. Let cool slightly. Top with the chopped chives and serve warm.

full-fat sour cream
  450 grams | 2 cups

eggs
  300 grams | 5 extra-large

extra virgin olive oil
  30 grams | 2 tablespoons

mushrooms, sliced
  225 grams | 8 ounces

leek, rinsed well and finely diced
  1 small

garlic, minced
  1 clove

white wine or vegetable stock
  2 tablespoons

Gluten-Free Egg Noodles (page 218)
  1 batch
    or
store-bought GF pasta or Thai wide rice noodles
  170 grams | 6 ounces

spinach, chopped (if using frozen, thawed and drained)
  285 grams | 10 ounces

chèvre (goat cheese), Cypress Grove preferred
  115 grams | one 4-ounce round

chopped fresh chives, for garnish
  3 or 4 chives

SAVORY HAND PIES

If a knish were a pie, it might be this. These are also sometimes referred to as empanadas, but they are just savory little hand pies and another great picnic food. Vary the filling by what you like. Make sure that the flavors are what you'd like together in a dish before putting them in a pie. Some surprises are not fun. My brother, for example, would add potato chips to anything if I let him.

SAVORY HAND PIECRUST

Cream Cheese Crust (page 108) or Dairy-Free Crust (page 109)
dough for 2 single crusts

Nosh AP GF flour (page 4), for dusting
2 teaspoons

egg
60 grams | 1 extra-large

coarse sea salt
2 teaspoons

mixed herbs: thyme, rosemary, basil, or oregano
2 teaspoons

MUSHROOM CHÈVRE FILLING (MAKES ENOUGH FOR 12 HAND PIES)

extra virgin olive oil
45 grams | 3 tablespoons

mixed mushrooms (white button and cremini), finely chopped
225 grams | 8 ounces

shallot, diced
1 tablespoon

white wine or vegetable stock
2 tablespoons

fresh thyme, chopped
1 tablespoon

garlic, minced
1 clove

lemon zest, freshly grated
5 grams | 1 tablespoon

spinach, chopped (if using frozen, thawed and drained)
210 grams | 7 ounces

chèvre (goat cheese), Cypress Grove preferred
113 grams | one 4-ounce round

SAVORY HAND PIECRUST

1. Roll out the chilled dough sandwiched between sheets of plastic wrap dusted with 2 teaspoons of flour until it is about ⅛ inch thick. Remove the top plastic wrap. Using a 5-inch round cutter dipped in flour, create as many circles as possible. Reroll the scraps of dough and continue to make crust rounds until you have a total of twelve.

2. Place the dough circles onto two parchment paper–lined baking sheets—six to each sheet—and refrigerate while preparing the filling.

3. Remove the crusts from the refrigerator and let sit at room temperature until the dough is pliable, 5 minutes.

MUSHROOM CHÈVRE FILLING

1. In a sauté pan, heat the olive oil over medium-low heat. Add the mushrooms and shallot. Cook until the mushrooms release their liquid. Add the white wine to deglaze the pan. Wait for the liquid to mostly evaporate and then add the thyme and garlic. Stir for 30 seconds.

2. Add the lemon zest, stir, and remove from the heat. Add the chopped spinach and stir. Let cool until just barely warm. Stir in the goat cheese until fully combined.

HARVEST VEGETABLE FILLING

1. In a sauté pan, heat the olive oil over medium-low heat. Add the celery, carrot, shallot, and seasonal vegetables. Cook until the vegetables are softened and beginning to caramelize. If using, add the white wine to deglaze the pan.

2. Add the thyme, parsley, salt, pepper, and garlic powder and cook for 30 seconds. Add the stock and milk and stir. Cook on medium heat for 2 to 3 minutes, until the liquid is reduced by half, then remove from the heat. Let cool until just barely warm.

ASSEMBLY

1. Preheat the oven to 350°F. Divide the filling into twelve equal portions. Beat the egg and brush each dough circle. Place the filling to one side of the circle and gently fold over the pastry to meet the other side. The dough should be warm enough to bend so it doesn't crack when you fold it over the filling.

2. Crimp the edges of each pie with a fork to seal. If the dough cracks, use a finger dipped in water to "paint" the dough until it seals. Use as little water as possible. Brush the top with egg wash. Slice two vents into the top of each hand pie. Sprinkle with sea salt and herbs. Chill the pies on their baking sheets for 15 minutes in either the freezer or the refrigerator.

3. Bake for 5 minutes and turn down the temperature to 325°F. Bake until the pastry is golden brown and the filling is bubbling though the vents, 25 to 30 minutes more. Let cool on the baking sheets for 5 minutes. Transfer to a rack and let cool completely. The hand pies are fragile when fresh from the oven but will become pretty sturdy as they cool.

HARVEST VEGETABLE FILLING
(MAKES ENOUGH FOR 12 HAND PIES)

extra virgin olive oil
  30 grams | 2 tablespoons

celery, finely diced
  25 grams | ¼ cup

carrot, finely diced
  65 grams | ½ cup

shallot, finely diced
  1 tablespoon

seasonal vegetable, your choice:
summer squash, mushrooms, or
asparagus, broccoli
  150 to 200 grams | 1 cup

white wine, dry Marsala, or
vegetable stock
  1 tablespoon

fresh thyme, chopped
  ½ teaspoon

fresh parsley, chopped
  ½ teaspoon

kosher salt
  ½ teaspoon

freshly ground black pepper
  ¼ teaspoon or 2 turns of the grinder

garlic powder
  ¼ teaspoon

vegetable stock
  100 grams | ½ cup

milk or nondairy milk
  40 grams | 4 tablespoons or ¼ cup

russet potatoes
3 large | 3 pounds

yellow onion
1 large | 225 grams | ½ pound

superfine brown rice flour
60 grams | ½ cup

eggs
180 grams | 3 extra-large

kosher salt
1½ teaspoons

freshly ground black pepper
½ teaspoon

safflower or other high-heat
vegetable oil
896 grams | 32 ounces

TOPPINGS
- applesauce
- sour cream or nondairy sour cream

POTATO LATKES

Nothing says tradition better than a well-seasoned, crispy potato latke topped with sour cream and chives or applesauce. No Hanukkah is complete without at least one potato latke meal. We have three variations that should please any latke fan: traditional, mixed potato, and mixed root vegetable. Be sure to use high-heat oil, which will help keep things from burning. Pay attention to the temperature of the oil—keep it between 325° and 350°F—and you'll be rewarded with extra crispy latkes that are not at all greasy, just tasty. Also, if you have a latke assistant, the recipe can be doubled, tripled, gazillioned for Hanukkah parties.

1. Preheat the oven to 170°F or your preferred keep-warm setting. Line a baking sheet with layers of paper towels.

2. Peel the potatoes, cut to fit a food processor chute, and place in cold water to keep them from turning brown. Cut the onion in half. Using a grater attachment, grate all the potatoes and onion together. Transfer the mixture to a large bowl. Using the cutting blade, finely grind half of the mixture. Return to the bowl with the remaining grated potato and onion and mix to combine. Alternatively, if grating by hand, coarsely grate half of the mixture and finely grate the other half, then combine the two mixtures in a large bowl.

3. Line a colander with a clean dish towel. Place the colander in a large bowl. Place the potato mixture in the lined colander. Squeeze the life out of the mixture to get the liquid out. It will be messy, but keep going until it is pretty dry, because too much liquid in the latke mixture spells greasy, icky, heavy, messy pancakes.

4. Empty the liquid from the large bowl. Place the potato mixture in the bowl and add the flour, eggs, salt, and pepper. Mix well.

5. Fill a cast-iron skillet with ¼ inch of oil. Heat the oil until a tiny bit of the mixture sizzles when dropped in. Maintain an oil level that is ¼ inch deep with a temperature of 325° to 350°F at all times.

6. Scoop ¼ cup of batter for each pancake, flatten to 4 inches in diameter, and fry over medium heat until nicely browned, 3 to 4 minutes. Flip and cook for 3 to 4 minutes more. If

the oil is not hot enough, the potatoes will absorb the oil and just be greasy; if the oil is too hot, the potatoes will be black on the outside and the inside will be raw—325°F is the right temperature.

7. Place the finished latkes on the paper towel–lined baking sheet. Place the sheet in the oven to keep warm while finishing up the other latkes.

8. Serve the latkes warm, topped with applesauce and/or sour cream.

LATKE VARIATIONS

- Mixed Potato Latke: Replace the russet potatoes with a combination of Yukon Gold, red, sweet, and purple potatoes (total 1360 grams/3 pounds).
- Mixed Root Vegetable Latkes: In addition to the three large russet potatoes, add no more than 45 grams (⅓ cup) of mixed shredded carrot, parsnip, and acorn or butternut squash.

nonstick spray, for greasing

red potatoes
6 medium | 1,130 grams | 2½ pounds

red onion
1 medium | ½ pound

extra virgin olive oil
50 grams | ¼ cup

kosher salt
2½ teaspoons

freshly ground black pepper, to taste
½ to 1 teaspoon

garlic powder
1 teaspoon

dried thyme
1 teaspoon

baking powder
½ teaspoon

baking soda
¼ teaspoon

eggs
240 grams | 4 extra-large

Nosh AP GF flour (page 4)
130 grams | 1 cup

chopped fresh chives, for garnish

RED POTATO KUGELETTES

Potato kugel was a staple in our house when I was a kid. It was an inexpensive way to feed a large family with very few boring white potatoes. Fortunately, these days we have access to an abundance of interesting potatoes. Red potatoes are a favorite in our house. This kugelettes recipe features the red potato, though it could be made with other potatoes: Yukon Gold, russet, purple, or white.

1. Preheat the oven to 350°F. Grease two 12-count muffin pans or eight to ten small ramekins with nonstick spray.
2. Peel the potatoes and cut to fit a food processor chute. Using the grater attachment, grate all the potatoes and onion. Transfer the mixture to a large bowl. Using the cutting blade, finely grind half of the mixture. Mix with the remaining grated potato and onion in a large bowl. Alternatively, if grating by hand, coarsely grate half of the mixture and finely grate the other half, then combine the two mixtures in a large bowl. Stir in the oil, salt, pepper, garlic powder, thyme, baking powder, and baking soda. Add the eggs and stir. Fold in the flour, making sure everything is well mixed.
3. Scoop into the prepared muffin pans or ramekins until they are filled halfway and smooth. Bake for 35 to 45 minutes, or until the tops are golden and the edges are browned. A knife inserted into the center should come out clean. Let cool slightly. Serve warm, topped with the freshly chopped chives.

THREE-CHEESE CHOUX BITES

These puffs are otherwise known as *gougères*. They are easy to prepare and will feed a small village. Enjoy them the same day for best flavor.

1. Preheat the oven to 400°F. Line two baking sheets with parchment paper.
2. Whisk the flour with the salt, pepper, and herbs. In a medium saucepan, heat the milk and butter over medium heat until it comes to a low simmer. Using a wooden spoon, add the flour mixture all at once and stir like crazy. A filmy layer will form on the bottom of the pan. Turn down the heat to low. Cook for a minute or two, until it all comes together and the spoon leaves an impression in the dough when pressed. The color will be boring beige. Remove from the heat and turn out the dough into a bowl.
3. Crack the eggs into a small bowl so they are easily at hand. Using an electric mixer on medium speed, beat in one egg at a time until fully incorporated. Make sure that the last one is really incorporated and give it one more stir. Stir in the cheeses and chives, if using, until incorporated. The dough should be a soft yellow.
4. Using a small scoop or piping bag fitted with a ½-inch plain tip, pipe small domes the size of walnuts onto the prepared baking sheet, spaced ½ inch apart. Make sure the dough goes up, not out, as you scoop or pipe. You should get twenty-five to thirty domes on each baking sheet.
5. As you place the baking sheets in the oven, using your fingers, sprinkle the dough with a few drops of water to help create an initial burst of steam, which helps the choux batter puff. Bake for 13 minutes and then turn down the temperature to 350°F. Continue to bake for 15 to 20 minutes, or until the puffs are very golden brown. Do not open the oven door at all during the baking time, or you may lose the lift in the choux pastry.
6. Transfer the cheese puffs to a rack to cool. Serve warm or at room temperature.

Nosh AP GF flour (page 4)
  130 grams | 1 cup

kosher salt
  1 teaspoon

freshly ground pepper, to taste
  ¼ to 1 teaspoon

dried parsley or thyme, to taste
  1 to 2 teaspoons

whole milk
  245 grams | 1 cup

unsalted butter
  150 grams | 10 tablespoons

eggs, at room temperature
  240 grams | 4 extra-large

mixed stinky hard cheeses: Cheddar, Romano, Asiago, or stinky blue, finely grated
  120 grams | 1 cup

chopped fresh chives or green onion, optional
  1 to 2 tablespoons

SEASONED CHALLAH CORN BREAD CUBES

Quick Corn Bread (page 180) and Quick Challah (page 185), dried and cubed
  450 grams combined | 5 cups combined

extra virgin olive oil
  45 grams | 3 tablespoons

poultry seasoning, Savory Spice brand preferred (see page 256)
  1 teaspoon

kosher salt | ½ teaspoon

freshly ground black pepper
  ½ teaspoon

onion powder | ½ teaspoon

garlic powder | ½ teaspoon

herbes de Provence | ½ teaspoon

STUFFING CASSEROLE

nonstick spray or extra virgin olive oil, for greasing

extra virgin olive oil
  60 to 90 grams | 4 to 6 tablespoons

celery, chopped
  1 to 2 stalks

shallot, finely chopped | 1 medium

fresh parsley, chopped | 1 tablespoon

poultry seasoning, Savory Spice brand preferred (see page 256), to taste
  1 to 2 teaspoons

fresh thyme, chopped | 1 teaspoon

kosher salt and freshly ground black pepper

Seasoned Challah Corn Bread Cubes (above) or stale corn bread and challah bread cubes | 5 cups

chicken or vegetable stock
  530 grams | 2¼ cups

egg
  60 grams | 1 extra-large

CHALLAH CORN BREAD STUFFING

This is a great stuffing for a crowd—and worthy of a seat at the Thanksgiving table. If you care to double the recipe, simply use all the bread at once—otherwise, dry out the cubes and freeze half for another use later on. If time isn't on your side, feel free to skip the Seasoned Challah Corn Bread Cubes step and go straight to preparing the Stuffing Casserole with just the stale corn bread and challah. The intermediate step, which can be made ahead, offers the stuffing another layer of flavor and is well worth the time. Everything but the final preparation with vegetables, stock, and egg can be done well ahead.

SEASONED CHALLAH CORN BREAD CUBES

1. Preheat the oven to 325°F. Line one or two baking sheets with parchment paper. Toss the corn bread and challah cubes with the olive oil in a large bowl. Add the poultry seasoning, salt, pepper, onion and garlic powders, and herbes de Provence and fold, making sure everything is well coated.

2. Spread the mixture on the prepared baking sheets. Bake for 15 to 20 minutes, until the cubes are lightly golden brown and look toasted. Turn down the temperature to 300°F if they seem to be browning too quickly. Let the mixture cool completely at room temperature before making the stuffing casserole. The bread cubes can be prepared a day or so ahead of time—leave uncovered at room temperature.

STUFFING CASSEROLE

1. Preheat the oven to 350°F. Grease a 9-inch square baking pan or cast-iron skillet (use oil in the cast-iron pan).

2. In a small sauté pan, heat the olive oil over medium-low heat and add the celery and shallot. Stir until the shallot is a nice golden color and the celery is slightly soft. Add the parsley, poultry seasoning, thyme, and salt and pepper to taste. Remove from the heat and toss with the stuffing cubes in a large bowl. Add the stock and fold gently until combined. Beat the egg and fold in gently to

combine. Let the mixture sit for 5 minutes to absorb the liquid. Fold again. Scrape everything from the bowl into the prepared pan. Bake for 30 to 40 minutes, or until the top is crunchy brown and the casserole looks set. Let cool slightly and serve.

Savory Crust (page 109)
  dough for 1 single crust

spinach, chopped (if using frozen,
thawed and drained), or asparagus or
zucchini, sautéed and drained
  285 grams | 10 ounces

extra virgin olive oil
  30 grams | 2 tablespoons

mushrooms, sliced: cremini, button,
or other mixed mushrooms
  225 grams | 8 ounces

leek, rinsed well and finely diced
  1 leek
    or
shallot or sweet onion, thinly sliced
and caramelized
  1 medium shallot | ½ medium sweet
  onion

kosher salt
  ¼ to ½ teaspoon, to taste

freshly ground black pepper
  ¼ teaspoon, or to taste

Emmental, Gruyère, or Jarlsberg
cheese
  120 grams | heaping ⅓ cup

eggs
  360 grams | 6 extra-large

full-fat kefir or crème fraîche
  285 grams | 1 cup

nutmeg, freshly grated preferred
  ¼ teaspoon

MUSHROOM AND LEEK QUICHE

You might want to make two of these, because one might not be enough after you taste it. Leftover quiche heats up nicely and makes an easy lunch or dinner. Kefir adds a flavor similar to crème fraîche, but without the huge amount of fat or calories—use whole-milk kefir, for best flavor. To keep the filling from becoming watery, be sure to squeeze all the liquid from the spinach, whether it is fresh or frozen. The cheese is totally up to you, but Emmental is a nice mellow yet flavorful quiche cheese. If you like quiche, you will love this.

1. Press the crust dough into a 9-inch tart pan. Save the leftover raw dough for patching. Place the pan on a baking sheet and freeze or refrigerate for 15 minutes. Preheat the oven to 350°F.

2. Place the chilled crust (still on the baking sheet) in the oven and bake for 20 minutes. Patch any cracks with the leftover raw dough and let the crust cool.

3. Squeeze the spinach dry. Repeat again to make sure it is thoroughly dry. Heat the olive oil in a sauté pan over medium-low heat. Add the mushrooms, leek, and salt and pepper. Caramelize the mushrooms until they are past that liquid stage and are nice and brown. Add the chopped spinach to the mushroom mixture and heat slightly. Grate the cheese and set aside.

4. When you are ready to assemble the quiche, mix the eggs with the kefir and whisk until the mixture is smooth. Add a pinch more salt and pepper and stir. Place the mushroom mixture in the bottom of the cooled tart crust. Add half of the grated cheese. Top with the nutmeg. Add a pinch of salt and pepper. Top with most of the remaining cheese, leaving a little behind to add to the top.

5. Pour the egg mixture into the crust through a strainer to leave behind little egg bits—you'd be surprised what lurks. Add the remaining cheese to the top of the quiche, with some more nutmeg on top if you wish. Bake for 35 to 40 minutes, or just until the top looks cooked and is golden brown and puffed. Let cool just slightly and serve.

SWEET STUFF

When the song starts up in my head and sings *I want candy*, it doesn't quit until I make one of these recipes. Because a lot of commercial candy is not gluten-free safe, the remedy is to learn how to make some over-the-top treats that even a nosher would find decadent. Homemade marshmallows, truffles, buckeyes, peanut butter cups, matzo rocky road, and meringue sandwich bites are a few of our favorite things. About the only skill these require is patience and the ability to not eat the ingredients before they get used in the recipe, no matter how tempting. I grew up in a house where my dad's sweet tooth was king. His favorite treats were well hidden from four children, or so he thought. Thankfully, he never checked the bottoms of the chocolates in his box of Fanny Farmer because there would be indents where little fingers checked out the filling. If he were with us today, I bet he would pronounce this chapter the perfect nosh.

SPECIAL EQUIPMENT
Parchment paper, mixer, instant-read digital thermometer, double boiler, silicone spatulas

TIPS
- When a recipe calls for chocolate chips, use the best you can find (see page 7).
- To temper chocolate so it hardens with a shine, follow the directions on page 236.
- Chocolate burns easily, so melt it slowly on low heat in a double boiler or for short bursts in the microwave.
- When taking the temperature of simmering chocolate or boiling sugar on the stove top, aim the thermometer for the middle of the mixture, to ensure an accurate reading.
- Moisture is not chocolate's friend and will make it seize, then make you cry.
- Also, never add liquid flavoring to melted chocolate because it will seize—flavored oils, however, will not make the mixture seize.
- Be aware that boiling sugar is very hot; take care to keep your hands protected.

THE STATE OF CHOCOLATE: TEMPERING CHOCOLATE 101

Tempering is all about controlling the temperature of the melted chocolate by heating and cooling it to just the right temperature, so it hardens with a shine and snap.

Special Ingredients and Equipment

- Choose the best-tasting discs (pistoles), melting wafers, or bar chocolate to temper—chocolate chips and lower-cost chocolate bars won't temper because they contain additives to hold their shape.
- Enrobing chocolate (see page 254) is an alternative to tempered chocolate and will set easily without a lot of fuss.
- Chocolate dipping tools (see page 252) are more deft than a fork and toothpicks, which will do in a pinch.
- An instant-read digital thermometer will take the real-time temperature of melting chocolate, avoiding any delay in getting an accurate measurement.

Microwave Tempering

While a little bit quicker, this method is also more challenging for anyone new to tempering. You have to know in advance what the chocolate ought to look like at any stage, to be really comfortable with tempering chocolate in a microwave. With a little practice and patience, anyone can learn.

Place three-quarters of the chopped chocolate (or pistoles, wafers, or discs) in a microwave-safe container. Melt for 20-second bursts on high, stirring after each interval, because the chocolate will continue to melt. Don't be tempted to go over 20 seconds each time. You want it to be shiny, smooth, and liquid.

The final temperature after melting the chocolate should be between 110° and 114°F. Once that is achieved and the chocolate is smooth and shiny, add the remaining chocolate and stir gently until it is fully incorporated and melted, without any more microwave action. The temperature of the chocolate should eventually fall to between 89° and 90°F. That's the tempered chocolate working temperature range. Dip. Quickly. No interruptions. With this method, you really don't want to reheat the chocolate in the microwave and risk the temperature's rising above 91°F, because that means starting all over again.

Double Boiler Method

In a double boiler over very low heat, melt three-quarters of the chocolate until it is between 110° and 114°F. Carefully remove the bowl from the heat, avoiding any contact with steam, and set it on a towel to insulate it from a cold countertop, then add the remaining chocolate. Stir until the chocolate is 88° to 90°F. You will have to reheat the chocolate again if it falls below 88°F, but don't heat it above 91°F, or you'll have to start the process all over again.

Dipping

Have the items to dip ready in advance and as crumb-free as possible. The tempered chocolate should be in a container that is deep enough to easily cover the item(s) you're dipping. Dunk the item with a dipping fork and slide it out of the chocolate bath. Let the excess chocolate drip

Annie's second birthday, where she is convinced all cakes are heart-shaped and chocolate.

back into the bowl by rapping the fork gently on the edge of the bowl. Slide the item onto the parchment paper, using another fork to push it off. Move quickly and avoid interruptions because tempered chocolate sets quickly. Tempered chocolate will release easily from parchment paper.

TIPS

- Avoid tempering on a humid day, in a hot kitchen, or near steamy water or a boiling teakettle.
- Limit the number of items to dip, to keep the process manageable.
- To keep the chocolate at 89° to 90°F, place the bowl on a towel-covered heating pad set on low or use a hair dryer to heat the bowl occasionally.
- Alternatively, keep the double boiler base on very low heat and, if needed, heat the chocolate for a few seconds to warm it up, but avoid the steam.
- To become proficient at tempering, practice dipping dried fruit, pretzels, or even cookies.
- Never add liquid flavoring to the chocolate (because it will seize), but you can add flavoring oils once the temperature is close to tempering range.
- Use GF enrobing chocolate as an alternative and follow the manufacturer's instructions for dipping.
- If the chocolate won't temper, place it in the refrigerator, where it will harden, and serve it cold.
- If it is streaky but tempered, just say you meant for it to look a bit arty.
- If it seizes, use the chocolate as a future ingredient (freeze and chop for easier handling).
- If you have the funds or the desire, there are tempering machines that can make dipping chocolate as painless as it gets, except for the initial purchase price (see page 252.

CHILLING TIME: 4 hours to overnight

FILLING

unsalted butter, slightly softened
  115 grams | 8 tablespoons or ½ cup

confectioners' sugar, sifted
  330 grams | 3 cups

creamy peanut butter, Skippy
Natural preferred
  380 grams | 1½ cups

kosher salt
  1 teaspoon

vanilla extract
  1 teaspoon

CHOCOLATE COATING

bittersweet or semisweet bar
chocolate, roughly chopped
  500 grams | 18 ounces | 4½ cups

PEANUT BUTTER CUPS
AND BUCKEYES

These treats should come with a warning label: highly addictive. Buckeyes are thought to be native to Ohio, where they are fashioned after a buckeye or horse chestnut—not the athletic teams. Most are made with crushed cookies but these are not, which happily makes them absolutely gluten-free. You can use the very same ingredients to prepare Peanut Butter Cups that are ridiculously way better than anything you've had from the candy counter.

FILLING

1. Line a baking sheet with parchment paper.
2. Cut the butter into tablespoon-size pieces. Combine the confectioners' sugar, peanut butter, and butter in a large bowl. Using an electric mixer, mix on low speed until the confectioners' sugar is incorporated. Turn the speed to medium and mix for 1 minute. With the mixer on low speed once again, slowly add the salt and vanilla.
3. FOR BUCKEYES: Using a tablespoon scoop, place round balls on the prepared baking sheet until you've used all the mixture. Using clean, wet hands, roll each ball into a smooth 1½-inch sphere. Rinse your hands periodically while forming the balls, otherwise they will not be smooth. Cover the pan with foil or plastic wrap and leave in the freezer overnight to both develop the flavor and set.
4. FOR PEANUT BUTTER CUPS: Roll the filling into ½-inch-wide logs and freeze overnight. When ready to assemble the peanut butter cups, slice the frozen logs into skimpy ¼-inch-thick rounds. Use standard muffin or specialty peanut butter cup candy liners (see page 252) for making the peanut butter cups. If using standard muffin cup liners, fill only one-quarter full in total.

CHOCOLATE COATING

1. When ready to dip the buckeye in chocolate, or to create the peanut butter cups, temper the bar chocolate (see page 236) and follow the instructions on the opposite page.

2. **FOR BUCKEYES:** Remove the buckeye balls from the freezer and one by one, using toothpicks or a chocolate dipping fork, dip each into the chocolate just until it is mostly covered—but letting the top peek through (think of chestnuts). Let the excess chocolate drip off. Place the buckeyes back on the (cold) parchment paper–lined baking sheet to set.

3. **FOR PEANUT BUTTER CUPS:** Fill each paper liner one-eighth full with melted chocolate. Place one peanut butter disk in the center, being sure to let the chocolate rise up around the edges as you press the disk down, just slightly. Fill with additional chocolate until the disk is covered and the liner is full (if using small candy liners; otherwise, just fill until you can't see the peanut butter disk and the chocolate is smooth, one quarter of the way up a standard muffin liner). Work rapidly because the cold filling will set the chocolate rather quickly.

4. Both keep at room temperature if tempered, but if the chocolate does not temper, they can be refrigerated and served cold.

CHOCOLATE-COVERED NUTELLA HEARTS

unsalted butter, slightly softened
  105 grams | 7 tablespoons or ¼ cup plus 3 tablespoons

confectioners' sugar, sifted
  330 grams | 3 cups

Nutella
  450 grams | 1½ cups

hazelnut liqueur, Frangelico preferred
  1 tablespoon
   or
  hazelnut or almond extract
  1 teaspoon

vanilla extract
  ½ teaspoon

kosher salt
  1 teaspoon

bittersweet or semisweet bar chocolate, roughly chopped
  500 grams | 18 ounces | 4½ cups

I am a late convert to Nutella, but these candies help make up for lost time and are a stylish Valentine's Day treat. Be sure to use a heart cookie cutter that measures 2½ inches wide by ¾ inch thick to achieve the same yield.

1. Line a baking sheet with parchment paper. Cut the butter into tablespoon-size pieces. In a large bowl, combine the sifted confectioners' sugar, Nutella, and butter. Using an electric mixer on low speed, beat just until incorporated. Add the hazelnut liqueur, vanilla, and salt. Mix until fully incorporated. The mixture should not be terribly sticky and should be somewhat easy to handle. If it is sticky, make sure your hands are slightly wet when handling the dough.

2. To make heart shapes, roll into small balls the size of Ping-Pong balls, flatten just slightly with your hand, and cut out 2½-inch-wide heart shapes with a sharp cookie cutter. Reroll the scraps. Transfer the hearts to the prepared baking sheet. Cover with plastic wrap and freeze for at least 4 hours or overnight.

3. When you are just about ready to remove the baking sheet from the freezer, temper the chocolate (see page 236).

4. One by one, using toothpicks or a chocolate dipping fork, dip each heart into the chocolate just until it is covered. Let the excess chocolate drip off. Place the hearts back onto the parchment-lined baking sheet. If desired, dip a toothpick or the fork back into the chocolate and flick it back and forth over the hearts once or twice to drizzle on decorative ribbons. If they don't temper perfectly, keep them chilled and serve directly from the freezer.

DRESSY CHOCOLATE TRUFFLES

MAKES THIRTY-SIX TO
FORTY-TWO 1½-INCH TRUFFLES

COOKING TIME:
6 minutes (plus setting time)

It used to be that sending someone truffles was the ultimate in chocolate-giving goodness. These days you can find truffles everywhere, including the drugstore candy counter, but nothing beats the quality of a homemade chocolate truffle. They're easy enough to make in under an hour and can be refrigerated until you're ready to give them away or serve them with coffee. The flavor variations are as limited as your imagination.

1. Line a baking sheet with parchment paper. Heat the cream and corn syrup in a double boiler. As soon as it is just warm, add the semisweet and bittersweet chocolate and stir until they are fully melted. Stir in the butter. Let the mixture cool for 5 minutes, then stir in your flavoring of choice. Stir well.

2. Let the mixture set for 3 hours at room temperature. Scoop into generous 1½-inch balls; roll in your hands until mostly round and smooth. Roll in cocoa powder, toasted chopped nuts, or coconut.

3. Place on the prepared pan. Refrigerate until hard. Store, covered, in the refrigerator but serve at room temperature, for best flavor.

heavy cream
240 grams | 1 cup

light corn syrup
1 tablespoon

semisweet bar chocolate, roughly chopped
225 grams | 8 ounces | 2 cups

bittersweet bar chocolate, roughly chopped
225 grams | 8 ounces | 2 cups

unsalted butter, slightly softened
15 grams | 1 tablespoon

FLAVOR VARIATIONS

any of the following: GF liqueur, brewed coffee, vanilla, orange or almond extract
1 teaspoon

COATING VARIATIONS
- unsweetened cocoa powder, sifted
  20 grams | 3 tablespoons
- nuts, finely chopped and toasted (see page 251)
  75 grams | ½ cup
- unsweetened shredded coconut, finely chopped
  55 grams | 1 cup

MAKES THIRTY-SIX
1½-INCH MARSHMALLOWS
(ABOUT 20 OUNCES)

COOKING TIME: 8 to 12 minutes
(plus setting time)
DAIRY-FREE

nonstick spray, for greasing

unflavored gelatin
14 grams | two ¼-ounce envelopes

cold water
235 grams | 1 cup

granulated sugar
200 grams | 1 cup

light corn syrup
110 grams | ⅓ cup

kosher salt
¼ teaspoon

vanilla extract
1 teaspoon

confectioners' sugar, sifted
30 grams | ¼ cup

tapioca starch
65 grams | ½ cup

FLUFFY MARSHMALLOWS

Marshmallows from a store and homemade marshmallows are worlds apart. If you've never made a homemade marshmallow, you are in for a surprise. They are easy to prepare and economical and store for a couple of weeks in a covered tin. Although they mix up in minutes, give them four hours to set properly; the flavor improves the second day. They also make an excellent gift alongside a tin of your favorite hot cocoa mix.

1. Generously grease a 9-inch square pan with nonstick spray. So you can easily remove the marshmallows once they have set, place a piece of parchment paper in the pan, with the edges overhanging like a sling. Spray the parchment generously with nonstick spray.

2. Place the gelatin in the bottom of a large bowl. Add 175 grams (¾ cup) of the cold water to the gelatin and let the mixture set without stirring or disturbing it for 10 minutes or so. You'll be using an electric mixer after the next step, so be sure to have it ready.

3. Meanwhile, in a small but deep saucepan, gently stir the granulated sugar with the corn syrup, salt, and 60 grams (¼ cup) of water once or twice just to combine. Without stirring it again, heat the mixture on medium heat, swirling the pan every once in a while, until it reaches 240°F and turns clear, about 5 minutes. Remove the saucepan from the heat and set aside.

4. Using the electric mixer on low speed, mix the gelatin mixture while pouring the heated sugar down the side of the large bowl, keeping it away from the mixer blades so it will not splash. Be careful—the mixture is very hot. As soon as the sugar is incorporated, turn up the mixer speed little by little until the mixture begins to get frothy and fluffy. It will stink to high heaven, and you might want to not breathe much at this point. Keep going and turn the speed to high. Keep going until it gets huge in volume and turns marshmallow white with giant fluffy white peaks. It should take anywhere from 5 to 8 minutes

in a stand mixer and 14 to 16 minutes with a hand mixer. Add the vanilla and whip just until mixed in thoroughly.

5. Spray a silicone spatula with nonstick spray so you can easily transfer the marshmallow goo into the prepared pan. Then use the spatula to even out the top and make it flat. Let the mixture set at room temperature, untouched, for at least 4 hours, but overnight is better because the flavors develop.

6. Whisk the confectioners' sugar and tapioca starch together and sprinkle generously on a cutting surface. Flip the marshmallow square onto the dusted surface. Remove the parchment paper. Cover generously with more of the sugar mixture. Dip a sharp knife into the sugar mixture, trim the uneven edges, and slice the marshmallow square into 1½-inch squares. Be sure to dip the sticky marshmallow edges into the excess sugar mixture so they won't stick together. These can be stored in a covered tin for up to 2 weeks.

COCONUT MATZO ROCKY ROAD

MAKES 12 TO 16 PIECES

BAKING TIME: 20 to 22 minutes (plus
3 to 4 hours cooling time)

DAIRY-FREE OPTION AVAILABLE

This recipe is an adaptation of Marcy Goldman's original Caramel Matzo Crunch from her book, *A Treasury of Jewish Holiday Baking*. If you are a fan of rocky road, this will make you very happy. Be sure to use the whole box of matzo and make as many layers as possible, which leads to an incredible flaky base. You'll never look at matzo the same way again. For those who buy matzo for Passover and then find three extra boxes in their cupboard when cleaning it out months later, this is for you. Be sure to make this well ahead of when you want to serve it—it takes a long time to cool.

nonstick spray or butter, for greasing

brown sugar
    200 grams | 1 cup

unsalted butter or kosher margarine
    230 grams | 16 tablespoons or 1 cup

Yehuda GF Matzo Style Squares (see page 255)
    one 300-gram box | 10½ ounces

bittersweet and semisweet chocolate chips, mixed (half and half)
    340 grams | 2 cups

unsweetened coconut flakes
    115 grams | 2 cups

nuts, toasted (see page 251) and roughly chopped
    300 grams | 2 cups

mini marshmallows, Paskesz kosher preferred
    135 grams | 2 cups

1. Preheat the oven to 350°F. Grease an 8-inch square baking pan with nonstick spray. Line the pan fully with foil that hangs over all sides like a handle (two long pieces lined crosswise). Spray or butter the foil generously (but not the handles).

2. In a deep saucepan over medium heat, melt the brown sugar with the butter to create the caramel. Once it is all dissolved and begins a low boil, time it for 3 minutes and don't stir the mixture.

3. Use one whole sheet of matzo for each layer in the pan. Place a matzo in the bottom of the greased pan. When the caramel is ready, pour on a thin layer and, using an offset spatula, spread it quickly. Be careful—it is quite hot. Quickly place another whole matzo on top and repeat until you run out of matzo or the caramel. Bake for 15 minutes.

4. While that bakes, get the other ingredients ready to go. Once the matzo comes out of the oven and while it is piping hot, top with half of the chocolate chips followed by half of the coconut flakes, and then half of the nuts and half of the mini marshmallows. Repeat. End with a few strategically placed marshmallows, coconut, chocolate chips, and nuts on top so it looks attractive.

5. Bake for 5 to 7 minutes more, or until the marshmallows just start to become golden. Remove from the oven. Let cool thoroughly in the pan for 3 to 4 hours. Using the foil handles, transfer from the pan onto a cutting board. Peel away the foil. Gently slice, using a serrated knife.

MERINGUE SANDWICH BITES

MAKES 40 TO 45 MERINGUE
SANDWICH BITES

BAKING TIME: 3 to 5 minutes (plus 8
hours or overnight resting in oven)

DAIRY-FREE OPTION AVAILABLE

No one would ever accuse these little meringue sandwich cookies of being ordinary. Filled with Nutella, melted chocolate, jam, or nut butter, these are not those dried-out, too-sweet counterparts in a plastic tub. The trick to keeping the cookies bright white is to place them in a hot oven, close the door, time them for three minutes, and turn the oven off. Leave them to dry for eight hours without opening the door and you'll be rewarded with very pretty meringues. Fair warning: If you bake them on a very humid day, they may be slightly chewy on the inside, which is not a bad thing at all.

egg whites, at room temperature
140 grams | 4 extra-large

cream of tartar
¼ teaspoon

kosher salt
¼ teaspoon

superfine sugar
100 grams | ½ cup

vanilla extract
½ teaspoon

almond extract
¼ teaspoon

FILLING OPTIONS
- Nutella
175 grams | ½ cup
- semisweet chocolate chips, melted
90 grams | ½ cup
- jam, Bonne Maman preferred
160 grams | ½ cup
- nut butter
130 grams | ½ cup

1. Preheat the oven to 350°F. Line two baking sheets with parchment paper.
2. In the bowl of a stand mixer or using a hand mixer, combine the egg whites with the cream of tartar and salt. Begin to whip the whites on high speed. When the whites are frothy, begin to add the sugar slowly down the side of the bowl, making sure it gets incorporated. Go slowly—the whites will absorb a little at a time. Whip the whites until they are bright white and the shiny peaks stand tall.
3. Add the vanilla and almond extract and whip for a few seconds to incorporate. Using a silicone spatula, transfer the whipped egg whites to a large piping bag fitted with a ½-inch star tip. Pipe small kisses or small rounds onto the prepared baking sheets—close together is fine; they don't spread. Alternatively, place 2-teaspoon-size scoops on the prepared pan, close together.
4. Bake for 3 to 5 minutes, then turn the oven off. Keep the oven light on and the door closed. The meringues will need to stay in the oven for 8 hours, or overnight if possible. The meringues should be dry, white, and cool in the morning. Depending on the weather, they might be crispy on the outside and somewhat chewy inside, and that's acceptable, too.
5. Place ½ teaspoon of your preferred filling on the flat side of one meringue and place the flat side of another against it to make a meringue sandwich. Repeat until you've used all of the meringues.

RESOURCES

MEASURING UNITS USED AND METRIC CONVERSIONS

TABLE 3: US VOLUME MEASURES AND METRIC EQUIVALENTS

US Measure	Gallons	Quarts	Pints	Cups	Fluid ounces	Tablespoons	Teaspoons	Milliliters
1 gallon	1	4	8	16	128	256	768	3785
1 quart	0.25	1	2	4	32	64	192	946
1 pint	0.125		1	2	16	32	96	473
1 cup	0.0625			1	8	16	48	237
1 fluid ounce	0.00781				1	2	6	30
1 tablespoon	0.00391					1	3	15
1 teaspoon	0.00130						1	5

"All mine? Why, thank you," says Cory on her fourth birthday.

THE 411 ON FREQUENTLY USED INGREDIENTS

BROWN SUGAR

Your choice—use light (golden) or dark

BUTTER, COLD

Directly from refrigerator, icy cold

BUTTER, SLIGHTLY SOFTENED

Let rest on counter for 20 minutes before using. Still chilly but can leave a finger indent, not melty.

BUTTER, MELTED

Melted until liquid and cooled slightly—but still liquid

BUTTERMILK SUBSTITUTES

245 grams (1 cup) of whole milk plus 1 tablespoon lemon juice or white vinegar; let sit for 10 minutes

or

180 grams (¾ cup) of plain yogurt mixed with 60 grams (¼ cup) of whole milk

CHILLING TIME

Amount of time (or range) in refrigerator or freezer for best results

COCONUT

Flakes are always unsweetened and look like large peels of coconut. Shredded looks like short or long pieces of string and can be sweetened or unsweetened, which is indicated in each recipe.

COCONUT MILK, CANNED

Full-fat, no additives (if possible), stirred thoroughly

CREAM CHEESE

Full-fat—brick-style only

EASY CRÈME FRAÎCHE

480 grams (1 pint) of heavy cream plus 3 tablespoons (no substitutes) of cultured buttermilk; let sit covered on the counter for 12 hours, then refrigerate

EGGS

All eggs are extra-large and weigh about 60 grams in the shell; whites are about 35 grams and yolks about 25 grams (slight variation is fine, as long as the eggs are extra-large). All eggs should be at room temperature unless otherwise specified.

HONEY	100% pure; local is best
LEMON JUICE	100% fresh juice squeezed from a lemon
MAPLE SYRUP	100% pure grade A or B amber
MILK, DAIRY AND NONDAIRY	Whole milk is the best choice for flavor, but nonfat will work; unsweetened almond milk is the best choice for nondairy unless the recipe specifies coconut.
NONSTICK SPRAY	High heat, no flour added
POMEGRANATE CONCENTRATE	100% pomegranate concentrate with no additives (not pomegranate molasses). Or simmer 100% pure pomegranate juice over low heat until reduced by half to create a homemade pomegranate concentrate suitable for these recipes.
ROASTED AND SALTED NUTS	Fresh, good-quality store-purchased roasted and salted nuts (should always be confirmed GF)
SHORTENING	Nonhydrogenated, solid vegetable
SPARKLING MINERAL WATER	Pellegrino preferred; it has the perfect level of acidity for bread making. Brands with a higher acidity level work better.
TOASTED COCONUT	Single layer on a baking sheet, toasted at 325°F for 5 to 10 minutes until golden
TOASTED NUTS	Single layer of raw nuts on a baking sheet, toasted at 350°F for 8 to 10 minutes until fragrant; let cool
WATER	Tap water is sufficient when called for as an ingredient. Hot water should always be between 95° and 110°F.

See Resources (page 249) for select ingredients and retailers.

LOCATING EQUIPMENT, INGREDIENTS, AND INFORMATION

Equipment	Retailers

BAKING PANS:
    CANOE, MUFFIN, BAKING SHEETS, BREAD,
    ANGEL CAKE, BAKING SHEETS, HALF-SHEET SIZE
    ENGLISH MUFFIN RINGS (NORPRO)
    METAL MIXING BOWLS, ASSORTED
    TART AND SPRINGFORM PANS
	Amazon
	 King Arthur Flour
	 Overstock.com
	 Sur la Table
	 USA Pans
	 Williams-Sonoma
	 The WEBstaurant Store

CAKE DECORATING TOOLS: BISMARCK AND OTHER PIPING TIPS DISPOSABLE PIPING BAGS, ASSORTED COUPLERS, ASSORTED SIZES GREASEPROOF CUPCAKE LINERS (STANDARD AND MINI)	Amazon Bake It Pretty Shop Sweet Lulu The WEBstaurant Store
CHOCOLATE DIPPING TOOLS & TEMPERING MACHINE	Amazon Chocoley Chocosphere
DIGITAL KITCHEN SCALES	Amazon Overstock.com The WEBstaurant Store
HAND MIXERS STAND MIXERS CUISINART FOOD PROCESSORS	Amazon Cuisinart KitchenAid Overstock.com Sur la Table The WEBstaurant Store Williams-Sonoma
PARCHMENT PAPER, BAKING SHEET-SIZE (QUANTITY)	King Arthur Flour The WEBstaurant Store
PLASTIC WRAP, FREEZE-TITE PLASTIC FREEZER WRAP PREFERRED	Amazon

STORAGE TINS	Amazon
	Container Store
	Kitchen supply stores
	Target
THERMAPEN INSTANT-READ DIGITAL THERMOMETER	Amazon
	King Arthur Flour
	Thermoworks
UTENSILS:	Amazon
SILICONE SPATULAS	King Arthur Flour
WHISKS	Overstock.com
PASTRY BLENDER TOOL	The WEBstaurant Store
BENCH SCRAPER	
ROLLING PINS, ROLLING DOCKING TOOL	
OFFSET SPATULAS, ASSORTED SIZES	
SCOOPS, VARIETY OF SIZES	

Ingredients	Retailers
BONNE MAMAN JAMS AND PRESERVES	Amazon Bonne Maman
BOYAJIAN CITRUS OILS	Amazon Boyajian
CANNED PUMPKIN, SWEET POTATO, FARMER'S FOODS PREFERRED	Amazon Farmer's Market Organic
CHÈVRE CHEESE, CYPRESS GROVE PREFERRED	Cypress Grove
CHOCOLATE: GUITTARD DISCS, PISTOLES, MELTING WAFERS BARS, CHIPS, AND MORE UNSWEETENED COCOA POWDER ENROBING CHOCOLATE (ALTERNATIVE TO TEMPERING)	Amazon Chocoley Chocosphere Hershey's Scharffen Berger
DAIRY WHEY POWDER, DRY BUTTERMILK POWDER, DRY MILK POWDER	Amazon Bob's Red Mill Saco Buttermilk Blend
EXPANDEX MODIFIED TAPIOCA STARCH	Celiac Specialties Gifts of Nature Rheinlander Bakery
FIORI DI SICILIA FLAVORING	King Arthur Flour
FLAVORINGS: ALMOND, HAZELNUT, LEMON, ORANGE, AND MORE	Penzeys Spices Savory Spice Shop
GLUTEN-FREE CAKE MIXES: BETTY CROCKER, GLUTEN-FREE PANTRY PREFERRED	Betty Crocker Glutino Gluten Free Pantry
GLUTEN-FREE SUPERFINE FLOURS: BROWN RICE, WHITE RICE, SWEET WHITE RICE TAPIOCA STARCH	Authentic Foods

GLUTEN-FREE MATZO, YEHUDA PREFERRED	Yehuda Gluten-Free Matzo
GLUTEN-FREE PASTA, THAI RICE NOODLES	Amazon
KOSHER GROCERIES ONLINE	All in Kosher Allergy Free Kosher
LOVE'N BAKE FILLINGS, ALMOND PASTE	Amazon AmericanAlmond.com Nuts.com
MAPLE SYRUP, HONEY, LYLE'S GOLDEN SYRUP	Amazon King Arthur Flour
NUTELLA	Amazon Nutella USA
NUTS: ALMONDS, PECANS, AND MORE DRIED FRUITS: APPLES, APRICOTS, FIGS, RAISINS, AND MORE	Nuts.com
PUMPKIN BUTTER	Amazon Trader Joe's Whole Foods Most grocery stores
RED STAR YEAST	Amazon Red Star Yeast
SEEDS: POPPY, CARAWAY, SESAME (BULK)	Nuts.com Penzeys Spices Savory Spice Shop
SOLO BRAND FILLINGS: ALMOND, POPPY SEED, AND MORE	Amazon Solo Foods
SPECIALTY GLUTEN-FREE FLOURS AND STARCHES, INCLUDING NUT, OAT, POTATO	Authentic Foods Bob's Red Mill Nuts.com

SPECTRUM ORGANIC VEGETABLE SHORTENING SPECTRUM ORGANIC OILS: CANOLA, COCONUT, OR SAFFLOWER	Amazon Spectrum Organics
SPICES: WHOLE NUTMEG, CINNAMON, CLOVES, AND MORE HERBS: POULTRY SEASONING, THYME, AND MORE	Penzeys Spices Savory Spice Shop
UNSWEETENED SHREDDED COCONUT AND FLAKES	Amazon Bob's Red Mill Edward and Sons
VANILLA EXTRACT, NIELSEN-MASSEY 32-OUNCE MADAGASCAR PREFERRED	Amazon Chefs Catalog Nielsen Massey Penzeys Spices Savory Spice Shop

CELIAC RESOURCES

Celiac Information, Resources, and Organizations

Celiac Disease Awareness Campaign of the National Institute of Health | celiac.nih.gov

Celiac Disease Center at Columbia University | www.celiacdiseasecenter.org

Celiac Disease Foundation | www.celiac.org

Coeliac Australia | www.coeliac.org.au

Canadian Celiac Association | www.celiac.ca

Coeliac UK | www.coeliac.org.uk

National Foundation for Celiac Awareness | www.celiaccentral.org

The University of Chicago Celiac Disease Center | www.cureceliacdisease.org

Living Without magazine | www.living without.org

Gluten Test Strips: Detecting Gluten in Food and Ingredients

EZ Gluten Test

Gluten Tox Pro

JEWISH BAKING RESOURCES

Books

Joan Nathan's *Jewish Holiday Cookbook*

Marcy Goldman's *A Treasury of Jewish Holiday Baking*

Arthur Schwartz's *Jewish Home Cooking*

Norene Gilletz's *The New Food Processor Bible*

Sara Kasdan's *Love and Knishes* (out of print)

Blogs

Joy of Kosher with Jamie Geller | www.JoyofKosher.com

The Shiksa in the Kitchen with Tori Avey | www.theShiksa.com

The History Kitchen with Tori Avey | www.thehistorykitchen.com

JEWISH HOLIDAY BAKING CHART

	SHABBAT	ROSH HASHANAH
Almond Mandelbrot (page 23)	✔	✔
Apple Butter Donuts (page 162)		✔
Apple Pomegranate Tart (page 113)	✔	✔
Apple Upside-Down Cake with Honey Pomegranate Syrup (page 72)		✔
Baked Honey Bites (page 138)		✔
Banana Maple Pecan Glazed Donuts (page 160)		
Big Fat Baked Sufganiyah Jelly Donuts (page 164)		
Black & White Angel Food Cake (page 82)	✔	✔
Black & White Cookies (page 30)		
Braided Challah (page 188)	✔	✔
Braided Challah in the Round (190)	✔	✔
Challah Corn Bread Stuffing (page 230)	✔	✔
Challah Rolls (page 194)	✔	✔
Cherry Chocolate Mandelbrot (page 21)	✔	✔
Chocolate Angel Cake Roll (page 90)	✔	
Chocolate Babka (page 78)	✔	
Chocolate Pecan Rugelach (page 132)	✔	
Cherry Chocolate Cupcakes (page 87)		
Chocolate Chip Macaroons (page 37)		✔
Chocolate Chunk Cherry Brownies (page 63)		
Dark Chocolate Cinnamon Cupcakes (page 85)		
Chocolate Drizzle Almond Macaroons (page 43)		✔
Chocolate Nut Two-Bite Tarts (page 124)		
Coconut Matzo Rocky Road (page 245)		
Cory-O Sandwich Cookies (page 28)		
Crostata for All Seasons (page 123)	✔	✔
Dark Chocolate Apricot Rugelach (page 134)	✔	

BREAKING YOM KIPPUR FAST	SUKKOT	HANUKKAH	PURIM	PASSOVER
✔		✔		
	✔			
	✔			
	✔			
	✔	✔		
	✔			
		✔		
		✔		✔
		✔		
✔				
✔				
		✔		
✔				
✔		✔		
		✔		✔
		✔		
✔				
		✔		
				✔
		✔		
		✔		
				✔
		✔		
		✔		✔
		✔		
	✔			
✔				

	SHABBAT	ROSH HASHANAH
Dorable Fudgies (page 39)		
Double Chocolate Chunk Mandelbrot (page 37)	✔	✔
Dressy Chocolate Truffles (page 241)		
Fast Mocha Whoopie Pies (page 208)		
Fig Tart (page 115)	✔	✔
Flourless Almond Puff Cookies (page 49)		
Flourless Chocolate Orange Cookies (page 46)	✔	
Frangelico Pear Tart (page 127)		
Goldie's Pound Cake (page 77)	✔	✔
Goldie's Quick Apple Cake (page 203)	✔	✔
Hamantashen (page 140)		
Honey Cake (page 71)		✔
Kichlach (page 26)	✔	✔
Lemon Jammer Donuts (page 166)		
Lemon Zest Macaroons (page 45)		✔
Linzer Berry Torte (page 146)	✔	✔
Mallo Bites (page 32)		
Marshmallow Swirl Cocoa Brownies (page 65)		
Marzipany Gooey Brownies (page 59)		
Matzo Squares (page 199)		
Meringue Sandwich Bites (page 247)	✔	
Mini Fruit Tarts (page 111)	✔	✔
Mom's Apple Pie (page 117)		✔
Mom's Brownies (page 57)		
Mom's Double Chocolate Gelt (page 37)		
Mom's Marble Chiffon Cake (page 88)	✔	✔
Nutella Chewy Bites (page 61)		
O'Figginz Bars (page 54)		✔
Passover Mini Berry Pavlovas (page 152)		
Pastry Cream–Filled Éclairs (page 145)		

BREAKING YOM KIPPUR FAST	SUKKOT	HANUKKAH	PURIM	PASSOVER
		✔		
✔		✔		
		✔		✔
		✔		
	✔			
	✔			✔
		✔		✔
✔	✔			
		✔		
✔	✔			
			✔	
	✔			
✔		✔		
		✔		
				✔
		✔		
		✔		
		✔		
				✔
		✔		✔
	✔			
	✔			
		✔		
		✔		
		✔		✔
		✔		
	✔			
				✔
			✔	

	SHABBAT	ROSH HASHANAH
Peanut Butter Cups and Buckeyes (page 238)		
Picnic Pies (page 118)		
Pineapple Raisin Noodle Kugel (page 221)	✔	✔
Potato Latkes (page 226)		
Potato Matzo (page 199)		
Pumpkin Corn Bread Streusel Muffins (page 175)		✔
Pumpkin Cupcakes with Honey Buttercream (page 75)		✔
Pumpkin Honey Bread (page 179)		✔
Quick Challah (page 185)	✔	✔
Quick Challah in the Round with Poolish (page 186)	✔	✔
Raisin Nut Strudel Bites (page 136)	✔	✔
Raisin Pecan Rugelach (page 131)	✔	✔
Red Potato Kugelettes (page 228)	✔	✔
Spinach Noodle Kugel (page 223)	✔	✔
Sweet Corn Bread Honey Donuts (page 163)		✔
Sweet Potato Kugel (page 218)	✔	✔
Sweet Potato Pumpkin Butter Pie (page 121)		✔
Turban Challah with Raisins (page 192)	✔	✔

BREAKING YOM KIPPUR FAST	SUKKOT	HANUKKAH	PURIM	PASSOVER
			✔	
✔	✔	✔		
✔		✔		
		✔		
				✔
✔	✔			
	✔			
✔	✔			
✔				
✔				
✔				
✔				
		✔		
✔	✔	✔		
	✔			
✔	✔	✔		
	✔			
✔				

Lisa's third birthday, with her mom and three (cookie-stealing, older) brothers

ACKNOWLEDGMENTS

MY MOTHER and my two backup spare moms, Ruth and Flo, might no longer be with us except in spirit, but they remain strong influences nonetheless. My mother was the one who introduced me to the family recipes. Ruth, the bossypants of the group and my mother's Hadassah colleague and best friend, carried on where my mother left off and made sure I amounted to something (or other) with a college degree. Flo was with us the longest, and she made sure I knew Jewish deli pastry better than, say, calculus. They are the force behind this book, those three. I owe them some pastry and whole lot of thanks.

Some moments in writing a book are like getting pushed into the abyss, but it all turns out to be just like Bloomingdale's on a sale day; slight chaos unfolds into order and maybe a great new pair of shoes. Fortunately for us, Cara Bedick, our wonderful and multitalented editor, was our fearless leader throughout. Without her, and without the team at The Experiment, this book would only be half a nosh, or maybe just a nibble. Cara, Matthew, Jack, Molly, and everyone at The Experiment (and Workman), from the designer to the copyeditor, played a role in helping make the book the best nosh it could be. For all their work on our book's behalf, and their belief in this project, a mighty big fat thank-you.

To our fabulously patient family, from the lemon-loving in-laws, to my little brother the rabbi, to my stepmother who owns the official second mom title, and to our siblings and siblings-in-law who were there through thick and thicker, thank you. To our kids and the ZZ boys, this is for you.

To our friends, those we know in person and those who are still virtual, but friends nonetheless—thank you for your support and your assistance. A big shout-out to Lisa K. and Marilyn T. for their literary assistance, and also to Kimberly and Mary and David for the loan of those stylish props.

To my cousin Ruthe—without you, the poppyseed cookies would not be possible. And thank you for not only being so generous with the recipe, but also for all the stories you shared about growing up with my mother.

We would be remiss in not thanking our crowd of testers. That they tasted these recipes endlessly with enthusiasm—some never realizing they were noshing on GF goodies—only encouraged us to feed them more. We apologize for those newly acquired elastic pants.

And last, but also important, while I learned some early lessons in Jewish baking from my mother and her Hadassah friends, as an adult I owe my continuing education to some of my favorite authors. Joan Nathan, Sara Kasdan, Arthur Schwartz, Marcy Goldman, and Norene Gilletz—each of them has a beloved place in our home. Links to their books are included in the Resources.

It takes a village. Thank you. And I have noshes. Want some?

INDEX

ABOUT THE AUTHORS

LISA STANDER-HOREL AND TIM HOREL are the writing and photography team behind the blog *Gluten Free Canteen*. They have been experimenting with gluten-free baking recipe development for over a decade. Their work has been published in *Living Without* magazine, Salon, Huffington Post, Joy of Kosher, GourmetLive.com, BlogHer Food, and BurdaFood.net/*Sweet Dreams* magazine (Germany).

Lisa comes from a long line of bakers who emigrated from Eastern Europe to America. She began baking with her mother at an early age, learning how to make many traditional Jewish holiday foods. Tim spent most of his youth falling out of trees and breaking bones, when he wasn't doing science experiments. He also learned to bake alongside his mother, who made all of their bread and baked goods from scratch. When they met at age fifteen in the French horn section of their high school orchestra, Lisa and Tim traded baking techniques while playing Mozart. Tim learned to bake rugelach and Lisa learned to make crusty boules. They were married at seventeen and, though unusual, it seemed

logical to them. During their college years they not only collected degrees but also became parents to two girls.

Lisa began a career in the nonprofit sector, developing and directing programs while writing grants to fund programs that served children and families. There was baking involved, because even funders enjoy a good brownie or rugelach. Tim worked as an engineer at IBM, followed by Sun Microsystems (now Oracle), as well as a couple of Silicon Valley start-ups. He began his photography career when he inherited some old SLR cameras from his photographer father-in-law. His subjects progressed from flowers to dogs, then dogs in Paris, then food in Paris, and finally gluten-free baked goods.

After the family left the northeast for northern California, Tim learned that the reason his bones continued to break was premature osteoporosis caused by celiac. Once their kitchen had become gluten-free and Lisa had begun converting all of their favorite recipes to gluten-free versions, it became apparent that Tim was not the only one benefiting. It turned out that Lisa's long battle with migraines and a host of other ailments were caused by sensitivity to gluten (and dairy). Once they were eating gluten-free, both her symptoms and Tim's osteoporosis cleared up.

Today, Lisa can usually be found in the kitchen wielding some sort of spatula while developing and testing new recipes. Rest assured, chocolate will be nearby. Engineer (geek) by day and photographer by night, Tim can often be spotted with a lens in one hand and a gluten-free cookie in the other.